COMPANION

TO

VERGI

By

Joseph Pearl,

Professor of Classical Languages, Brooklyn College.
Author of "Companions to Caesar and to Cicero"

COLLEGE ENTRANCE BOOK COMPANY
104 FIFTH AVENUE NEW YORK CITY

Revised Edition

Companion to Vergil

PRINTED IN THE UNITED STATES OF AMERICA

PREFACE

TEACHERS of Latin have come to realize more and more the necessity of so enriching the course of study that there will be no doubt about the cultural advantages derived from the pursuit of that subject. Particularly is this enrichment necessary in a course in Vergil, which is so essentially literary and cultural. The student entering upon the study of Latin poetry through the medium of Vergil's Aeneid requires information on various topics. To make this information readily available, I have included, among other features, an account of the life and work of the poet; a treatment of the mythological background, the characters and the story of the Aeneid; a chapter dealing with the scansion of Latin hexameter poetry; a summary of the chief features of Vergil's grammatical usage; a detailed account of Latin word formation; and numerous exercises for translation from Latin to English and English to Latin.

In the selection of this material I have been guided by the more recent syllabi which embody the results of the Report of the Classical Investigation, and by the needs of the large number of students who begin the study of Vergil in college.

The favorable reception accorded to my COMPANIONS TO CAESAR and CICERO influenced me to write the COMPANION TO VERGIL. I offer it in the hope that it will prove helpful to those who are studying the work of this great poet.

I wish to express my gratitude to Dr. I. E. Drabkin, Instructor in Latin, the College of the City of New York, for his valuable suggestions.

LIST OF ILLUSTRATIONS

All illustrations in this book are authentic copies from Ancient Greek Vases, and are reproduced from Griechische Vasenbilder by Eduard Gerhard.

CONTENTS

MUSA MIHI CAUSAS MEMORA ❋❋ QUO NUMINE LAESO ❋❋

THIS mosaic, made in the second century A. D., was discovered in an ancient villa in Tunis, Africa. It is the oldest portrait of Vergil in existence and shows Vergil with Clio, the Muse of History, on his right and Melpomene, the Muse of Tragedy, on his left. The inscription on the roll he holds is reprinted at the left of the picture. The mosaic is at present in the Bardo Museum in Tunis.

THIS ancient bust of Vergil is in the Capitoline Museum in Rome.

CHAPTER I

VERGIL'S LIFE AND WORKS

B.C.

70 Publius Vergilius Maro was born October 15, 70 B.C., in the township of Andes, near Mantua, in Cisalpine Gaul. His father, first a hired assistant of a certain Magius, later became an independent landowner. His mother was Magia Polla, the daughter of his father's employer. Studied at first in his native town, later in Mantua, and later still in Cremona, about fifty miles west of Mantua.

55 Assumed the **toga virīlis.** Moved to Milan, the capital of Cisalpine Gaul, to continue his studies.

53 Removed to Rome, where he studied rhetoric, philosophy, mathematics, and medicine. Some of his teachers were Parthenius, a poet of some note; Epidius, the rhetorician; and Siro, a distinguished Epicurean.

42 Back in his native district. Composition of the *Eclogues* begun.

41 Evicted from his farm by the members of the Second Triumvirate.

40 Through the aid of C. Asinius Pollio, governor of Cisalpine Gaul, Cornelius Gallus, and Alfenus Varus, Vergil's farm was restored to him.
Beginning of Vergil's friendship with Maecenas, one of the chief advisers of Augustus, and a noted patron of literature.

38 Vergil accompanied Maecenas to Brundisium.

37 Completion and publication of the *Eclogues*.
Composition of the *Georgics* begun.

B.C.

29 The *Georgics* published.
The *Aeneid* begun.

23 Death of Marcellus, son of Octavia (sister of Augustus).
Portion of the *Aeneid* read by Vergil to Augustus and Octavia.

19 Vergil went to Greece, where he intended to spend three years in putting the finishing touches to the *Aeneid*, and then to devote his remaining days to philosophy. At Athens he met Augustus, and was persuaded by him to return to Italy. On the way, Vergil fell ill of a fever, and a few days after reaching Brundisium he died, on September 21, in his fifty-first year. He was buried near Naples, and on his tomb was inscribed the following epitaph, which briefly summarizes his life and works:

Mantua mē genuit; Calabrī rapuēre; tenet nunc
Parthenopē. Cecinī pascua, rūra, ducēs.

Mantua gave me birth; Calabria took me off; now Parthenope (Naples) holds me. I sang of pastures, fields, and heroes.

VERGIL'S WORKS

1. **The Minor Poems.** — Ancient biographers of Vergil give the following list: *Catalepton*, a collection of fourteen short poems, most of which are supposed to have been written by the poet in his youth; the *Culex* (*The Gnat*), the *Cīris*, the *Morētum* (*The Salad*), and the *Cōpa* (*The Hostess*).

2. **The Eclogues** (**Selections**), also called **Bucolics** (**Pastorals**). These consist of ten short pastoral poems, which treat of the life and the occupations of herdsmen. In most of these Vergil imitates the Idyls of Theocritus, a Greek poet of Sicily in the third century B.C. However, while Theocritus describes the life of actual shepherds, Vergil in his *Eclogues* introduces himself and his friends as characters in the rather thin guise of shepherds. Later pastoral poetry, as that of Spenser and Milton, followed the Vergilian style. The *Eclogues* are known for " the charming way in which Vergil describes country scenes, and for the smoothness and grace of their

language and the music of their verse." They were published in 37.

3. **The Georgics.** — This work was undertaken at the request of Maecenas, who was desirous of arousing greater interest in rural life, and of restoring the old Roman virtues of thrift and industry. It is a didactic poem on husbandry, for which Vergil used as his model a very ancient poem of the Greek poet Hesiod, called *Works and Days*. It was published in 29, and dedicated to Maecenas. It consists of four books:

   1. Cultivation of the fields and the crops
   2. Cultivation of trees
   3. Cattle-raising
   4. Bee culture

   This poem is Vergil's most finished production; in fact, it is considered the most finished poem in the Latin language.

4. **The Aeneid,** the greatest Roman epic. Vergil devoted ten years to it, and then intended to devote three years more. Since it lacked the finishing touches, the poet begged Varius to destroy his poem; however, at the order of Augustus, Vergil's literary executors, Varius and Tucca, published the *Aeneid* practically as Vergil left it.

Subject of the Aeneid:

The first six books tell of the fall of Troy, the seven years' wandering of Aeneas and of his followers, and their final landing in Italy, with the help of the gods. This part is sometimes called Vergil's *Odyssey*, from a resemblance to Homer's *Odyssey*, which contains an account of the wanderings of Odysseus.

The last six books tell of Aeneas's successful contest with the native princes for the possession of Italy. This part is sometimes called Vergil's *Iliad*, because, like Homer's *Iliad*, it treats of wars and battles.

Sources of the Aeneid:

1. Homer's *Iliad* and *Odyssey*
2. Cyclic Poets of Greece

3. Tragedies of Aeschylus, Sophocles, and Euripides
4. *Bellum Pūnicum* of Naevius
5. *Annālēs* of Ennius

Purpose of the Aeneid:

Vergil, in writing the *Aeneid*, wished not merely to create a literary masterpiece which would give pleasure to his readers, but also to glorify the new régime of Augustus Caesar and to arouse interest in the state religion and in the old mythology. He reveals in the *Aeneid* the origins of the Roman race and the divine lineage of its rulers.

VERGIL'S FAME

1. Vergil is considered "one of the five or six chief poets of the world."
2. He was largely read in his own day, and his works at once became the leading text-book in the Roman schools.
3. No Latin author was quoted more extensively than Vergil by ancient scholars and grammarians; nearly every line of his works may be found somewhere in the works of later Roman writers.
4. Vergil exerted a very great influence on his successors in Latin literature, in both poetry and prose.
5. From the beginning of the second century A.D., it was customary among the superstitious to consult Vergil's works as oracles by opening them at random and accepting the first lines the eye fell upon as prophetic. These oracles were called **Sortēs Vergiliānae.**
6. In the Middle Ages Vergil was regarded by the people as a magician and as a saint. It was at this period that the poet's name was associated with the wand (**virga**) of the magician; and so the spelling Virgil came into vogue.
7. Dante, the author of the *Divine Comedy*, claims Vergil as his master, and makes him his guide through the world below.
8. Vergil was studied and imitated by Chaucer, Spenser, Shakespeare, Milton, Dryden, Tennyson, and others. He was "one of the most direct, powerful, continuous sources of the whole splendid body of English poetry from the fourteenth to the twentieth centuries."

CHAPTER II

OVID'S LIFE AND WORKS

Publius Ovidius Naso, the last great writer of the Augustan Age, was born on March 20, 43 B.C., at Sulmo, a city about ninety miles east of Rome, in the country of the Paeligni. His father was a knight of good social standing.

At an early age, Ovid was taken to Rome, where he was placed under the care of the best instructors. There he devoted himself especially to the study of rhetoric. To complete his education, he went to Athens, and, in the company of his life-long friend, the poet Aemilius Macer of Verona, he visited Asia Minor and Sicily, where he spent nearly a year.

Upon his return to Rome, he held several minor civil and judicial offices, but, as he soon tired of official duties, he gave up all thought of a public career, and devoted himself henceforth to a life of pleasure and to the pursuit of a literary career.

Of the poet's three matrimonial unions the first two led quickly to divorce; the last, however, with a lady of one of the oldest and most respected families of Rome, the Fabii, lasted till the poet's death.

Among his friends Ovid numbered the poets Sextus Propertius and Aemilius Macer. He was likewise fortunate in having as his patrons M. Valerius Messala Corvinus, Cotta Messalinus, and Fabius Maximus.

Towards the close of 8 A.D., Ovid was suddenly banished — without loss of his property, however — by the Emperor Augustus to Tomi, a little, cold, bleak town on the Black Sea, near the mouth of the Danube. The pretext of the banishment was the poet's licentious poem on the *Art of Love* (*Ars Amātōria*), which had been published nearly ten years earlier; but it is more likely that the banishment had some connection with the scandalous conduct of the Emperor's granddaughter Julia, who was banished in the same year as Ovid.

From Tomi Ovid wrote many pathetic letters to his friends in Rome in which he begged them to intercede in his behalf, but all to no avail. And so here in lonely retirement he passed the rest of his days until his death in 17 or 18 A.D.

OVID'S WORKS

First Period. The works of his youth. These are for the most part of an amatory nature:

1. **Amōrēs.** Three books of elegies, most of which deal with the poet's love for a certain Corinna.
2. **Hērōidēs,** or **Epistulae Hērōidum.** Twenty-one letters in elegiac verse, supposedly written by famous heroines of mythology — as Penelope, Medea, Dido — to absent husbands or lovers.
3. **Ars Amātōria,** consisting of three books, in the first two of which the poet tells men how they may win and keep the love of women, and in the third of which he advises women how they may win and keep the love of men.
4. **Remedia Amōris,** containing instructions on how to overcome the passion of love.

Second Period. To this period belong Ovid's most important poems, viz. the **Metamorphōsēs** and the **Fāstī.**

1. The **Metamorphōsēs.** In this work, which consists of fifteen books, it is the poet's purpose, as he tells us in the first two verses, **In nova . . . mūtātās dīcere formās corpora,** i.e., *to tell of bodies changed into new forms*, and the work receives its name from the different **transformations,** usually of human beings into animals, birds, trees, rocks, or other things, which it describes. The poet begins with the story of the Creation of the World out of Chaos, then passes to the description of more than two hundred transformations, and finally ends with the deification of Caesar.
2. The **Fāstī.** This poem, consisting of six books, has been well characterized as **"A Religious Calendar in Verse."** It is a collection of stories and legends connected with the religious

festivals of the first six months of the Roman year. One book is devoted to each month.

Third Period. The works of this period are in the nature of laments.

1. **Trīstia.** This work, consisting of five books, contains much biographical material. In this the poet describes his journey to Tomi and his life there. It also serves as the poet's appeal for a remission of his sentence of banishment.
2. **Epistulae ex Pontō.** Four books of letters addressed to different persons at Rome whom Ovid begs to intercede in his behalf.

Besides all the above mentioned works, Ovid wrote also a tragedy, **Mēdēa,** which has unfortunately been lost.

OVID'S ART

"It is agreed that his style is easier and more fluent than Vergil's. While he does not rise often to the grandeur of the *Aeneid*, his poetry does not show the mechanical difficulties and harsh effects which one meets at times in Vergil. His verses flow of themselves without any visible effort. He is usually interesting and always charming; and as a spinner of yarns, a maker of light verses to be read before the fashion and beauty of Rome, he had no equal. Much, however, that he wrote, especially in the years at Tomi, was really noble; and if a good part of his earlier work was unrefined, and some of it even immoral, it was quite in keeping with the social standards of polite society at that time."

Gleason, *A Term of Ovid.*

CHAPTER III

THE TROJAN WAR

The Apple of Discord. The Judgment of Paris.
The Abduction of Helen.

Eris, the goddess of Strife, who alone of all the gods and goddesses had not been invited to the marriage of Peleus and Thetis, enraged at this slight, threw among the assembled guests a golden apple, the Apple of Discord, with the inscription " To the Fairest." Thereupon the leading goddesses, viz. Juno, the queen of the gods, Minerva, the goddess of wisdom, and Venus, the goddess of love and beauty, each claimed the apple for herself. Jupiter, discreetly refusing to act as judge, referred the case to the second son of Priam, Paris, who was then dwelling as a shepherd on Mount Ida, near Troy. When the three goddesses appeared before him, each tried to bribe him to award the prize of beauty to her. Juno offered him the rule of Asia and great riches, Minerva great wisdom, and Venus the most beautiful woman in the world as his wife. Paris thereupon awarded the prize to Venus, thereby incurring the fierce and unforgiving hatred of both Juno and Minerva. Paris's decision in favor of Venus is known as " The Judgment of Paris."

Paris now sailed to Greece, and was hospitably received by Menelaus, King of Sparta. With the help of Venus, the young Trojan prince succeeded in carrying off the wife of Menelaus, Helen, who was the most beautiful woman in the world at that time. The Greeks, incensed at the insult, arose in arms. The command of the allied forces was given to the brother of Menelaus, Agamemnon, King of Mycenae. The Greek forces assembled at Aulis, a seaport in eastern Greece, where Agamemnon, while hunting, killed a deer sacred to Diana. Because of this the Greek fleet was detained by unfavorable winds, until at last Calchas, the priest and seer of the expedition, announced that only the sacrifice of Iphigenia, the daughter of the commander-in-chief, could appease the goddess. But when the princess was led to the altar, Diana substituted a hind in her place, and carried her off to Tauris, where she became the priestess of the goddess. Now the winds changed and the expedition could set out against Troy.

Besides the two leaders, Agamemnon and Menelaus, the following famous men joined the expedition against Troy: the swift-footed Achilles of Phthia; the wily Ulysses of Ithaca; the strong but dull-witted Ajax; and brave Diomedes, next to Achilles in prowess.

Among the Trojan defenders were: the dauntless Hector, eldest son of Priam; Paris, the abductor of Helen; and faithful Aeneas, the hero of the Aeneid.

For the events and the results of the war see Chapter IV, Story of the Aeneid.

THE EDUCATION OF ACHILLES

Achilles is being presented by his father, Peleus, to the centaur, Chiron, at whose hands he is to receive his education. His mother, Thetis, stands at the left.

MEDIOLANUM
CREMONA
PATAVIUM
MANTUA
ANDES
TIMAVUS FL.
PADUS FL.
GENUA
MONOECUS
CORYTHUS
ETRURIA
TIBERIS FL.
UMBRIA
APENNINUS M.
PICENUM
ITALIA
HADRIATICUM MA
LIBURNI
ILLYRICU
CORSICA
SARDINIA
FIDENAE
ROMA
LATIUM
LAURENTUM
LAVINIUM
ALBA LONGA
CAIETA
L. Avernus
APULIA
CUMAE
Misenum Pr.
Vesuvius M.
CAMPANIA
VELIA
Palinuri Pr.
TARENTUM
MARE TYRRHENUM
DREPANUM
CAULON
LOCRI
Pelorus Pr.
AEOLIAE INSVLAE
IO
M
SEGESTA
Eryx M.
Lilybaeum Pr.
SELINUS
Aetna M.
MEGARA
THAPSUS
SYRACUSAE
HELORUS
ACRAGAS
GELA
CAMARINA
CARTHAGO
AFRICA
MARE
SYRTIS MINOR
THE VOYAGE OF

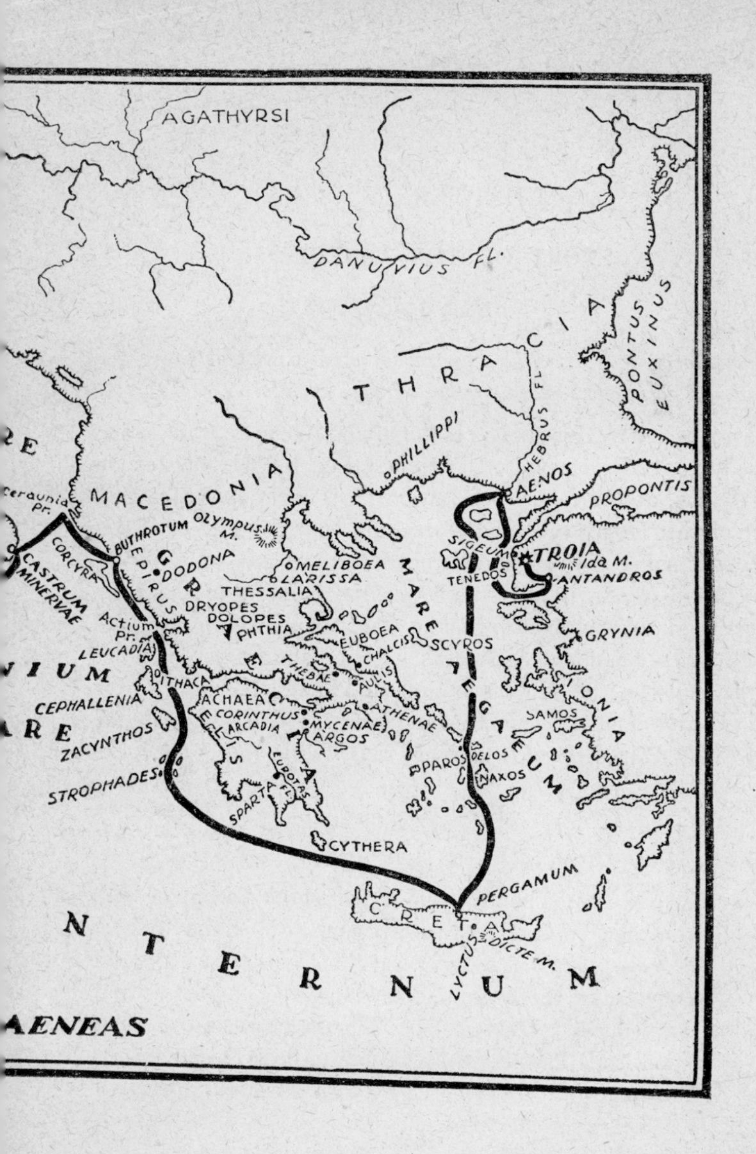
AGATHYRSI
DANUVIUS FL.
THRACIA
PONTUS EUXINUS
PHILLIPPI
HEBRUS FL.
AENOS
PROPONTIS
MACEDONIA
Ceraunia Pr.
CASTRUM MINERVAE
CORCYRA
BUTHROTUM
EPIRUS
DODONA
Olympus M.
MELIBOEA
LARISSA
THESSALIA
DRYOPES
DOLOPES
PHTHIA
Actium Pr.
LEUCADIA
ITHACA
CEPHALLENIA
ZACYNTHOS
STROPHADES
GRAECIA
EUBOEA
CHALCIS
THEBAE
AULIS
ACHAEA
CORINTHUS
ARCADIA
ELIS
MYCENAE
ARGOS
ATHENAE
SPARTA
EUROTAS FL.
CYTHERA
MARE AEGAEUM
SIGEUM
TROIA
Ida M.
TENEDOS
ANTANDROS
SCYROS
GRYNIA
IONIA
SAMOS
PAROS
DELOS
NAXOS
PERGAMUM
CRETA
LYCTUS
DICTE M.
RE
NIUM
ARE
NTERNUM
AENEAS

CHAPTER IV

STORY OF THE AENEID

Book I

The Storm at Sea. The Landing of Aeneas at Carthage. His Reception at the Palace of Dido.

The Trojans, led by Aeneas, son of Venus and Anchises, while sailing from Sicily to Italy, encounter a storm raised by the king of the Winds, Aeolus, at the request of Juno, who is eager to destroy the remnant of the Trojan race and so prevent the founding of Rome. The Trojans suffer shipwreck on the African coast, where Dido, the Phoenician queen, is just completing the building of Carthage. They are hospitably received by Dido, who, through the schemes of Venus, becomes enamored of Aeneas. At a banquet given in his honor, the leader of the Trojans is requested to tell the story of the fall of Troy and of his subsequent wanderings. (This story fills the whole of Books II and III of the Aeneid.)

Book II

The Wooden Horse. The Capture and Sack of Troy.

The Greeks, now in the tenth year of the siege, discouraged by their inability to take Troy, resort to stratagem. Pretending to have abandoned the siege, they sail away toward Tenedos, a small island near Troy, leaving before the walls of Troy a huge wooden horse within which are concealed many Greek chiefs. The ingeniously contrived tale of wily Sinon leads Priam and his people to drag the horse into the city. At night, the Greeks enclosed within the horse are released by Sinon, the Greek fleet returns from the island of Tenedos, and the slaughter and the pillage begin. As Aeneas and his followers are powerless to resist the enemy, they are forced to flee. In his flight, Aeneas takes with him his father Anchises, his little son Ascanius (also called Iulus), and a band of faithful Trojans. His wife Creusa, who is to follow him at a distance, fails to appear at the appointed place of meeting.

Book III

The Wanderings of Aeneas.

First Aeneas sails to Thrace, where he plans to found a new city, but, warned by the ghost of Polydorus, a son of Priam, who had been treacherously slain by the Thracian king Polymestor, he sails to Delos. Here a divine voice bids him seek his ancient motherland, which Anchises interprets to mean Crete, the motherland of Teucer, the founder of the Trojan race. Driven from here by a pestilence, Aeneas and his followers sail toward Hesperia, or Italy, the land which the Phrygian Penates told Aeneas was meant by Apollo. During a storm, they take refuge on one of the Strophades islands, the abode of the Harpies. From here they sail to Buthrotum in Epirus, where Priam's son Helenus instructs them as to their future course. They then reach Sicily and land at Drepanum, where they are hospitably received by King Acestes and where Anchises dies. On resuming their voyage, they encounter the storm already described in Book I, as a result of which they land on the coast of Africa.

Book IV

The Love and Death of Dido.

The hero, enthralled by the charms of Dido, lingers in Carthage, unmindful of his quest. Reminded by Mercury of his lofty mission, Aeneas refuses to listen to Dido's pleading and leaves Carthage. Dido, invoking a solemn curse upon Aeneas and praying that there may be eternal hatred between her people and his, mounts a funeral pyre and stabs herself with the sword given her by Aeneas.

Book V

Aeneas in Sicily. Funeral Games in Honor of Anchises. Departure for Italy.

Threatened by a storm, Aeneas lands in Sicily on the anniversary of his father's death, in whose honor he celebrates elaborate funeral games. At Juno's instigation, the Trojan women set fire to the ships. In answer to Aeneas's prayer, Jupiter sends a heavy rain which stays the flames. Then, leaving behind the weakest part of his followers, Aeneas sets sail for Italy. On the way, Palinurus, the pilot of Aeneas's ship, is overcome by the god of sleep and thrown overboard.

Book VI

Arrival of Aeneas at Cumae. His Descent to the Lower World. His Interview with the Shade of Anchises.

Aeneas lands at Cumae, in Campania, and mindful of his father's advice that before founding his Italian city he should visit him in the Lower World, he invokes the aid of Apollo and that of his priestess, the Sibyl. With her aid, he discovers the Golden Bough which makes it possible for him to visit the Lower World. There he finds his father Anchises, who describes the future fortunes of the great Romans to be born in later times and the glories of Rome. Aeneas returns safely to the upper air, and the exiles reach the harbor of Caieta.

Book VII

Arrival of Aeneas in Latium.

Aeneas reaches the Tiber and is well received by Latinus, king of Laurentum in Latium, who, mindful of the oracle at Albunea which had declared that his daughter should marry a foreign prince, offers him his daughter Lavinia in marriage. Relentless Juno, determined to prevent the proposed marriage, calls upon the Fury Allecto to sow discord between the Latins and the Trojans. Turnus, king of the Rutuli, and former suitor for Lavinia's hand, is roused by the hateful Fury against Aeneas, and he summons his followers to war against the Trojans. With the aid of Allecto Juno kindles strife also between the Trojans and the Latins.

Book VIII

The Alliance of Aeneas and Evander. The Armor and Shield of Aeneas.

Aeneas secures the alliance of Evander, a Greek from Arcadia, who reigns in Pallanteum, on the site afterwards occupied by Rome. Upon

Evander's suggestion, he also secures the alliance of the Etruscans, who are eager to make war upon Turnus, because he has welcomed into his kingdom their deposed tyrant, Mezentius, the scorner of the gods.

Venus, fearful for her son's safety, prevails upon Vulcan to make him a suit of divine armor.

Book IX

The Attack of Turnus on the Trojan Camp.

The Rutuli, led by Turnus, attack the Trojan camp and try to fire the ships in the absence of Aeneas. Cybele, the Great Mother of the gods, prevails on Jupiter to save the ships; he turns them into sea-nymphs.

Nisus and his devoted friend Euryalus plan to summon Aeneas from Pallanteum. They pass through the camp of the Rutuli and slay many of the enemy in their sleep. But, as they are leaving the hostile camp, they are surprised by a party of Latin horsemen and both are slain.

Book X

Council of the Gods. Pallas, Lausus, Mezentius.

Jupiter calls the gods to a council in Olympus, and tries to persuade them to put an end to discord.

Pallas, son of Evander, seeing the Arcadians in flight, hastens to rally them to the fight. In single combat he is slain by Turnus, who restores his body to the Arcadians, but keeps the young hero's belt, an act which later proves his undoing.

Mezentius, an ally of Turnus, and Aeneas meet in single combat; Mezentius is wounded; his son Lausus comes to his father's aid, but is himself slain by Aeneas. Mezentius returns to the fight, attacks Aeneas, and is slain by him.

Book XI

Funeral Honors to the Dead. The Truce. Renewal of Hostilities. Death of Camilla.

Aeneas bids his followers pay the last rites to the dead, and sends the body of Pallas with an escort of a thousand men to Pallanteum, the home of Evander.

The Latins ask for a truce in order to perform funeral ceremonies in honor of their fallen soldiers; they are granted a truce of twelve days. Latinus summons a council during which Drances, Turnus's chief opponent, advises the king to give his daughter in marriage to Aeneas; he also calls on Turnus either to give up the contest or to decide it by single combat with Aeneas. Turnus agrees to meet Aeneas in single combat.

When news is brought that the Trojans are advancing upon Laurentum, a town on the coast of Latium, the Latins rush to arms. Turnus meets Camilla, the Volscian heroine, at the gate of the city, and gives her the command of the cavalry. She performs many valiant deeds both on horseback and on foot, but is treacherously slain by an Etruscan ally of Aeneas, Arruns by name, who is himself killed by the nymph Opis, at the command of Diana.

Book XII

The Final Conflict between Aeneas and Turnus.

A treaty is made, providing that the war shall be settled by single combat between Aeneas and Turnus. Juturna, sister of Turnus, is urged by Juno to prevent the proposed duel, as it will prove fatal to Turnus. Accordingly, she excites the compassion of the Latins for Turnus, and, when in the ensuing excitement one of the Trojans is slain, both parties rush to arms. When news reaches Turnus that the city is surrounded, he hastens to meet Aeneas in single combat. Aeneas wounds him, and is on the point of sparing his life when he catches sight of Pallas's belt on Turnus's shoulder and slays him.

CHAPTER V

CHARACTERS AND MYTHOLOGICAL FIGURES IN THE AENEID

Acestes: son of the river-god Crinisus and a Trojan woman, Egesta or Segesta. King of western Sicily.

Achates: the armor-bearer and faithful friend of Aeneas.

Achilles: son of Peleus (hence **Pelides**) and Thetis; bravest of the Greeks before Troy. The hero of the Iliad.

Aeneas: son of Venus and Anchises. The hero of the Aeneid.

Aeolus: the god of the winds, who dwelt in Aeolia.

Ajax: son of Oileus. On the night of Troy's fall, he offered violence to Cassandra in Minerva's temple, and was punished by the goddess.

Anchises: son of Capys and Themis, grandson of Assaracus, and father of Aeneas. Jupiter crippled him with a thunderbolt because he had boasted of Venus's love.

Andromache: daughter of King Eetion, and wife of Hector.

Anna: sister of Dido.

Antenor: a Trojan leader who, after the fall of the Troy, went to Italy and founded Patavium (Padua).

Apollo: son of Jupiter and Latona, twin brother of Diana; god of the sun, of prophecy, of music, of medicine, and of archery. Born on the island of Delos. His chief oracles were at Delphi, in Greece, and at Cumae, in Italy. Called also **Phoebus.**

Ascanius: son of Aeneas and Creusa; called also **Iulus.** The founder of Alba Longa.

Atrides: son of Atreus, King of Mycenae. There were two sons, Agamemnon and Menelaus, the leaders of the Greeks at Troy.

Augustus: title bestowed on Octavianus by the Senate, B.C. 27, as emperor of Rome.

Aurora: goddess of the dawn, daughter of Hyperion, wife of Tithonus, and mother of Memnon.

Bacchus: son of Jupiter and Semele; god of wine and of poets. Called also **Lyaeus.**

Calchas: son of Thestor; a priest and the most famous seer among the Greeks at Troy.

Cassandra: daughter of Priam and Hecuba; priestess of Apollo. Beloved by Apollo and endowed by him with the power of prophecy; as she did not requite his love, Apollo decreed that she should proclaim the downfall of Troy, but that no one should believe her utterances.

Cerberus: the three-headed dog that guarded the entrance to the Lower World.

Ceres: daughter of Saturn and Ops, sister of Jupiter, and mother of Proserpina; goddess of agriculture.

Charon: the ferryman of the shades over the river Styx.

Creusa: daughter of Priam, wife of Aeneas.

Cupid: son of Venus; god of love. Called also **Amor.**

Cybele: a Phrygian goddess, daughter of Coelus and Terra, wife of Saturn, and mother of the gods. The Magna Mater of the Romans.

Cyclops: one of the Cyclopes who were giants with one eye in the middle of the forehead.

Daedalus: a famous artisan of Athens, the builder of the Labyrinth for King Minos of Crete. For having helped Theseus to thread the Labyrinth, he was imprisoned by Minos, but with the aid of artificial wings fastened on by wax he escaped to Cumae.

Dardanus: son of Jupiter and Electra, son-in-law of Teucer, founder of the royal house of Troy.

Diana: daughter of Jupiter and Latona, sister of Apollo; goddess of the moon; identified also with Hecate, goddess of the Lower World.

Dido: daughter of Belus, King of Tyre, wife of Sychaeus, sister of Pygmalion and Anna; founder and queen of Carthage. Called also **Elissa.**

Diomedes: son of Tydeus (hence **Tydides**); one of the most valiant Greek warriors before Troy.

Eumenides: the Wellwishers (a conciliatory name applied to the Furies for the purpose of propitiating them).

Ganymedes: son of Laomedon or of Tros. On account of his beauty he was carried off by an eagle to be the cupbearer of Jupiter in place of Hebe, the daughter of Juno.

Hector: the eldest son of Priam and Hecuba, the most valiant warrior of the Trojans. Slain by Achilles and dragged round the walls of Troy.

Hecuba: wife of Priam.

Helen: daughter of Jupiter and Leda, wife of Menelaus of Sparta; carried off to Troy by Paris. This brought on the Trojan War.

Hercules: son of Jupiter and Alcmene, grandson of Alceus (hence **Alcides**); the most famous demigod, renowned for his prodigious strength and for the Twelve Labors imposed upon him by King Eurystheus.

Iris: daughter of Thaumas and Electra; messenger of the gods, particularly of Juno; goddess of the rainbow.

Janus: a two-faced Italian god of doorways and beginnings. His temple was shut in time of peace.

Juno: daughter of Saturn, wife and sister of Jupiter. The queen of the gods. Bitter enemy of the Trojans on account of the judgment of Paris. Her favorite places were Argos, Carthage, and Samos.

Jupiter: son of Saturn and Rhea. The king of the gods, identified with the Greek Zeus. Divum pater atque hominum rex. His weapons are the lightning and the thunderbolt, made by Vulcan with the aid of the Cyclopes.

Laocoön: son of Priam, priest of Neptune; killed by two serpents after he had driven a spear into the Wooden Horse.

Lavinia: daughter of Latinus, King of Latium; married Aeneas.

Marcellus: son of Octavia, and adopted son of Augustus; died in early youth.

Mars: son of Jupiter and Juno; god of war. Father of Romulus and Remus, hence the special protector of the Roman race.

Menelaus: son of Atreus, brother of Agamemnon, and husband of Helen. King of Sparta, and one of the Greek leaders in the Trojan War.

Mercury: son of Jupiter and Maia, grandson of Atlas; messenger of the gods, and god of trade and gain; conductor of souls to the Lower World. Identified with the Greek Hermes.

Minerva: daughter of Jupiter, an Italian goddess identified with the Greek Pallas Athene. The goddess of wisdom, of the arts and sciences, and of warfare.

Minos: King of Crete, son of Jupiter and Europa. After death became a judge in the Lower World.

Neptune: son of Saturn, brother of Jupiter, Juno, and Pluto. Identified with the Greek god of the sea, Poseidon.

Parcae: the three Fates, goddesses of birth and death, identified with the Greek deities Clotho (who spun the thread of life), Lachesis (who allotted to each mortal his portion of the thread), and Atropos (who cut the thread of life).

Paris: son of Priam and Hecuba. Awarded the prize of beauty (the Apple of Discord) to Venus; brought about the Trojan War by carrying off Helen from Sparta. Slain by Philoctetes.

Penates: old Italian deities of the household and of the state.

Pluto: brother of Jupiter and Neptune, husband of Proserpina. King of the Lower World.

Priam: son of Laomedon, and husband of Hecuba. King of Troy; slain at the fall of Troy by Pyrrhus.

Proserpina: daughter of Jupiter and Ceres; wife of Pluto, by whom she was carried away and made queen of the Lower World.

Pygmalion: son of Belus, King of Tyre; brother of Dido. King of Phoenicia. Killed Sychaeus, the husband of Dido.

Pyrrhus: son of Achilles and Deidamia; called also **Neoptolemus**. King of a part of Epirus; slain by Orestes.

Romulus: son of Mars and Rhea Silvia; twin brother of Remus; mythical founder of Rome.

Saturn: son of Uranus; father of Jupiter, Juno, Neptune, and Pluto. An ancient Italian god of agriculture. His reign was the "Golden Age" of primitive virtue and simplicity. Identified with the Greek Cronos.

Sibyl: a prophetess. One of the most famous was the Cumaean, Deiphobe, by whom Aeneas was conducted through the Lower World.

Sinon: A Greek spy who induced the Trojans to take the Wooden Horse into Troy.

Sychaeus: the husband of Dido; slain by Pygmalion, brother of Dido.

Teucer: son of Scamander and the nymph Idaea. First King of Troy, father-in-law of Dardanus.

Titans: the twelve sons of Heaven and Earth, who warred against Jupiter.

Tithonus: son of Laomedon, brother of Priam, husband of Aurora, and father of Memnon.

Turnus: son of Daunus and the nymph Venilia. King of the Rutulians; slain by Aeneas in single combat.

Venus: daughter of Jupiter and Dione; sometimes identified with the Greek Aphrodite. Goddess of love and beauty. Mother of Aeneas, hence friend of the Trojans.

Vesta: daughter of Saturn, goddess of the hearth and of the household. In her temple the holy fire was kept always burning by the Vestal Virgins.

Vulcan: the husband of Venus. God of fire. With the aid of the Cyclopes fashions the thunderbolts of Jupiter.

CHAPTER VI

PLACES, RIVERS, ETC.

Acheron: a river of Hades; also the Lower World.

Argi: the capital of Argolis in the Peloponnesus, Greece, a place dear to Juno.

Avernus: a lake near Cumae, in Campania. Near it was one of the fabled entrances to the Lower World and also the grotto of the Cumaean Sibyl.

Carthage: a Phoenician city on the northern coast of Africa, near modern Tunis, opposite Sicily; the famous rival of Rome.

Cocytus: a river of the Lower World.

Cumae: an ancient town on the coast of Campania, in Italy; the home of the Sibyl. Founded by Greeks from Chalcis in Euboea.

Cynthus: a mountain of Delos, on which Apollo and Diana were born.

Cyprus: a large island in the eastern Mediterranean.

Cythera: an island in the Aegean Sea, near which Venus was said to have been born from the foam of the sea.

Delos: a small island in the Aegean Sea, famous as the birthplace of Apollo and Diana.

Elysium: the home of the blessed in the Lower World.

Erebus: son of Chaos, and brother of Night; god of darkness; also the Lower World.

Hesperia: the Western Land; a poetic name of Italy.

Ithaca: an island off the west coast of Greece, in the Ionian Sea; the home of Ulysses.

Libya: a country of northern Africa; also Africa.

Mycenae: a city of Argolis; the home of Agamemnon.

Oceanus: a river flowing round the whole world.

Olympus: a mountain in the northeastern part of Thessaly; the home of the gods.

Orcus: a god of the Lower World; also the Lower World.

Pergama: the citadel of Troy.

Phlegethon: a river of fire of the Lower World.

Phthia: a city in Thessaly, Greece; the home of Achilles.

Samos: an island off the coast of Asia Minor, famous for its temple of Juno.

Sidon: an ancient city of Phoenicia, from which Tyre was colonized.

Simois: a river near Troy.

Sparta: also called **Lacedaemon**; the capital of Laconia, in Greece.

Styx: a river which surrounded the Lower World.

Tartarus: the abode of the wicked in the Lower World; also the Lower World.

Tenedos: an island in the Aegean Sea, about five miles off the Trojan coast.

Troia: a city in the western part of Asia Minor, captured by stratagem by the Greeks, after a siege of ten years. Also called **Ilium.**

Tyros: a celebrated city of Phoenicia.

Xanthus: a river near Troy.

DEFENSE OF A GREEK SHIP

Ajax, at the left, defends the Greek ship against Hector, who is followed by a Trojan carrying a torch with which he attempts to set the ship afire.

CHAPTER VII

FAMOUS PASSAGES IN THE AENEID

I, *1–7:* Arma virumque canō, Trōiae quī prīmus ab ōrīs
Ītaliam, fātō profugus, Lāvīniaque vēnit
lītora, multum ille et terrīs iactātus et altō
vī superum, saevae memorem Iūnōnis ob īram,
multa quoque et bellō passus, dum conderet urbem,
īnferretque deōs Latiō, genus unde Latīnum,
Albānīque patrēs, atque altae moenia Rōmae.

I, *33:* Tantae mōlis erat Rōmānam condere gentem!

I, *94–96:* Ō terque quaterque beātī,
quīs ante ōra patrum Trōiae sub moenibus altīs
contigit oppetere!

I, *135:* Quōs ego! sed mōtōs praestat compōnere flūctūs.

I, *198–207:* Ō sociī (neque enim ignārī sumus ante malōrum),
ō passī graviōra, dabit deus hīs quoque fīnem.
Vōs et Scyllaeam rabiem penitusque sonantīs
accestis scopulōs, vōs et Cyclōpia saxa
expertī; revocāte animōs, maestumque timōrem
mittite; forsan et haec ōlim meminisse iuvābit.
Per variōs cāsūs, per tot discrīmina rērum
tendimus in Latium, sēdīs ubi Fāta quiētās
ostendunt; illīc fās rēgna resurgere Trōiae.
Dūrāte, et vōsmet rēbus servāte secundīs.

I, *461–462:* Ēn Priamus! Sunt hīc etiam sua praemia laudī,
sunt lacrimae rērum, et mentem mortālia tangunt.

I, *574:* Trōs Tyriusque mihī nūllō discrīmine agētur.

I, *607–609:* In freta dum fluviī current, dum montibus umbrae
lūstrābunt convexa, polus dum sīdera pāscet,
semper honōs nōmenque tuum laudēsque manēbunt.

I, *630:* Nōn ignāra malī, miserīs succurrere discō.

II, *3:* Īnfandum, rēgīna, iubēs renovāre dolōrem.

II, *48–49:* Equō nē crēdite, Teucrī.
Quidquid id est, timeō Danaōs et dōna ferentīs.

II, *311–312:* Iam proximus ārdet
Ūcalegōn.

II, *324–326:* Vēnit summa diēs et inēluctābile tempus
Dardaniae. Fuimus Trōes, fuit Īlium et ingēns
glōria Teucrōrum.

II, *354:* Ūna salūs victīs nūllam spērāre salūtem.

II, *367:* Quondam etiam victīs redit in praecordia virtūs.

II, *390:* Dolus an virtūs, quis in hoste requīrat?

II, *428:* Dīs aliter vīsum.

II, *774:* Obstipuī, steteruntque comae, et vōx faucibus haesit.

III, *56–57:* Quid nōn mortālia pectora cōgis,
aurī sacra famēs!

IV, *13:* Dēgenerēs animōs timor arguit.

IV, *173–177:* Extemplō Libyae magnās it Fāma per urbīs,
Fāma, malum quā non aliud vēlōcius ūllum.
Mōbilitāte viget vīrīsque adquīrit eundō;
parva metū prīmō, mox sēsē attollit in aurās,
ingrediturque solō, et caput inter nūbila condit.

IV, *296:* Quis fallere possit amantem?

IV, *412:* Improbe Amor, quid nōn mortālia pectora cōgis!

IV, *522–532:* Nox erat, et placidum carpēbant fessa sopōrem
corpora per terrās, silvaeque et saeva quiērant
aequora, cum mediō volvuntur sīdera lāpsū,
cum tacet omnis ager, pecudēs pictaeque volucrēs,
quaeque lacūs lātē liquidōs quaeque aspera dūmīs
rūra tenent, somnō positae sub nocte silentī.
Lēnībant cūrās et corda oblīta labōrum.
At nōn īnfēlīx animī Phoenissa nec umquam
solvitur in somnōs oculīsve aut pectore noctem
accipit; ingeminant cūrae, rūrsusque resurgēns
saevit amor, magnōque īrārum flūctuat aestū.

IV, *569–570:* Varium et mūtābile semper
fēmina.

IV, *625*: Exoriāre aliquis nostrīs ex ossibus ultor!

IV, *700–705*: Ergō Īris croceīs per caelum rōscida pinnīs
mīlle trahēns variōs adversō sōle colōrēs
dēvolat, et suprā caput adstitit. "Hunc ego Dītī
sacrum iussa ferō, tēque istō corpore solvō."
Sic ait, et dextrā crīnem secat; omnis et ūnā
dīlāpsus calor, atque in ventōs vīta recessit.

V, *231*: Possunt, quia posse videntur.

V, *710*: Quidquid erit, superanda omnis fortūna ferendō est.

VI, *95–96*: Tū nē cēde malīs, sed contrā audentior ītō
quam tua tē fortūna sinet.

VI, *126–129*: Trōs Anchīsiadē, facilis dēscēnsus Avernō
(noctīs atque diēs patet ātrī iānua Dītis);
sed revocāre gradum superāsque ēvādere ad aurās,
hoc opus, hic labor est.

VI, *620*: Discite iūstitiam monitī et nōn temnere dīvōs.

VI, *847–853*: Excūdent aliī spīrantia mollius aera
(crēdō equidem), vīvōs dūcent dē marmore vultūs,
ōrābunt causās melius, caelīque meātūs
dēscrībent radiō, et surgentia sīdera dīcent:
tū regere imperiō populōs, Rōmāne, mementō
(hae tibi erunt artēs), pācisque impōnere mōrem,
parcere subiectīs, et dēbellāre superbōs.

VII, *312*: Flectere sī nequeō superōs, Acheronta movēbō.

X, *467–469*: Stat sua cuique diēs; breve et irreparābile tempus
omnibus est vītae; sed fāmam extendere factīs,
hoc virtūtis opus.

X, *501*: Nescia mēns hominum fātī sortisque futūrae
et servāre modum, rēbus sublāta secundīs!

XII, *153*: Forsan miserōs meliōra sequentur.

CHAPTER VIII

SCANSION

The *Aeneid* and the *Metamorphoses* are written in **dactylic hexameter;** that is, each verse consists of six feet, the first four of which may be either dactyls (— ⏑ ⏑) or spondees (— —), the fifth regularly a dactyl, and the last either a spondee or a trochee (— ⏑). A complete line may therefore be represented thus:

´— ⏑ ⏑	´— ⏑ ⏑	´— ⏑ ⏑	´— ⏑ ⏑	´— ⏑ ⏑	´— —
´— —	´— —	´— —	´— —	´— ⏑ ⏑	´— ⏑

The fifth foot is occasionally a spondee, in which case the verse is termed **spondaic.**

" A preponderance of dactyls gives to a verse a light, graceful, rapid movement; a preponderance of spondees gives a slow, solemn, stately movement." " Rapid movement accords with joy, excitement, and passion, while slow movement harmonizes with solemnity, sadness, weariness, and kindred ideas." Contrast, for example, the following verses:

(*a*) torquet a | gens cir | cum, et rapi | dus vorat | aequore | vertex

(*b*) appa | rent ra | ri nan | tes in | gurgite | vasto

The following hints will help the student **scan** the *Aeneid* and the *Metamorphoses:*

1. Elide syllables wherever elision is possible; *i.e.* whenever a word ends with a vowel, diphthong, or **m** preceded by a vowel, and the following word begins with a vowel or **h,** elide the first vowel, diphthong, or final **m** with its preceding vowel.
2. Mark by a macron (—) those vowels that are naturally long and those that are long by position, *i.e.* short vowels that are followed

by two consonants. But if the two consonants are a mute followed by **l** or **r**, the syllable may be either long or short (in Vergil it is regularly short).

3. Mark all diphthongs long.
4. Mark all other vowels short.
5. Remember that a vowel followed by another vowel is short.
6. Remember that the last foot is always a spondee or a trochee, and that the fifth is regularly a dactyl.

Applying the above hints to the first seven verses of the Aeneid we have the following scheme:

Arma vi | rumque ca | nō, Trō | iae quī | prīmus ab | ōrīs

Ītali | am, fā | tō profu | gus, Lā | vīniaque | vēnit

lītora | , multum il | le et ter | rīs iac | tātus et | altō

vī supe | rum, sae | vae memo | rem Iū | nōnis ob | īram,

multa quo | que et bel | lō pas | sus, dum | conderet | urbem,

īnfer | retque de | ōs Lati | ō, genus | unde La | tīnum,

Albā | nīque pa | trēs, at | que altae | moenia | Rōmae.

TERMS OF PROSODY

Arsis: the unaccented part of a foot (*i.e.* that part of a foot other than the initial long syllable).

Caesura: the pause occasioned by the ending of a word within a metrical foot.

Dactyl: a metrical foot of three syllables, a long syllable followed by two short syllables (– ⏑ ⏑, lītŏră).

Diaeresis: the pause occasioned by the ending of a word at the end of a metrical foot.

Diastole: the lengthening of a short syllable (vidēt).

Elision: the slurring together of a final vowel or diphthong (or final **m** and its preceding vowel) with the first syllable of a following word beginning with a vowel or **h.**

Hexameter: a verse of six metrical feet.

Hiatus: the omission of elision, where elision would be expected (Sămō hīc).

Ictus: the stress of voice placed upon syllables at regular intervals in a metrical system. It is usually marked by ʹ.

Spondee: a metrical foot of two long syllables (– –, lātē).

Syllaba anceps: the last syllable of a dactylic hexameter, because such a syllable may be either long or short.

Synizesis: the slurring together of vowels within a word so as to form one syllable (de͡inde; aure͡a).

Systole: the shortening of a long syllable (stetĕrunt).

Thesis: The accented part of a foot (*i.e.* the initial long syllable).

DEATH OF ACHILLES

Ajax, in the center, supports the corpse of Achilles. He is looking at Aeneas, who is fighting with Neoptolemus, the son of Achilles. The right side of the picture shows Menelaus engaged in combat with Paris.

CHAPTER IX

DEVICES OF STYLE AND GRAMMAR

Alliteration: the repetition of the same letter, generally at the beginning of successive words.

magnō cum **m**urmure **m**ontis

Ille **p**atris magnī **p**ārēre **p**arābat

imperiō, et **p**rīmum **p**edibus tālāria nectit.

Anaphora: the repetition of the same word at the beginning of successive clauses or phrases.

saevus **ubi** Aeacidae tēlō iacet Hector, **ubi** ingēns

Sarpēdōn, **ubi** tot Simoīs. . . .

Hīc Dolopum manus, **hīc** saevus tendēbat Achillēs;

classibus **hīc** locus; **hīc** aciē certāre solēbant.

Anastrophe: the placing of a preposition after the word it governs.

Fronte **sub** adversā

maria omnia **circum**

Quōs **inter** medius vēnit furor.

Aposiopesis: an abrupt pause in a sentence.

quōs ego —! sed mōtōs praestat compōnere flūctūs.

(The punishment which Neptune will inflict is left to the imagination of the winds.)

Asyndeton: the omission of the connective.

urbe, domō sociās.

Nāvem in cōnspectū nūllam, trīs lītore cervōs

prōspicit errantīs.

Chiasmus: the arrangement of words in inverse order.

luctantīs ventōs tempestātēsque sonōrās

(Adjective Noun Noun Adjective)

Īlionēa petit dextrā laevāque Serestum

(Accusative Ablative Ablative Accusative)

Hendiadys: The expression of an idea by two nouns connected by a conjunction, instead of a noun modified by an adjective or by another noun in the genitive.

mōlemque et montīs īnsuper altōs
imposuit (instead of **mōlem montium**)

Hysteron proteron: a reversal of the natural or logical order of ideas.

disiēcitque ratīs ēvertitque aequora ventīs.

Litotes: the expression of an affirmative by the negative of its opposite.

operum **haud ignāra** Minervae

Metaphor: an implied comparison.

lūce sedet custōs

Metonymy: the use of one word for another that it suggests.

Cerēs = frūmentum
Bacchus = vīnum

Onomatopeia: the adaptation of sound to sense in the use of words.

īnsequitur clāmorque virum strīdorque rudentum.
quadrupedante putrem sonitū quatit ungula campum
(representing the galloping of a horse).

Oxymoron: the use of contradictory terms.

via invia = *a trackless track*

Personification: the treatment of inanimate things as if they were persons.

gaudet pater Appennīnus
vocat iam carbasus aurās

Polysyndeton: frequent repetition of the connective with several words.

Thessandrus Sthenelus**que** ducēs, **et** dīrus Ulixēs,
dēmissum lāpsī per fūnem, Acamās**que**, Thoās**que**,
Pēlīdēs**que** Neoptolemus, prīmus**que** Machāōn,
et Menelāus, **et** ipse dolī fabricātor Epēos.

Prolepsis: the use of a word before the action makes it logically appropriate.

submersās obrue puppīs = *overwhelm and sink the ships.*

Simile: an expressed comparison.

Ac velutī magnō in populō, etc., etc.

Synchysis: interlocked word order.

saevae *memorem* **Iūnōnis** ob *īram*

Synecdoche: the use of a part for the whole.

puppis (*stern*) for nāvis (*ship*)

tēctum (*roof*) for domus (*house*)

Tmesis: the separation of the two parts of a compound word by another word or words.

circum dea **fūdit** amictū

quae mē **cumque** vocant terrae

Zeugma: the use of a verb with two words to only one of which it strictly applies.

iūra magistrātūsque legunt sānctumque senātum.

THE DISAGREEING GODDESSES

The three goddesses, Aphrodite, Athena, and Hera, are being led by Hermes to Paris.

CHAPTER X

SUMMARY OF THE MOST IMPORTANT CHARACTERISTICS OF THE GRAMMAR OF VERGIL

NOUNS

Genitive

1. **Appositional.**

   urbem **Patavī,** *the city of Patavium,* instead of **Patavium** in apposition with **urbem**

2. **Specification with Adjectives.**

   fessī **rērum,** *weary of troubles*

   dīves **opum,** *rich in resources*

3. **Partitive.**

   (*a*) With the positive of an adjective

   sāncte **deōrum,** *holy deity* (of the gods)

   (*b*) With neuter adjectives or neuter participles used substantively

   opāca **locōrum,** *dark places*

   strāta **viārum,** *the pavements of the streets*

4. **With Verbs of Plenty and Want.**

   implentur **veteris Bacchī,** *they fill themselves with old wine.*

Dative

5. **Dative of Agent with the Passive Voice in Any Tense.**

   Quippe vetor **Fātīs,** *to be sure, I am forbidden by the Fates.*

   ōra, deī iussū nōn umquam crēdita **Teucrīs,** *lips which by order of the god were never believed by the Trojans*

6. **Dative of Limit of Motion.**

   īnferretque deōs **Latiō,** *and bring the gods to Latium*

   it clāmor **caelō,** *the shout mounts upward to the sky.*

   (In prose this construction is usually expressed by the Accusative with **in** or **ad.**)

7. **Dative of Association with Verbs.**

placitōne etiam pugnābis **amōrī**? *will you struggle even against a pleasing love?*

ACCUSATIVE

8. **Accusative of Specification.**

nūda **genū**, *with knee bare* (*bare as to the knee*)

ōs umerōsque deō similis, *in face and shoulders like a god*

NOTE. — This construction is often called the *Greek Accusative.*

9. **Accusative with the Middle Voice** (*i.e.* the Passive Voice with a Reflexive Meaning).

lacrimīs **oculōs** suffūsa, *having drenched her eyes with tears*

nōdōque **sinūs** collēcta **fluentīs**, *having gathered her flowing robes in a knot*

tūnsae **pectora**, *beating their breasts*

exuviās indūtus Achillī, *clad in the spoils of Achilles*

inūtile ferrum cingitur, *he girds on the useless steel.*

10. **Accusative of Limit of Motion without a Preposition.**

Ītaliam vēnit, *he came to Italy.*

11. **Accusative with Intransitive Verbs.**

nec vōx **hominem** sonat, *and your voice has no human ring.*

ABLATIVE

12. **Locative Ablative without a Preposition.**

terrīs et **altō**, *on land and sea*

lītore aēna locant aliī, *others place the brazen caldrons on the shore.*

13. **Ablative of the Place from Which without a Preposition.**

dētrūdunt nāvīs **scopulō**, *they shove off the ships from the rock.*

Tyriā urbe profecta, *who set out from the city of Tyre*

14. **Ablative of Manner without *cum*.**

turbine, *in a whirlwind*

cumulō, *in a mass*

VERBS

15. **Simple Verb for Compound Verb.**
    vertere for **ēvertere**
    volvere for **ēvolvere**
    temnere for **contemnere**
16. **Periphrasis with *dare*.**
    ruīnam dare instead of **ruere**
    sonitum dare instead of **resonāre**
    gemitum dare instead of **gemere**
17. **The Perfect Participle of Deponents Used with Passive Force.**
    pelagō **remēnsō**, *having recrossed the sea*
    comitātus Achātē, *attended by Achates*
18. **Infinitive of Purpose, especially with Verbs of Motion.**
    Nōn nōs **populāre** vēnimus, *we have not come to lay waste.*
19. **Infinitive instead of a Substantive Clause with the Subjunctive introduced by *ut*.**
    tot **adīre** labōrēs impulerit, *forced to face so many toils*
    hortāmur **fārī**, *we urge him to speak.*
    celerāre fugam suādet, *he urges her to hasten flight.*
20. **Infinitive with Nouns.**
    amor cāsūs **cognōscere** nostrōs, *desire to learn our disasters*
    quae cūra nitentīs **pāscere** equōs, *what care in keeping sleek steeds*
21. **Infinitive with Adjectives.**
    certa **morī**, *bent on death*
    maior **vidērī**, *taller to behold (to be seen)*
22. **Infinitive in Exclamations.**
    Mēne inceptō **dēsistere**, *what! I desist from my purpose!*
23. **Perfect Infinitive instead of the Present for Metrical Convenience.**
    magnum sī pectore possit **excussisse** deum, *if perchance she may shake off the mighty god from off her breast*
24. **Prohibitions with *nē* and the Imperative instead of *nōlī* (*nōlīte*) with the Infinitive.**
    Nē saevī, *be not angry.*
    Equō **nē crēdite**, *do not trust the horse.*

MISCELLANEOUS DIFFERENCES

25. **Perfect Participle with Present Force.**
    caelō **invectus** apertō, *riding under a clear sky*
    tūnsae pectora, *beating their breasts*
26. **Plural of a Noun for the Singular.**
    (*a*) For metrical convenience:
    montīs, silentia, incendia
    (*b*) To denote repeated instances of the quality:
    īrae, furiās, morae
    (*c*) To describe places fully:
    ōstia, Pergama, templa
27. **Collective Singular for the Plural.**
    custōde = **custōdibus**
    sine **rēmige** = sine **rēmigibus**
28. **The Neuter of Adjectives and Participles Used Substantively.**
    altō, *the sea*
    inceptō, *purpose*
    ultima, *death*
    meritīs, *services*
29. **The Use of *et* for *etiam*.**
    Sunt **et** (= **etiam**) Siculīs regiōnibus urbēs

ARCHAIC AND POETIC FORMS

Nouns

1. **First Declension.**
   -āī for **-ae** in the Genitive Singular:
   aulāī for **aulae**
   aurāī for **aurae**
   -um for **-ārum** in the Genitive Plural:
   Aeneadum for **Aeneadārum**
   caelicolum for **caelicolārum**
2. **Second Declension.**
   -um for **-ōrum** in the Genitive Plural:
   superum for **superōrum**
   deum for **deōrum**

3. **Fourth Declension.**

-ū for **-uī** in the Dative Singular:

currū for **curruī**

metū for **metuī**

-um for **-uum** in the Genitive Plural:

currum for **curruum**

Pronouns

4. **ollī** for **illī**
ollīs for **illīs**
quīs for **quibus**
mī for **mihi**

Verbs

5. The Ending **-ier** for **-ī** in the Present Infinitive Passive.

accingier for **accingī**

-ībat for **-iēbat,** and **-ībant** for **-iēbant** in the Imperfect Indicative Active of the Fourth Conjugation:

lēnībat for **lēniēbat**
lēnībant for **lēniēbant**

-ēre for **-ērunt** in the Third Person Plural of the Perfect Indicative Active:

tenuēre for **tenuērunt**

latuēre for **latuērunt**

6. **Syncopated Forms in the Perfect and Pluperfect:**

accestis = **accessistis**
exstīnxtī = **exstīnxistī**
exstīnxem = **exstīnxissem**
dīrēxti = **dīrēxistī**
trāxe = **trāxisse**

CHAPTER XI

SELECTIONS FOR TRANSLATION AT SIGHT

1

Jupiter tells of the transformation of the impious tyrant Lycaon.

Contigerat nostras infamia temporis aures;
quam cupiens falsam summo delabor Olympo
et deus humana lustro sub imagine terras.
Longa mora est, quantum noxae [1] sit ubique repertum
enumerare. Minor fuit ipsa infamia vero.
Maenala [2] transieram latebris horrenda ferarum;
Arcadis [3] hinc sedes et inhospita tecta tyranni
ingredior, traherent cum sera crepuscula [4] noctem.
Signa dedi venisse deum, vulgusque precari
coeperat. Inridet primo pia vota Lycaon,
mox ait: " Experiar, deus hic, discrimine aperto,
an sit mortalis. Nec erit dubitabile verum."
Nocte gravem somno necopina [5] perdere morte
me parat; haec illi placet experientia veri.
. . . . Ego vindice [6] flamma
in dominum dignosque everti tecta Penates.
Territus ipse fugit, nactusque silentia ruris
exululat frustraque loqui conatur; ab ipso
colligit os rabiem, solitaeque cupidine caedis
vertitur in pecudes, et nunc quoque sanguine gaudet;
fit lupus et veteris servat vestigia formae.

Ovid, *Metamorphoses*, i, 211–225, 230–237.

[1] *noxae*, from *noxa*, 'sin.'
[2] *Maenala*, *-orum*, a mountain range.
[3] *Arcadis*, gen. of *Arcas*, 'Arcadian.'
[4] *crepuscula*, from *crepusculum*, 'twilight.'
[5] *necopina*, from *necopinus*, 'unexpected.'
[6] *vindice*, from *vindex*, 'avenging.'

2

Proserpina, while gathering flowers, is carried off by Dis.

Quo dum Proserpina luco
ludit, et aut violas aut candida lilia carpit,
dumque puellari studio calathosque [1] sinumque
implet, et aequales certat superare legendo,
paene simul visa est dilectaque raptaque Diti:
usque adeo [2] est properatus amor. Dea territa maesto
et matrem et comites, sed matrem saepius, ore
clamat. Et, ut summa vestem laniarat [3] ab ora,
collecti flores tunicis cecidere remissis.
Tantaque simplicitas puerilibus affuit annis:
haec quoque virgineum movit iactura [4] dolorem.

Ovid, *Metamorphoses*, v, 391–401.

3

Scylla betrays her father, Nisus, to Minos, by cutting the lock of hair on which his life depends.

Talia dicenti, curarum maxima nutrix,
nox intervenit; tenebrisque audacia crevit.
Prima quies aderat, qua curis fessa diurnis
pectora somnus habet. Thalamos taciturna paternos
intrat, et (heu facinus!) fatali nata parentem
crine suum spoliat, praedaque potita nefanda
per medios hostes — meriti fiducia tanta est —
pervenit ad regem. Quem sic adfata paventem est:
" Suasit amor facinus. Proles ego regia Nisi
Scylla tibi trado patriaeque meosque Penates.
Praemia nulla peto, nisi te. Cape pignus amoris
purpureum crinem, nec me nunc tradere crinem
sed patrium tibi crede caput," scelerataque dextra
munera porrexit.[5] Minos porrecta refugit:

[1] *calathos*, 'baskets.' [2] *usque adeo*, 'to such a degree.' [3] *laniare*, 'to tear.' [4] *iactura*, 'loss.' [5] *porrigere*, 'present.'

"Di te summoveant, o nostri infamia saecli,
orbe suo; tellusque tibi pontusque negetur.
Certe ego non patiar Iovis incunabula,[1] Creten,
qui meus est orbis, tantum contingere monstrum."

Ovid, *Metamorphoses*, viii, 81–100.

4

Orpheus begs Pluto and Persephone to allow the return of Eurydice to life.

"Si licet, et falsi positis [2] ambagibus oris [3]
vera loqui sinitis, non huc, ut opaca viderem
Tartara, descendi, nec uti villosa [4] colubris
terna Medusaei vincirem guttura monstri.[5]
Causa viae coniunx, in quam calcata [6] venenum
vipera diffudit, crescentesque abstulit annos.
Posse pati volui, nec me temptasse negabo:
vicit Amor. Supera deus hic bene notus in ora est:
an sit et hic, dubito, sed hic tamen auguror [7] esse.
Famaque si veteris non est mentita rapinae,
vos quoque iunxit Amor. Per ego haec loca plena timoris,
per Chaos hoc ingens, vastique silentia regni,
Eurydices, oro, properata retexite [8] fata.
Omnia debentur vobis, paulumque morati
serius aut citius sedem properamus ad unam.
Tendimus huc omnes, haec est domus ultima; vosque
humani generis longissima regna tenetis.
Haec quoque, cum iustos matura peregerit annos,
iuris erit vestri. Pro munere poscimus usum.[9]
Quod si fata negant veniam pro coniuge, certum est
nolle redire mihi: leto gaudete duorum."

Ovid, *Metamorphoses*, x, 19–39.

[1] *incunabula*, 'cradle.' [2] *positis ambagibus*, 'without circumlocution.' [3] from *os*. [4] shaggy. [5] refers to Cerberus. [6] trodden on. [7] suppose. [8] spin backward. [9] a loan.

5

Two instances of the perjury of Laomedon.

Inde novae primum moliri moenia Troiae
Laomedonta videt, susceptaque magna labore
crescere difficili nec opes exposcere parvas;
cumque tridentigero tumidi genitore profundi
mortalem induitur formam, Phrygiaeque tyranno
aedificat muros pactus [1] pro moenibus aurum.
Stabat opus; pretium rex infitiatur et addit,
perfidiae cumulum,[2] falsis periuria verbis.
"Non impune feres," rector maris inquit, et omnes
inclinavit aquas ad avarae litora Troiae;
inque freti formam terras complevit, opesque
abstulit agricolis et fluctibus obruit agros.
Poena neque haec satis est; regis quoque filia monstro
poscitur aequoreo. Quam dura ad saxa revinctam
vindicat [3] Alcides, promissaque munera, dictos
poscit equos; tantique operis mercede [4] negata
bis periura capit superatae moenia Troiae.
Nec pars [5] militiae, Telamon sine honore recessit,
Hesioneque [6] data potitur.

Ovid, *Metamorphoses*, xi, 199–217.

6

Ulysses pleads that the arms of the dead Achilles be presented to him rather than to Ajax, who has not brains enough to appreciate their beauty.

"Me miserum, quanto cogor meminisse dolore
temporis illius, quo, Graium murus, Achilles
procubuit! Nec me lacrimae luctusve timorve
tardarunt quin corpus humo sublime referrem.
His umeris, his, inquam, umeris ego corpus Achillis

[1] *pactus*, from *paciscor*, 'make a bargain for.'
[2] *cumulum*, from *cumulus*, 'crowning act.'
[3] *vindicat*, from *vindico*, 'loose.'
[4] *mercede*, from *merces*, 'pay.'
[5] *pars*, 'partner.'
[6] *Hesione* is the *regis filia*.

et simul arma tuli, quae nunc quoque ferre laboro.
Sunt mihi, quae valeant in talia pondera, vires;
est animus certe vestros sensurus honores.
Scilicet idcirco [1] pro nato caerula mater [2]
ambitiosa suo fuit, ut caelestia dona,
artis opus tantae, rudis [3] et sine pectore miles
indueret? Neque enim clipei caelamina [4] norit,[5]
Oceanum et terras cumque alto sidera caelo,
diversasque urbes nitidumque Orionis ensem.
Per spes nunc socias casuraque moenia Troum,
perque deos oro quos hosti nuper ademi,[6]
per si quid superest quod sit sapienter agendum,
este mei memores! Aut si mihi non datis arma,
huic date!" — et ostendit signum fatale Minervae.

Ovid, *Metamorphoses*, xiii, 280–294, 375–381.

7

Hecuba's lament after Polyxena has been sacrificed on the tomb of Achilles.

"Nata, tuae (quid enim superest?) dolor ultime matri,
nata, iaces; videoque tuum, mea vulnera, vulnus.
En, ne perdiderim quemquam sine caede meorum,
tu quoque vulnus habes. At te, quia femina, rebar
a ferro tutam. Cecidisti et femina ferro;
totque tuos idem fratres, te perdidit idem,
exitium Troiae nostrique orbator,[7] Achilles.
At postquam cecidit Paridis Phoebique sagittis,
nunc certe, dixi, non est metuendus Achilles.
Nunc quoque mi metuendus erat, cinis ipse sepulti
in genus hoc saevit, tumulo quoque sensimus hostem.
Nunc trahor exsul, inops, tumulis avulsa meorum,

[1] *idcirco*, 'for this.'
[2] *caerula mater*, she was a sea goddess.
[3] *rudis*, 'rough.'
[4] *caelamina*, 'figures' (on the shield).
[5] *norit*, shortened form of *noverit*.
[6] *ademi*, from *adimo*, 'take away.'
[7] *nostri orbator*, 'the one who has deprived me of my children.'

Penelopae munus. Quae me data pensa trahentem [1]
matribus ostendens Ithacis ' haec Hectoris illa est
clara parens, haec est,' dicet, ' Priameia coniunx.'
Postque tot amissos tu nunc, quae sola levabas
maternos luctus, hostilia busta [2] piasti.
Inferias [3] hosti peperi. Quo [4] ferrea resto?
Quidve moror? Quo [4] me servas, annosa senectus?"

Ovid, *Metamorphoses*, xiii, 494–517.

8

Aeneas consults the Sibyl and enters the Lower World.

Has [5] ubi praeteriit et Parthenopeia [6] dextra
moenia deseruit, laeva de parte canori
Aeolidae tumulum et loca feta palustribus undis,
litora Cumarum, vivacisque [7] antra Sibyllae
intrat, et ad Manis veniat per Averna paternos
orat. At illa diu vultum tellure moratum
erexit, tandemque deo furibunda recepto.
" Magna petis," dixit, " vir factis maxime, cuius
dextera per ferrum, pietas spectata [8] per ignes.
Pone tamen, Troiane, metum; potiere petitis,
Elysiasque domos et regna novissima mundi [9]
me duce cognosces simulacraque cara parentis.
Invia virtuti nulla est via." Dixit, et auro
fulgentem ramum silva Iunonis Avernae
monstravit, iussitque suo divellere trunco.
Paruit Aeneas, et formidabilis Orci
vidit opes atavosque [10] suos umbramque senilem
magnanimi Anchisae. Didicit quoque iura locorum,
quaeque novis essent adeunda pericula bellis.

Ovid, *Metamorphoses*, xiv, 101–119.

[1] *data pensa trahere*, 'to spin the allotted wool.' [2] *busta*, from *bustum*, 'tomb.'
[3] *inferias*, 'funeral offerings.' [4] *quo*, 'for what.'
[5] *Has* refers to scenes previously described.
[6] Adjective from *Parthenope*, an early name of Naples.
[7] long-lived, venerable. [8] tested. [9] world. [10] ancestors.

9

Achaemenides tells Macareus of his gratitude to the Trojans for rescue from a cruel death.

Macareus, comes experientis Ulixei,
desertum quondam mediis sub rupibus Aetnae
noscit Achaemeniden, improvisoque repertum
vivere miratus, "Qui te casusve deusve
servat, Achaemenide? Cur," inquit, "barbara Graium
prora vehit? Petitur vestra quae terra carina?"
Talia quaerenti, iam non hirsutus [1] amictu,
fatur Achaemenides: "Iterum Polyphemon et illos
aspiciam fluidos humano sanguine rictus,[2]
si minus Aenean veneror genitore. Nec umquam
esse satis potero, praestem [3] licet omnia, gratus.
Quod loquor et spiro caelumque et sidera solis
respicio, possimne ingratus et immemor esse?
Ille dedit quod non anima haec Cyclopis in ora
venit.
Talia fingebam misero mihi fata parari.
Perque dies multos latitans,[4] omnemque tremescens
ad strepitum, mortemque timens, cupidusque moriri,
solus, inops, exspes, leto poenaeque relictus,
hanc procul aspexi longo post tempore navem,
oravique fugam gestu, ad litusque cucurri,
et movi; Graiumque ratis Troiana recepit."

Ovid, *Metamorphoses*, xiv, 159–175, 213–220.

10

A Greek tells how he and his companions, coming to the palace of Circe, were frightened, but not hurt, by the beasts in front of it.

Sorte sumus lecti. Sors me fidumque Politen,
bisque novem socios Circaea ad moenia misit.

[1] *hirsutus*, 'squalid.'
[2] *rictus*, 'jaws.'
[3] *praestem*, 'do.'
[4] *latitans*, compare *lateo*.

Quae simul attigimus, stetimusque in limine tecti,
mille lupi mixtaeque lupis ursaeque leaeque [1]
occursu fecere metum. Sed nulla timenda,
nullaque erat nostro factura in corpore vulnus.
Quin etiam blandas movere per aera caudas,
nostraque adulantes [2] comitant vestigia, donec
excipiunt famulae, perque atria marmore tecta
ad dominam ducunt. Pulchro sedet illa recessu.

Ovid, *Metamorphoses*, xiv, 251–261.

11

The Sibyl and Scipio see the shade of Homer.

Atque hic Elysio tendentem limite [3] cernens
effigiem iuvenis, caste cui vitta ligabat [4]
purpurea effusos per colla nitentia crines,
"Dic," ait, "hic quisnam, virgo? Nam luce refulget
praecipua frons sacra viro, multaeque sequuntur
mirantes animae et laeto clamore frequentant.
Qui vultus! Quam, si Stygia non esset in umbra,
dixissem facile esse deum!" "Non falleris," inquit
docta comes Triviae; "meruit deus esse videri,
et fuit in tanto non parvum pectore numen.
Carmine complexus terram, mare, sidera, Manis
et cantu Musas et Phoebum aequavit honore.
Atque haec cuncta, prius quam cerneret, ordine terris
prodidit [5] ac vestram tulit usque ad sidera Troiam."
Scipio perlustrans oculis laetantibus umbram,
"Si nunc fata darent ut Romula facta per orbem
hic caneret vates, quanto maiora futuros
facta eadem intrarent [6] hoc," inquit, "teste nepotes!
Felix Aeacide, cui tali contigit ore
gentibus ostendi! Crevit tua carmine virtus."

Silius Italicus, *Punica*, xiii, 778–797.

[1] *lea*, 'a lioness.'
[2] *adulari*, 'to fawn.'
[3] *limite*, 'path.'
[4] *ligare*, 'bind.'
[5] *prodere*, 'describe.'
[6] *intrare*, 'inspire.'

12

Jason asks Medea's help in gaining the golden fleece.

At ille
excepit [1] blandoque prior sic ore locutus:
" O decus in nostros magnum ventura Penates,
solaque tantarum virgo haud indigna viarum
causa reperta mihi, iam iam non ulla requiro
vellera teque meae satis est quaesisse carinae.
Verum age et hoc etiam, quando potes, adice tantis
muneribus meritisque tuis; namque aurea iussi
terga referre sumus, socios ea gloria tangit."
Sic ait, et primis supplex dedit oscula palmis.
Contra virgo novis iterum singultibus [2] orsa est:
" Linquo domos patrias te propter opesque meorum;
nec iam nunc regina loquor, sceptrisque relictis
vota sequor. Serva hanc profugae, prior ipse dedisti
quam (scis nempe [3]) fidem. Di nostris vocibus adsunt,
sidera et haec te meque vident. Tecum aequora, tecum
experiar quascumque vias, modo ne quis abactam
huc referat me forte dies oculisque parentis
ingerar.[4] Hoc superos, hoc te quoque deprecor, hospes."

Valerius Flaccus, *Argonautica*, viii, 35–53.

13

The Colchians discover the flight of Medea and Jason.

Interea patrias [5] saevus venit horror ad aures,
fata domus ductumque ferens, fraudemque fugamque
virginis. Hinc subitis infelix frater in armis,
urbs etiam mox tota coit; volat ipse senectae
immemor Aeetes. Complentur litora bello
nequiquam; fugit immissis nam puppis habenis.
Mater adhuc ambas tendebat in aequora palmas,

[1] *excepit*, supply *Medeam*. [2] *singultibus*, 'sobs.' [3] *nempe*, 'certainly.'
[4] *ingerar*, 'thrust upon.' [5] *patrias* refers to Aeetes.

et soror, atque omnes aliae matresque nurusque
Colchides, aequalesque tibi, Medea, puellae.
Exstat sola parens, impletque ululatibus auras:
"Siste fugam, medio refer huc ex aequore puppim;
nata, potes. Quo," clamat, "abis? Hic turba tuorum
omnis, et iratus nondum pater; haec tua tellus
sceptraque. Quid terris solam te credis Achaeis?
Quis locus Inachias [1] inter tibi, barbara, natas?"
Ipsa fugit, tantoque (nefas!) ipsa ardet amore.

Valerius Flaccus, *Argonautica*, viii, 134–148, 159.

14

Hector upbraids Paris, and urges that he fight in single combat with Menelaus.

Iamque duae stabant acies fulgentibus armis,
cum Paris, exitium Troiae funestaque flamma,
armatum adverso Menelaum ex agmine cernit,
seque velut viso perterritus angue recepit
ad socios amens. Quem postquam turpiter Hector
confusum terrore videt, "O dedecus,[2]" inquit,
"aeternum patriae generisque infamia nostri,
terga refers? Ubi sunt vires, ubi cognita nobis
ludorum quondam vario in certamine virtus?
Hic animos ostende tuos; nihil adiuvat arma
nobilitas formae; duro Mars milite gaudet."
Dixit. Quem contra paucis Priameius heros,
"Quid nimis indignis," inquit, "me vocibus urges,
O patriae, germane, decus? Nam nec mihi coniunx
privaque luxuria [3] est potior virtutis honore,
nec vires temptare viri dextramque recuso,
dum modo victorem coniunx cum pace sequatur."

Ilias Latina, 252–268.

[1] *Inachias*, 'of Inachus.' [2] *dedecus*, opposite of *decus*.
[3] *priva luxuria*, 'self-indulgence.'

15

Diomedes and Ulysses surprise Dolon, a Trojan scout.

Dumque iter horrendum loca per nota paventes
carpebant,[1] venit ecce Dolon, quem Troia pubes
miserat, ut Danaum sollerti[2] pectore vires
perspiceret sensusque ducum plebisque referret.
Quem procul ut vidit socius Diomedis Ulixes,
abdiderunt occultantes sua corpora furtim
post densos frutices,[3] dum spe percussus[4] inani
Tros Eumediades[5] cursu praecederet illos.
Post ubi transierat fidens animoque manuque,
prosiluere[6] viri iuvenemque evadere cursu
conantem capiunt ferroque manuque minantur.
Ille timore pavens "Vitam concedite" dixit,
"hoc unum satis est; quod si perstatis in ira,
quanta ex morte mea capietis praemia laudis?
At si cur veniam tacitis exquiritis umbris:
maxima Troia mihi currum promisit Achillis,
si vestras cepisset opes. Haec dona secutus
in dubios casus, coram quod cernitis ipsi,
infelix cecidi."

Ilias Latina, 703–722.

16

The Trojans mourn Hector. King Priam begs Achilles to give him the body of his son.

Flent miseri amissum Phryges Hectora, totaque maesto
Troia sonat planctu![7] Fundit miseranda querelas[8]
infelix Hecube[9] saevisque arat unguibus[10] ora,
Andromacheque suas scindit de pectore vestes,
heu tanto spoliata viro! Ruit omnis in uno
Hectore causa Phrygum; ruit et defessa senectus
adflicti miseranda patris, quem nec sua coniunx

[1] *carpere*, 'to pursue.' [2] shrewd. [3] bushes. [4] dazzled.
[5] Eumedes was the father of Dolon. [6] *prosilire*, 'to leap out.' [7] lamentation.
[8] complaints. [9] = Hecuba [10] nails

turbaque natorum nec magni gloria regni
oblitum tenuit vitae, quin iret inermis
et solum invicti castris se redderet hostis.
Mirantur Danaum proceres, miratur et ipse
Aeacides animum miseri senis. Ille trementes,
adfusus [1] genibus, tendens ad sidera palmas
haec ait: "O Graiae gentis fortissime Achilles,
O regnis inimice meis, te Dardana solum
victa tremit pubes, te sensit nostra senectus
crudelem nimium. Nunc sis mitissimus, oro,
et patris adflicti genibus miserere precantis
donaque quae porto miseri pro corpore nati
accipias."

Ilias Latina, 1015–1034.

17

Pluto, carrying away Proserpina to the Lower World, strives to console her.

"Desine funestis [2] animum, Proserpina, curis
et vano vexare metu. Maiora dabuntur
sceptra nec indigni taedas patiere mariti.
Amissum ne crede diem; sunt altera nobis
sidera, sunt orbes alii, lumenque videbis
purius Elysiumque magis mirabere solem.
Parva loquor; quidquid liquidus complectitur aer,
quidquid alit tellus, quidquid maris aequora verrunt,
quod fluvii volvunt, quod nutrivere paludes,
cuncta tuis pariter cedent animalia regnis.
Sub tua purpurei venient vestigia reges,
deposito luxu, turba cum paupere mixti
(omnia mors aequat); tu damnatura nocentes,
tu requiem latura piis; te iudice, sontes [3]
improba cogentur vitae commissa fateri.
Accipe Lethaeo famulas cum gurgite Parcas,
sitque ratum [4] quodcumque voles."

Claudian, *De Raptu Proserpinae*, ii, 277–293.

[1] casting himself down. [2] gloomy. [3] guilty. [4] ratified.

18

Ilioneus gives reasons why King Latinus should welcome the Trojans.

Dixerat, et dicta Ilioneus sic voce secutus:
"Rex, genus egregium Fauni, nec fluctibus actos
atra subegit hiems vestris succedere terris,
nec sidus regione viae litusve fefellit;
consilio hanc omnes animisque volentibus urbem
adferimur pulsi regnis, quae maxima quondam
extremo veniens Sol aspiciebat Olympo.
Ab Iove principium generis, Iove Dardana pubes
gaudet avo, rex ipse Iovis de gente suprema
Troius Aeneas tua nos ad limina misit.
Non erimus regno indecores, nec vestra feretur
fama levis tantive abolescet [1] gratia facti,
nec Troiam Ausonios gremio excepisse pigebit.[2]
Fata per Aeneae iuro dextramque potentem,
sive fide seu quis bello est expertus et armis:
multi nos populi, multae (ne temne, quod ultro
praeferimus manibus vittas ac verba precantia)
et petiere sibi et voluere adiungere gentes;
sed nos fata deum vestras exquirere terras
imperiis egere suis."

Aeneid, vii, 212–221, 231–240.

19

Iulus, while hunting, wounds a pet stag.

Cervus erat forma praestanti et cornibus ingens,
Tyrrhidae pueri quem matris ab ubere raptum
nutribant Tyrrhusque pater, cui regia parent
armenta et late custodia credita campi.
Adsuetum imperiis soror omni Silvia cura
mollibus intexens ornabat cornua sertis,
pectebatque [3] ferum puroque in fonte lavabat.

[1] fade away. [2] repent. [3] *pectebat*, from *pecto*, 'comb.'

Ille, manum patiens mensaeque adsuetus erili,[1]
errabat silvis, rursusque ad limina nota
ipse domum sera quamvis [2] se nocte ferebat.
Hunc procul errantem rabidae venantis Iuli
commovere canes . . . .
Ipse etiam, eximiae laudis succensus amore,
Ascanius curvo direxit spicula [3] cornu.[4]
Saucius at quadrupes nota intra tecta refugit
successitque gemens stabulis, questuque cruentus
atque imploranti similis tectum omne replebat.
Silvia prima soror, palmis percussa lacertos,[5]
auxilium vocat et duros conclamat agrestis.

Aeneid, vii, 483–504.

20

The Gates of War.

Mos erat Hesperio in Latio, quem protinus urbes
Albanae coluere sacrum — nunc maxima rerum
Roma colit — cum prima movent in proelia Martem.
Sunt geminae Belli portae (sic nomine dicunt),
religione sacrae et saevi formidine Martis;
centum aerei claudunt vectes [6] aeternaque ferri
robora, nec custos absistit limine Ianus:
haec, ubi certa sedet patribus sententia pugnae,
insignis [7] reserat [8] stridentia limina consul,
ipse vocat pugnas; sequitur tum cetera pubes,
aereaque adsensu conspirant cornua rauco.
Hoc et tum Aeneadis indicere bella Latinus
more iubebatur tristisque recludere portas.
Abstinuit tactu pater aversusque refugit
foeda ministeria, et caecis se condidit umbris.
Tum regina deum caelo delapsa morantis

[1] *erili*, adjective derived from *erus*, 'master.' [2] *sera quamvis*, 'however late.' [3] *spicula*, 'arrows.' [4] *cornu*, 'bow.' [5] *lacertos*, 'arms.' [6] bars. [7] *i.e.*, in robes of state. [8] unbars.

impulit ipsa manu portas, et cardine verso
belli ferratos rumpit Saturnia postis.

Aeneid, vii, 601–603, 607–611, 613–622.

21

The river-god Tiber appears to the sleeping Aeneas and encourages him.

"O sate gente deum, Troianam ex hostibus urbem
qui revehis nobis aeternaque Pergama servas,
exspectate solo Laurenti arvisque Latinis,
hic tibi certa domus, certi — ne absiste — Penates;
ne belli terrere minis; tumor omnis et irae
concessere deum.
Haud incerta cano. Nunc qua ratione quod instat
expedias victor, paucis, adverte, docebo.
Arcades his oris, genus a Pallante profectum,
delegere locum et posuere in montibus urbem
Pallantis proavi de nomine Pallanteum:
Hos castris adhibe socios, et foedera iunge.
Surge age, nate dea, primisque cadentibus astris
Iunoni fer rite preces, iramque minasque
supplicibus supera votis. Mihi victor honorem
persolves. Ego sum, pleno quem flumine cernis
stringentem [1] ripas et pinguia culta secantem,
caeruleus Thybris, caelo gratissimus amnis."

Aeneid, viii, 36–64 (adapted).

22

The Trojan embassy arrives at the court of Evander.

Forte die sollemnem illo rex Arcas honorem
Amphitryoniadae [2] magno divisque ferebat
ante urbem in luco. Pallas huic filius una,
una omnes iuvenum primi pauperque senatus

[1] lightly-laving. [2] *i.e.*, Hercules.

tura dabant, tepidusque cruor fumabat ad aras.
Ut celsas videre rates atque inter opacum
adlabi nemus et tacitis incumbere [1] remis,
terrentur visu subito cunctique relictis
consurgunt mensis. Audax quos rumpere Pallas
sacra vetat, raptoque volat telo obvius ipse,
et procul e tumulo: "Iuvenes, quae causa subegit
ignotas temptare vias? quo tenditis?" inquit.
"Qui genus? unde domo? pacemne huc fertis an arma?"
Tum pater Aeneas puppi sic fatur ab alta
paciferaeque manu ramum praetendit olivae:
"Troiugenas ac tela vides inimica Latinis,
quos illi bello profugos egere superbo.
Euandrum petimus. Ferte haec et dicite lectos
Dardaniae venisse duces, socia arma rogantis."
Obstipuit tanto percussus nomine Pallas:
"Egredere o quicumque es," ait, "coramque parentem
adloquere ac nostris succede penatibus hospes."

Aeneid, viii, 102–123.

23

Evander recalls meeting Anchises at Pheneus in Arcadia.

Dixerat Aeneas. Ille [2] os oculosque loquentis
iamdudum et totum lustrabat lumine corpus.
Tum sic pauca refert: "Ut te, fortissime Teucrum,
accipio agnoscoque libens! Ut verba parentis
et vocem Anchisae magni vultumque recordor!
Nam memini Hesionae visentem regna sororis
Laomedontiaden Priamum, Salamina petentem,
protinus Arcadiae gelidos invisere [3] finis.
Tum mihi prima genas vestibat flore iuventas,
mirabarque duces Teucros, mirabar et ipsum
Laomedontiaden; sed cunctis altior ibat
Anchises. Mihi mens iuvenali ardebat amore

[1] Supply a personal subject. [2] *ille* refers to Evander. [3] *invisere*, 'come to see.'

compellare virum et dextrae coniungere dextram.
Accessi et cupidus Phenei sub moenia duxi.
Ille mihi insignem pharetram Lyciasque sagittas
discedens chlamydemque auro dedit intertextam,
frenaque bina meus quae nunc habet aurea Pallas.[1]
Ergo et quam petitis iuncta est mihi foedere dextra,
et lux cum primum terris se crastina [2] reddet,
auxilio laetos dimittam opibusque iuvabo."

Aeneid, viii, 152–171.

24

King Evander relates to Aeneas the traditions of early Rome.

Ibat rex obsitus aevo,
et comitem Aenean iuxta natumque tenebat
ingrediens, varioque viam sermone levabat.
Miratur facilisque oculos fert omnia circum
Aeneas, capiturque locis, et singula laetus
exquiritque auditque virum monumenta priorum.
Tum rex Euandrus, Romanae conditor arcis:
"Haec nemora indigenae [3] Fauni Nymphaeque tenebant,
gensque virum truncis et duro robore nata,
quis [4] neque mos neque cultus erat, nec iungere tauros,
aut componere opes norant, aut parcere parto,
sed rami atque asper victu venatus [5] alebat.
Primus ab aetherio venit Saturnus Olympo,
arma Iovis fugiens et regnis exsul ademptis.
Is genus indocile ac dispersum montibus altis
composuit, legesque dedit, Latiumque vocari
maluit, his quoniam latuisset tutus in oris.
Aurea quae perhibent,[6] illo sub rege fuere
saecula: sic placida populos in pace regebat;
deterior donec paulatim ac decolor [7] aetas
et belli rabies et amor successit habendi."

Aeneid, viii, 307–327.

[1] *Pallas*, son of Evander. [2] *crastina*, 'tomorrow's.' [3] native-born.
[4] = quibus. [5] game. [6] call. [7] less brilliant.

25

Venus begs Vulcan to forge armor for Aeneas.

At Venus haud animo nequiquam exterrita mater,
Laurentumque minis et duro mota tumultu,
Volcanum adloquitur, thalamoque haec coniugis aureo
incipit, et dictis divinum adspirat amorem:
"Dum bello Argolici vastabant Pergama reges
debita [1] casurasque inimicis ignibus arces,
non ullum auxilium miseris, non arma rogavi
artis opisque tuae; nec te, carissime coniunx,
incassumve [2] tuos volui exercere labores,
quamvis et Priami deberem plurima natis,
et durum Aeneae flevissem saepe laborem.
Nunc Iovis imperiis Rutulorum constitit oris:
ergo eadem supplex venio, et sanctum mihi numen [3]
arma rogo, genetrix nato. Te filia Nerei,
te potuit lacrimis Tithonia flectere coniunx.
Aspice qui coeant populi, quae moenia clausis
ferrum acuant portis in me exscidiumque meorum."

Aeneid, viii, 370–386.

26

Evander, the Arcadian king, bids farewell to his son Pallas.

Tum pater Euandrus dextram complexus euntis [4]
haeret, inexpletus lacrimans, ac talia fatur:
"O mihi praeteritos referat si Iuppiter annos,
qualis eram, cum primam aciem Praeneste sub ipsa
stravi scutorumque incendi victor acervos
et regem hac Erulum dextra sub Tartara misi,
nascenti cui tris animas Feronia mater
(horrendum dictu) dederat, terna arma movenda
ter leto sternendus erat; cui tum tamen omnis
abstulit haec animas dextra et totidem exuit armis:
non ego nunc dulci amplexu divellerer usquam,

[1] doomed. [2] *incassum*, 'in vain.' [3] *numen* refers to Vulcan. [4] supply *filii.*

nate, tuo, neque finitimo Mezentius umquam
huic capiti insultans tot ferro saeva dedisset
funera, tam multis viduasset [1] civibus urbem.
At vos, o superi, et divum tu maxime rector
Iuppiter, Arcadii, quaeso, miserescite regis
et patrias audite preces: si numina vestra
incolumem Pallanta mihi, si fata reservant,
si visurus eum vivo et venturus in unum,
vitam oro, patior quemvis durare laborem.
Sin aliquem infandum casum, Fortuna, minaris,
nunc, nunc o liceat crudelem abrumpere vitam,
dum te, care puer, mea sola et sera voluptas,
complexu teneo."

Aeneid, viii, 558–582.

27

Juno urges Turnus to attack the Trojans during the absence of Aeneas, who is seeking the aid of Evander.

Atque ea diversa penitus dum parte geruntur,
Irim de caelo misit Saturnia Iuno
audacem ad Turnum. Luco tum forte parentis
Pilumni Turnus sacrata valle sedebat.
Ad quem sic roseo Thaumantias [2] ore locuta est:
"Turne, quod optanti divum promittere nemo
auderet, volvenda dies, en, attulit ultro.
Aeneas, urbe et sociis et classe relicta,
sceptra Palatini sedemque petit Euandri.
Nec satis: extremas Corythi penetravit ad urbes
Lydorumque manum, collectos armat agrestis.
Quid dubitas? nunc tempus equos, nunc poscere currus.
Rumpe moras omnis et turbata arripe castra."
Dixit, et in caelum paribus se sustulit alis
ingentemque fuga secuit sub nubibus arcum.
Agnovit iuvenis duplicisque ad sidera palmas

[1] deprived. [2] *i.e.*, Iris.

sustulit ac tali fugientem est voce secutus:
"Iri, decus caeli, quis te mihi nubibus actam
detulit in terras? Unde haec tam clara repente
tempestas? Medium video discedere caelum
palantisque [1] polo stellas. Sequor omina tanta,
quisquis [2] in arma vocas."

Aeneid, ix, 1–22

28

The Mother of the Gods, by a miracle, saves the Trojan ships from Turnus.

Ergo aderat promissa dies et tempora Parcae
debita complerant, cum Turni iniuria Matrem
admonuit ratibus sacris depellere taedas.
Hic primum nova lux oculis offulsit et ingens
visus ab Aurora caelum transcurrere nimbus
Idaeique chori; tum vox horrenda per auras
excidit et Troum Rutulorumque agmina complet:
"Ne trepidate meas, Teucri, defendere navis,
neve armate manus; maria ante exurere Turno
quam sacras dabitur pinus. Vos ite solutae,
ite deae pelagi; genetrix iubet." Et sua quaeque
continuo puppes abrumpunt vincula ripis
delphinumque [3] modo demersis aequora rostris
ima petunt. Hinc virgineae (mirabile monstrum)
reddunt se totidem facies pontoque feruntur.
Obstipuere animis Rutuli, conterritus ipse
turbatis Messapus equis, cunctatur et amnis
rauca sonans revocatque pedem Tiberinus ab alto.
At non audaci Turno fiducia cessit;
ultro animos tollit dictis atque increpat ultro:
"Troianos haec monstra petunt, his Iuppiter ipse
auxilium solitum eripuit, non tela neque ignis
exspectant Rutulos."

Aeneid, ix, 107–130.

[1] *palari*, 'to wander.' [2] Supply *es qui*. [3] dolphin.

29

Nisus confides to his fellow-sentinel, Euryalus, his purpose of stealing through the Rutulian lines with a message for Aeneas.

Nisus erat portae custos, acerrimus armis,
Hyrtacides, comitem Aeneae quem miserat Ida
venatrix iaculo celerem levibusque sagittis;
et iuxta comes Euryalus, quo pulchrior alter
non fuit Aeneadum Troiana neque induit arma.
His armor unus erat pariterque in bella ruebant:
tum quoque communi portam statione tenebant.
Nisus ait: "Dine hunc ardorem mentibus addunt,
Euryale, an sua cuique deus fit dira cupido?
Aut pugnam aut aliquid iamdudum invadere magnum
mens agitat mihi, nec placida contenta quiete est.
Cernis, quae Rutulos habeat fiducia rerum.
Lumina rara micant, somno vinoque soluti
procubuere, silent lata loca. Percipe porro,
quid dubitem [1] et quae nunc animo sententia surgat.
Aenean acciri [2] omnes, populusque patresque,
exposcunt mittique viros, qui certa reportent.
Si tibi quae posco promittunt (nam mihi facti
fama sat est), tumulo videor reperire sub illo
posse viam ad muros et moenia Pallantea."

Aeneid, ix, 176–196.

30

Euryalus and Nisus are discovered by horsemen of the Latins.

Interea praemissi equites ex urbe Latina,
cetera dum legio campis instructa moratur,
ibant et Turno regi responsa ferebant,
ter centum, scutati [3] omnes, Volcente magistro.
Iamque propinquabant castris murosque subibant

[1] am pondering. [2] i.e., *arcessi.* [3] Compare *scutum*, 'shield.'

cum procul hos laevo flectentis limite cernunt,
et galea Euryalum sublustri [1] noctis in umbra
prodidit immemorem radiisque adversa refulsit.
Haud temere est visum. Conclamat ab agmine Volcens:
"State, viri. Quae causa viae? Quive estis in armis?
Quove tenetis iter?" Nihil illi tendere contra,
sed celerare fugam in silvas et fidere nocti.
Obiciunt equites sese ad divortia [2] nota
hinc atque hinc, omnemque abitum custode coronant.
Silva fuit late dumis atque ilice nigra
horrida, quam densi complerant undique sentes; [3]
rara per occultos lucebat semita callis.[4]
Euryalum tenebrae ramorum onerosaque praeda
impediunt fallitque timor regione viarum.
Nisus abit; iamque imprudens evaserat hostis
atque locos, qui post Albae de nomine dicti
Albani.

Aeneid, ix, 367–388.

31

Numanus utters a defiance.

Tum primum bello celerem intendisse sagittam
dicitur, ante feras solitus terrere fugacis,
Ascanius, fortemque manu fudisse Numanum,
cui Remulo cognomen erat, Turnique minorem
germanam nuper thalamo sociatus habebat.
Is primam ante aciem digna atque indigna relatu
vociferans tumidusque novo praecordia regno
ibat et ingentem sese clamore ferebat:
"Non pudet obsidione iterum valloque teneri,
bis capti Phryges, et morti praetendere muros?
En, qui nostra sibi bello conubia poscunt!
Quis deus Italiam, quae vos dementia adegit?
Non hic Atridae, nec fandi fictor Ulixes.

[1] dim. [2] forks in the roads. [3] brambles. [4] paths, ways.

Durum ab stirpe genus natos ad flumina primum
deferimus saevoque gelu duramus et undis;
venatu invigilant pueri silvasque fatigant;
flectere ludus equos et spicula tendere cornu.
At patiens operum parvoque adsueta iuventus
aut rastris [1] terram domat, aut quatit oppida bello."

Aeneid, ix, 590-608

32

Ascanius in his first fight has just killed Numanus.

Teucri clamore sequuntur
laetitiaque fremunt animosque ad sidera tollunt.
Aetheria tum forte plaga [2] crinitus [3] Apollo
desuper Ausonias acies urbemque videbat,
nube sedens, atque his victorem adfatur Iulum:
"Macte [4] nova virtute, puer: sic itur ad astra,
dis genite et geniture deos. Iure omnia bella
gente sub Assaraci fato ventura resident,
nec te Troia capit." [5] Simul haec effatus ab alto
aethere se misit, spirantis dimovet auras
Ascaniumque petit. Formam tum vertitur oris
antiquum in Buten. Hic Dardanio Anchisae
armiger ante fuit fidusque ad limina custos;
tum comitem Ascanio pater addidit. Ibat Apollo
omnia longaevo similis, vocemque coloremque
et crinis albos et saeva sonoribus arma,
atque his ardentem dictis adfatur Iulum:
"Sit satis, Aenide, telis impune [6] Numanum
oppetiisse [7] tuis; primam hanc tibi magnus Apollo
concedit laudem et paribus non invidet armis:
cetera parce, puer, bello."

Aeneid, ix, 636-656.

[1] rakes. [2] region, quarter. [3] adjective from *crinis*. [4] blessings on.
[5] hold, contain. [6] without harm to you. [7] supply *mortem*.

33

Mars aids the Latins against the Teucri.

Hic Mars armipotens animum virisque Latinis
addidit et stimulos acris sub pectore vertit,
immisitque Fugam Teucris atrumque Timorem.
Undique conveniunt, quoniam data copia pugnae,
bellatorque animo deus incidit.
Pandarus, ut fuso [1] germanum corpore cernit
et quo sit fortuna loco, qui casus agat res,
portam vi magna converso cardine torquet,
obnixus latis umeris, multosque suorum
moenibus exclusos duro in certamine linquit;
ast alios secum includit recipitque ruentis,
demens, qui Rutulum in medio non agmine regem
viderit irrumpentem ultroque incluserit urbi,
immanem veluti pecora inter inertia tigrim.
Continuo nova lux oculis effulsit et arma
horrendum sonuere; tremunt in vertice cristae
sanguineae clipeoque micantia fulmina mittit.
Agnoscunt faciem invisam atque immania membra
turbati subito Aeneadae. Tum Pandarus ingens
emicat et mortis fraternae fervidus ira
effatur: "Non haec dotalis [2] regia [3] Amatae,
nec muris cohibet patriis media Ardea Turnum.
Castra inimica vides; nulla hinc exire potestas."

Aeneid, ix, 717–739.

34

The council of the gods.

Panditur interea domus omnipotentis Olympi,
conciliumque vocat divom pater atque hominum rex
sideream in sedem, terras unde arduus omnis
castraque Dardanidum adspectat populosque Latinos.

[1] laid low, stretched on the ground. [2] adjective from *dos*, 'dowry.' [3] palace.

Considunt tectis bipatentibus;[1] incipit ipse:
"Caelicolae magni, quianam[2] sententia vobis
versa retro, tantumque animis certatis iniquis?
Abnueram bello Italiam concurrere Teucris.
Quae contra vetitum[3] discordia? Quis metus aut hos
aut hos arma sequi ferrumque lacessere suasit?
Adveniet iustum pugnae, ne arcessite, tempus,
cum fera Carthago Romanis arcibus olim
exitium magnum atque Alpes immittet apertas;[4]
tum certare odiis, tum res rapuisse licebit.
Nunc sinite, et placitum laeti componite foedus."

Aeneid, x, 1–15.

35

Venus in despair asks Jupiter to save the remaining Trojans.

"Nil super imperio movear; speravimus ista,
dum fortuna fuit; vincant, quos vincere mavis.
Si nulla est regio, Teucris quam det tua coniunx
dura, per eversae, genitor, fumantia Troiae
excidia obtestor, liceat dimittere ab armis
incolumem Ascanium, liceat superesse nepotem.
Aeneas sane ignotis iactetur in undis
et quacumque viam dederit Fortuna sequatur:
hunc[5] tegere et dirae valeam subducere pugnae.
Est Amathus, est celsa mihi Paphus atque Cythera
Idaliaeque domus: positis inglorius armis
exigat hic aevum. Magna dicione iubeto
Carthago premat Ausoniam; nihil urbibus inde
obstabit Tyriis. Quid pestem evadere belli
iuvit et Argolicos medium fugisse per ignis
totque maris vastaeque exhausta pericula terrae,
dum Latium Teucri recidivaque[6] Pergama quaerunt?

[1] *i.e.*, with doors at either end. [2] why? [3] against my command.
[4] Equivalent to *exitium immittet per Alpes apertas*. [5] *i.e.*, Ascanius.
[6] *recidiva*, 'restored.'

Non satius[1] cineres patriae insedisse supremos
atque solum, quo Troia fuit? Xanthum et Simoenta
redde, oro, miseris iterumque revolvere casus
da, pater, Iliacos Teucris."

Aeneid, x, 42–62.

36

Jupiter refuses to favor either the Trojans or the Rutulians.

Talibus orabat Iuno cunctique fremebant
caelicolae adsensu vario, ceu flamina prima
cum deprensa fremunt silvis et caeca volutant
murmura, venturos nautis prodentia ventos.
Tum pater omnipotens, rerum cui prima potestas,
infit[2] (eo dicente deum domus alta silescit
et tremefacta solo tellus, silet arduus aether,
tum Zephyri posuere,[3] premit placida aequora pontus):
"Accipite ergo animis haec atque mea figite dicta.
Quandoquidem Ausonios coniungi foedere Teucris
haud licitum, nec vestra capit discordia finem:
quae cuique est fortuna hodie, quam quisque secat[4] spem,
Tros Rutulusne fuat,[5] nullo discrimine habebo."
Hic finis fandi. Solio tum Iuppiter aureo
surgit, caelicolae medium quem ad limina ducunt.

Aeneid, x, 96–108, 116–117.

37

Pallas' prayer to Hercules and Jupiter's answer.

Desiluit Turnus biiugis, pedes[6] apparat ire
comminus; utque leo, specula cum vidit ab alta
stare procul campis meditantem in proelia taurum,
advolat: haud alia est Turni venientis imago.
Hunc ubi contiguum missae fore credidit hastae,
ire prior Pallas, si qua fors adiuvet ausum
viribus imparibus, magnumque ita ad aethera fatur:

[1] = *melius*. [2] begins. [3] supply *se*. [4] gains. [5] = *sit*. [6] on foot.

"Per patris hospitium et mensas, quas advena [1] adisti,
te precor, Alcide, coeptis ingentibus adsis.
Cernat semineci sibi me rapere arma cruenta
victoremque ferant morientia lumina Turni."
Audiit Alcides iuvenem magnumque sub imo
corde premit gemitum lacrimasque effundit inanis.
Tum genitor natum dictis adfatur amicis:
"Stat sua cuique dies, breve et irreparabile tempus
omnibus est vitae; sed famam extendere factis,
hoc virtutis opus. Troiae sub moenibus altis
tot nati cecidere deum; quin occidit una
Sarpedon, mea progenies. Etiam sua Turnum
fata vocant metasque dati pervenit ad aevi."
Sic ait, atque oculos Rutulorum reicit arvis.
At Pallas magnis emittit viribus hastam
vaginaque cava fulgentem deripit ensem.

Aeneid, x, 453–475.

38

Juno resigns Turnus to his fate.

Iunonem interea compellat Iuppiter ultro:
"O germana mihi atque eadem gratissima coniunx,
ut rebare, Venus (nec te sententia fallit)
Troianas sustentat opes, non vivida bello
dextra viris animusque ferox patiensque pericli."
Cui Iuno submissa: "Quid, O pulcherrime coniunx,
sollicitas aegram et tua tristia dicta timentem?
Si mihi, quae quondam fuerat, quamque esse decebat,
vis in amore foret, non hoc mihi namque negares,
omnipotens, quin et pugnae subducere Turnum
et Dauno possem incolumem servare parenti.
Nunc pereat, Teucrisque pio det sanguine poenas.
Ille tamen nostra deducit origine nomen,
Pilumnusque illi quartus pater, et tua larga
saepe manu multisque oneravit limina donis."

Aeneid, x, 606–620.

[1] stranger.

39

Aeneas has wounded the father of young Lausus. Furious, the boy attacks Aeneas.

Aeneas nubem belli, dum detonet [1] omnis,
sustinet, et Lausum increpitat Lausoque minatur:
"Quo moriture ruis, maioraque viribus audes?
Fallit te incautum pietas tua." Nec minus ille
exsultat demens; saevae iamque altius irae
Dardanio surgunt ductori, extremaque Lauso
Parcae fila [2] legunt: validum namque exigit ensem
per medium Aeneas iuvenem, totumque recondit.
At vero ut voltum vidit morientis et ora,
ora modis Anchisiades pallentia miris,
ingemuit miserans graviter, dextramque tetendit.
"Quid tibi nunc, miserande puer, pro laudibus istis,
quid pius Aeneas tanta dabit indole [3] dignum?
Arma, quibus laetatus, habe tua; teque parentum
manibus [4] et cineri, si qua est ea cura, remitto.
Hoc tamen infelix miseram solabere mortem:
Aeneae magni dextra cadis."

Aeneid, x, 809–816, 821–823, 825–830.

40

The grief of Aeneas at the death of Pallas.

Sic ait inlacrimans recipitque ad limina gressum,
corpus ubi exanimi positum Pallantis Acoetes
servabat senior, qui Parrhasio [5] Euandro
armiger ante fuit, sed non felicibus aeque
tum comes auspiciis caro datus ibat alumno.
Circum omnis famulumque manus Troianaque turba
et maestum Iliades crinem de more solutae.
Ut vero Aeneas foribus sese intulit altis,
ingentem gemitum tunsis ad sidera tollunt

[1] *detonare*, 'cease thundering.' [2] threads. [3] *indole* = *ingenio*.
[4] not from *manus*. [5] *i.e.*, Arcadian.

pectoribus, maestoque immugit regia luctu.
Ipse caput nivei fultum [1] Pallantis et ora
ut vidit levique patens in pectore vulnus
cuspidis Ausoniae, lacrimis ita fatur obortis:
"Tene," inquit, "miserande puer, cum laeta veniret,
invidit Fortuna mihi, ne regna videres
nostra neque ad sedes victor veherere paternas?
Non haec Euandro de te promissa parenti
discedens dederam, cum me complexus euntem
mitteret in magnum imperium metuensque moneret
acris esse viros, cum dura proelia gente."

Aeneid, xi, 29–48.

41

Aeneas and his ally, Tarchon, burn the bodies of their dead warriors.

Aurora interea miseris mortalibus almam
extulerat lucem, referens opera atque labores:
iam pater Aeneas, iam curvo in litore Tarchon
constituere pyras. Huc corpora quisque suorum
more tulere patrum, subiectisque ignibus atris
conditur in tenebras altum caligine [2] caelum.
Ter circum accensos cincti fulgentibus armis
decurrere rogos, ter maestum funeris ignem
lustravere in equis ululatusque ore dedere.
Spargitur et tellus lacrimis, sparguntur et arma;
it caelo clamorque virum clangorque tubarum.
Hic alii spolia occisis derepta Latinis
coniciunt igni, galeas ensesque decoros
frenaque ferventisque rotas; pars munera nota,
ipsorum clipeos et non felicia tela.
Multa boum circa [3] mactantur corpore Marti,
saetigerosque [4] sues raptasque ex omnibus agris
in flammam iugulant [5] pecudes.

Aeneid, xi, 182–199.

[1] from *fulcio*, 'support.' [2] smoke. [3] equivalent to *circum*. [4] bristly.
[5] slaughter.

42

Ambassadors report to Latinus their failure to gain the help of King Diomedes against Aeneas.

"Postquam introgressi et coram data copia fandi,
munera praeferimus, nomen patriamque docemus,
qui bellum intulerint, quae causa attraxerit Arpos.[1]
Auditis ille haec placido sic reddidit ore:
'O fortunatae gentes, Saturnia regna,
antiqui Ausonii, quae vos fortuna quietos
sollicitat suadetque ignota lacessere bella?
Ne vero, ne me ad talis impellite pugnas.
Munera, quae patriis ad me portatis ab oris,
vertite ad Aenean. Stetimus tela aspera contra
contulimusque manus: experto credite, quantus
in clipeum adsurgat, quo turbine torqueat hastam.
Si duo praeterea talis Idaea tulisset
terra viros, ultro Inachias venisset ad urbes
Dardanus, et versis lugeret Graecia fatis.
Quidquid apud durae cessatum est moenia Troiae,
Hectoris Aeneaeque manu victoria Graium
haesit et in decimum vestigia rettulit annum.
Ambo animis, ambo insignes praestantibus armis;
hic pietate prior. Coeant in foedera dextrae,
qua datur; ast armis concurrant arma cavete.'"

Aeneid, xi, 248–254, 278, 281–293.

43

In a council of war King Latinus suggests making two proposals of peace to Aeneas.

"Ante equidem summa de re statuisse, Latini,
et vellem et fuerat melius, non tempore tali
cogere concilium, cum muros obsidet hostis.
Nunc adeo [2] quae sit dubiae sententia menti,

[1] *Arpi, -orum*, a town. [2] *adeo*, 'indeed.'

expediam et paucis (animos adhibete) docebo.
Est antiquus ager Tusco mihi proximus amni.
Haec omnis regio et celsi plaga pinea [1] montis
cedat amicitiae Teucrorum, et foederis aequas
dicamus leges sociosque in regna vocemus;
considant, si tantus amor, et moenia condant.
Sin alios fines aliamque capessere gentem
est animus, possuntque solo decedere nostro,
bis denas Italo texamus robore naves,
seu plures complere valent; iacet omnis ad undam
materies. Ipsi numerumque modumque carinis
praecipiant; nos aera, manus, navalia [2] demus.
Praeterea, qui dicta ferant et foedera firment,
centum oratores prima de gente Latinos
ire placet pacisque manu praetendere ramos."

Aeneid, xi. 302–304, 314–316, 320–332.

44

Turnus replies angrily to Drances.

Talibus exarsit dictis violentia Turni;
dat gemitum rumpitque has imo pectore voces:
"Larga quidem, Drance, semper tibi copia fandi
tum, cum bella manus poscunt, patribusque vocatis
primus ades. Sed non replenda est curia verbis,
quae tuto tibi magna volant, dum distinet hostem
agger murorum nec inundant sanguine fossae.
Proinde tona eloquio (solitum tibi) meque timoris
argue tu, Drance, quando tot stragis [3] acervos
Teucrorum tua dextra dedit passimque tropaeis
insignis [4] agros. Possit quid vivida virtus,
experiare licet: nec longe scilicet hostes
quaerendi nobis; circumstant undique muros.
Imus in adversos — quid cessas? an tibi Mavors

[1] *plaga pinea*, 'tract of pine.'
[2] *navalia*, 'equipment.'
[3] dead bodies.
[4] *insignire*, 'to mark,' 'to decorate.'

ventosa in lingua pedibusque fugacibus istis
semper erit?
pulsus ego? aut quisquam merito, foedissime, pulsum
arguet, Iliaco tumidum qui crescere Thybrim
sanguine et Euandri totam cum stirpe videbit
procubuisse domum atque exutos Arcadas armis?
haud ita me experti Bitias et Pandarus ingens
et quos mille die victor sub Tartara misi,
inclusus muris hostilique aggere saeptus.

Aeneid, xi, 376–398.

45

Turnus answers the old king's counsels of war.

"Nunc ad te et tua magna, pater, consulta revertor.
Si nullam nostris ultra spem ponis in armis,
si tam deserti sumus et semel agmine verso
funditus occidimus neque habet Fortuna regressum,
oremus pacem et dextras tendamus inertis.
Quamquam o si solitae quicquam virtutis adesset!
Ille mihi ante alios fortunatusque laborum
egregiusque animi, qui, ne quid tale videret,
procubuit moriens et humum semel ore momordit.[1]
Sin et opes nobis et adhuc intacta iuventus
auxilioque urbes Italae populique supersunt,
sin et Troianis cum multo gloria venit
sanguine (sunt illis sua funera, parque per omnis
tempestas [2]) — cur indecores in limine primo
deficimus? cur ante tubam tremor occupat artus?"

Aeneid, xi, 410–424.

46

The alarm in the city of Latinus when the approach of the Trojans is reported.

Nuntius ingenti per regia tecta tumultu
ecce ruit magnisque urbem terroribus implet;

[1] *mordere*, 'to bite.' [2] used figuratively for the destruction wrought by war.

instructos acie Tiberino a flumine Teucros
Tyrrhenamque manum totis descendere campis.
Extemplo turbati animi concussaque vulgi
pectora et arrectae stimulis haud mollibus irae.
Ilicet [1] in muros tota discurritur urbe.
Concilium ipse pater et magna incepta Latinus
deserit ac tristi turbatus tempore differt,
multaque se incusat, qui non acceperit ultro
Dardanium Aenean generumque adsciverit [2] urbi.
Praefodiunt [3] alii portas aut saxa sudesque [4]
subvectant. Bello dat signum rauca cruentum
bucina. Tum muros varia cinxere corona [5]
matronae puerique; vocat labor ultimus omnes.
Nec non ad templum summasque ad Palladis arces
subvehitur magna matrum regina caterva
dona ferens, iuxtaque comes Lavinia virgo,
causa mali tanti, oculos deiecta decoros.
Succedunt matres et templum ture vaporant [6]
et maestas alto fundunt de limine voces.

Aeneid, xi, 447–452, 468–482.

47

The warrior maiden Camilla, while pursuing an enemy clad in gold, arouses the wrath of the cowardly Arruns.

Hunc virgo, sive ut templis praefigeret arma
Troia, captivo sive ut se ferret in auro
venatrix, unum ex omni certamine pugnae
caeca sequebatur totumque incauta per agmen
femineo praedae et spoliorum ardebat amore,
telum ex insidiis cum tandem tempore [7] capto
concitat et superos Arruns sic voce precatur:
"Summe deum, sancti custos Soractis Apollo,

[1] *ilicet*, 'forthwith.'
[2] *adsciverit*, from *adscisco*, 'welcome to.'
[3] *praefodiunt*, from *praefodio*, 'dig ditches in front of.'
[4] *sudes*, 'stakes.'
[5] *corona*, 'multitude.'
[6] *vaporant*, from *vaporo*, 'perfume.'
[7] *tempore*, 'opportunity.'

da, pater, hoc nostris aboleri dedecus armis,
omnipotens. Non exuvias pulsaeque tropaeum
virginis aut spolia ulla peto, mihi cetera laudem
facta ferent; haec dira meo dum vulnere pestis
pulsa cadat, patrias remeabo [1] inglorius urbes."
  Audiit et voti Phoebus succedere partem
mente dedit, partem volucres dispersit in auras:
sterneret ut subita turbatam morte Camillam
adnuit oranti; reducem ut patria alta videret,
non dedit, inque Notos vocem vertere procellae.

Aeneid, xi, 778–785, 789–798.

48

The rout of the Rutuli after the death of Camilla.

Prima fugit domina amissa levis ala Camillae,
turbati fugiunt Rutuli, fugit acer Atinas,
disiectique duces desolatique manipli
tuta petunt et equis aversi ad moenia tendunt.
Nec quisquam instantis Teucros letumque ferentis
sustentare valet telis aut sistere contra,
sed laxos referunt umeris languentibus arcus,
quadripedumque putrem [2] cursu quatit ungula [3] campum.
Volvitur ad muros caligine turbidus atra
pulvis, et e speculis [4] percussae pectora matres
femineum clamorem ad caeli sidera tollunt.
Qui cursu portas primi irrupere patentis,
hos inimica super [5] mixto premit agmine turba,
nec miseram effugiunt mortem, sed limine in ipso,
moenibus in patriis atque inter tuta domorum
confixi exspirant animas. Pars claudere portas,
nec sociis aperire viam nec moenibus audent
accipere orantis, oriturque miserrima caedes
defendentum armis aditus inque arma ruentum.

[1] *remeabo*, from *remeo*, 'return.' [2] dusty. [3] literally, hoof.
[4] watch-towers. [5] adverb.

Exclusi ante oculos lacrimantumque ora parentum
pars in praecipitis fossas urgente ruina
volvitur, immissis pars caeca et concita frenis
arietat [1] in portas et duros obice [2] postis.

Aeneid, xi, 868–890.

49

Turnus asks King Latinus to sanction his resolve to meet Aeneas in single combat.

"Nulla mora in Turno; nihil est quod dicta retractent
ignavi Aeneadae, nec quae pepigere [3] recusent.
Congredior. Fer sacra, pater, et concipe foedus.[4]
Aut hac Dardanium dextra sub Tartara mittam,
desertorem Asiae — sedeant spectentque Latini —
et solus ferro crimen commune refellam,
aut habeat victos, cedat Lavinia coniunx."
Olli sedato respondit corde Latinus:
"O praestans animi iuvenis, quantum ipse feroci
virtute exsuperas, tanto me impensius [5] aequum est
consulere atque omnes metuentem expendere casus.
Sunt tibi regna patris Dauni, sunt oppida capta
multa manu, nec non aurumque animusque Latino est.
Sunt aliae innuptae Latio et Laurentibus agris,
nec genus indecores.[6] Sine me haec haud mollia factu
sublatis aperire dolis, simul hoc animo hauri;
me natam nulli veterum sociare procorum [7]
fas erat, idque omnes divique hominesque canebant."

Aeneid, xii, 11–28.

50

King Latinus swears loyalty to the Trojans.

Sic prior Aeneas; sequitur sic deinde Latinus,
suspiciens caelum, tenditque ad sidera dextram:
"Haec eadem, Aenea, terram, mare, sidera, iuro,

[1] for the meaning compare *aries*, 'ram.' [2] barrier. [3] *pangere*, 'to agree upon.
[4] seal the compact. [5] more earnestly. [6] = *ignobiles*. [7] suitors.

Latonaeque genus duplex Ianumque bifrontem,
vimque deum infernam et duri sacraria Ditis;
audiat haec Genitor, qui foedera fulmine sancit.
Tango aras, medios ignis et numina testor:
nulla dies pacem hanc Italis nec foedera rumpet,
quo res cumque cadent; nec me vis ulla volentem
avertet, non, si tellurem effundat in undas,
diluvio [1] miscens, caelumque in Tartara solvat;
ut sceptrum hoc" — dextra sceptrum nam forte gerebat —
"numquam fronde levi fundet virgulta [2] nec umbras,
cum semel in silvis imo de stirpe recisum
matre [3] caret, posuitque comas et bracchia [4] ferro;
olim arbos, nunc artificis manus aere decoro
inclusit patribusque dedit gestare Latinis."
Talibus inter se firmabant foedera dictis
conspectu in medio procerum. Tum rite sacratas
in flammam iugulant pecudes et viscera vivis
eripiunt, cumulantque oneratis lancibus [5] aras.

Aeneid, xii, 195–216.

51

A treaty has been made, by which Aeneas and Turnus are to engage in single combat. Juturna prevents this by her words and an omen.

Talibus incensa est iuvenum sententia dictis
iam magis atque magis, serpitque per agmina murmur;
ipsi Laurentes mutati ipsique Latini.
Qui sibi iam requiem pugnae rebusque salutem
sperabant, nunc arma volunt foedusque precantur
infectum,[6] et Turni sortem miserantur iniquam.
His aliud maius Iuturna adiungit, et alto
dat signum caelo, quo non praesentius [7] ullum
turbavit mentes Italas monstroque fefellit.

[1] in deluge. [2] i.e., *ramos*. [3] parent-stalk.
[4] *comas et bracchia:* used metaphorically. [5] platters. [6] *infectum*, 'undone.'
[7] *praesentius*, 'more potent.'

Namque volans rubra [1] fulvus Iovis ales [2] in aethra
litoreas agitabat aves turbamque sonantem
agminis aligeri,[3] subito cum lapsus ad undas
cycnum [2] excellentem pedibus rapit improbus uncis.
Arrexere animos Itali, cunctaeque volucres [2]
convertunt clamore fugam (mirabile visu),
aetheraque obscurant pennis, hostemque per auras
facta nube premunt, donec vi victus et ipso
pondere defecit praedamque ex unguibus ales
proiecit fluvio, penitusque in nubila fugit.

Aeneid, xii, 238-256.

52

The wounding of Aeneas.

At pius Aeneas dextram tendebat inermem
nudato capite atque suos clamore vocabat:
"Quo ruitis? quaeve ista repens discordia surgit?
o cohibete iras! ictum iam foedus et omnes
compositae leges; mihi ius concurrere soli;
me sinite atque auferte metus; ego foedera faxo [4]
firma manu; Turnum debent haec iam mihi sacra." [5]
Has inter voces, media inter talia verba,
ecce viro stridens alis adlapsa sagitta est.
Nec sese Aeneae iactavit vulnere quisquam.
Turnus ut Aenean cedentem ex agmine vidit
turbatosque duces, subita spe fervidus ardet;
poscit equos atque arma simul, saltuque superbus
emicat in currum et manibus molitur [6] habenas.
Multa virum volitans dat fortia corpora leto,
seminecis [7] volvit multos aut agmina curru
proterit [8] aut raptas fugientibus ingerit hastas.

Aeneid, xii, 311-319, 323-330.

[1] *rubra*, 'red.'
[2] *Iovis ales* signifies Aeneas, *cycnum*, 'swan,' Turnus, and *volucres*, the followers of Turnus.
[3] *aligeri*, 'winged.'
[4] *faxo = faciam.*
[5] rites.
[6] manages.
[7] half-dead.
[8] crushes.

53

The doctor, Iapyx, disclaims credit for the miraculous healing of the wound of Aeneas.

Fovit [1] ea vulnus lympha longaevus Iapyx
ignorans, subitoque omnis de corpore fugit
quippe dolor, omnis stetit imo vulnere sanguis.
Iamque secuta manum nullo cogente sagitta
excidit, atque novae rediere in pristina vires.
"Arma citi properate viro. Quid statis?" Iapyx
conclamat primusque animos accendit in hostem.
"Non haec humanis opibus, non arte magistra
proveniunt, neque te, Aenea, mea dextera servat;
maior agit deus atque opera ad maiora remittit."
Ille avidus pugnae suras [2] incluserat auro
hinc atque hinc oditque moras hastamque coruscat.
Postquam habilis [3] lateri clipeus loricaque tergo est,
Ascanium fusis circum complectitur armis:
"Disce, puer, virtutem ex me verumque laborem,
fortunam ex aliis. Nunc te mea dextera bello
defensum dabit [4] et magna inter praemia ducet.
Tu facito, mox cum matura adoleverit [5] aetas,
sis memor, et te animo repetentem exempla tuorum
et pater Aeneas et avunculus excitet Hector."

Aeneid, xii, 420–440.

54

Aeneas returns to battle, searching for Turnus, king of the Rutulians.

Haec ubi dicta dedit, portis sese extulit ingens,
telum immane manu quatiens; simul agmine denso
Antheusque Mnestheusque ruunt, omnisque relictis
turba fluit castris. Tum caeco pulvere campus
miscetur pulsuque pedum tremit excita tellus.

[1] *fovit*, from *foveo*, 'bathe.' [2] *suras*, from *sura*, 'leg'; *i.e.*, he puts on his greaves.
[3] *habilis*, 'fitted to.' [4] *defensum dabit* is equivalent to *defendet*.
[5] *adoleverit*, from *adolesco*, 'grow.'

Vidit ab adverso venientes aggere Turnus,
videre Ausonii, gelidusque per ima cucurrit
ossa tremor; prima ante omnes Iuturna [1] Latinos
audiit agnovitque sonum et tremefacta refugit.
Ille volat campoque atrum rapit agmen aperto.
Qualis ubi ad terras abrupto sidere [2] nimbus
it mare per medium; miseris, heu, praescia longe
horrescunt corda agricolis; dabit ille ruinas
arboribus stragemque [3] satis, ruet omnia late;
ante volant sonitumque ferunt ad litora venti:
talis in adversos ductor Rhoeteius [4] hostes
agmen agit, densi cuneis [5] se quisque coactis
adglomerant.
Tollitur in caelum clamor, versique vicissim
pulverulenta fuga Rutuli dant terga per agros.

Aeneid, xii, 441–458, 462–463.

55

Venus suggests to Aeneas that he shall attack Laurentum.

Hic mentem [6] Aeneae genetrix pulcherrima misit,
iret ut ad muros, urbique adverteret agmen
ocius et subita turbaret clade Latinos.
Ille, ut vestigans diversa per agmina Turnum
huc atque huc acies [7] circumtulit, aspicit urbem.
Continuo pugnae accendit maioris imago;
Mnesthea Sergestumque vocat fortemque Serestum
ductores, tumulumque capit, quo cetera Teucrum
concurrit legio, nec scuta aut spicula [8] densi
deponunt. Celso medius stans aggere fatur:
"Ne qua meis esto dictis mora; Iuppiter hac stat;
neu quis ob inceptum subitum mihi segnior ito.
Urbem hodie, causam belli, regna ipsa Latini,

[1] *Iuturna*, sister of Turnus. [2] *sidere*, 'a storm.' [3] *stragem*, 'destruction.'
[4] *Rhoeteius*, i.e., 'Trojan.' [5] *cuneis*, from *cuneus*, 'a column' (of attack).
[6] = *consilium*. [7] supply *oculorum*. [8] darts.

ni frenum accipere et victi parere fatentur,
eruam et aequa solo fumantia culmina ponam."

Aeneid, xii, 554–558, 560–569.

56

Turnus attempts to strike down Aeneas with a stone, but his strength fails him.

Nec plura effatus saxum circumspicit ingens,
saxum antiquum, ingens, campo quod forte iacebat.
Vix illud lecti bis sex cervice subirent,
qualia nunc hominum producit corpora tellus;
ille manu raptum trepida torquebat in hostem,
altior insurgens et cursu concitus heros.
Sed neque currentem se cognoscit euntem
tollentemve manu saxumque immane moventem;
genua labant, gelidus concrevit frigore sanguis.
Tum lapis ipse viri, vacuum per inane volutus,
nec spatium evasit totum, neque pertulit ictum.
Ac velut in somnis, oculos ubi languida pressit
nocte quies, nequiquam avidos extendere cursus
velle videmur, et in mediis conatibus aegri
succidimus (non lingua valet, non corpore notae
sufficiunt vires, nec vox aut verba sequuntur),
sic Turno, quacumque viam virtute petivit,
successum dea dira negat. Tum pectore sensus
vertuntur varii; Rutulos aspectat et urbem,
cunctaturque metu, letumque instare tremescit.

Aeneid, xii, 896–916.

57

The omens at Caesar's death.

Sol tibi signa dabit. Solem quis dicere falsum
audeat? Ille etiam caecos instare tumultus
saepe monet, fraudemque et operta tumescere bella.
Ille etiam exstincto miseratus Caesare Romam,

cum caput obscura nitidum ferrugine [1] texit
impiaque aeternam timuerunt saecula noctem.
Tempore quamquam illo tellus quoque et aequore ponti,
obscenaeque canes, inportunaeque volucres
signa dabant. Quotiens Cyclopum effervere in agros
vidimus undantem ruptis fornacibus [2] Aetnam,
flammarumque globos liquefactaque volvere saxa!
Armorum sonitum tota Germania caelo
audiit; insolitis tremuerunt motibus Alpes.
Vox quoque per lucos volgo exaudita silentis
ingens, et simulacra modis pallentia miris
visa sub obscurum noctis, pecudesque locutae
(infandum!); sistunt amnes terraeque dehiscunt,
et maestum inlacrimat templis ebur aeraque sudant.
Proluit insano contorquens vertice silvas
fluviorum rex Eridanus, camposque per omnis
cum stabulis armenta tulit.

Georgics, i, 463–483.

58

The blessings of a farmer's life.

Fortunatus et ille, deos qui novit agrestis,
Panaque Silvanumque senem Nymphasque sorores.
Illum non populi fasces, non purpura regum
flexit et infidos agitans discordia fratres,
non res Romanae perituraque regna; neque ille
aut doluit miserans inopem aut invidit habenti.
Quos rami fructus, quos ipsa volentia rura
sponte tulere sua, carpsit, nec ferrea iura
insanumque forum aut populi tabularia [3] vidit.
Sollicitant alii remis freta caeca, ruuntque
in ferrum, penetrant aulas et limina regum;
hic petit excidiis urbem miserosque Penatis;
condit opes alius defossoque incubat auro;

[1] lurid hue. [2] furnaces; here, crater. [3] record-halls.

hic stupet attonitus Rostris, hunc plausus hiantem [1]
per cuneos [2] geminatus enim plebisque patrumque
corripuit; gaudent perfusi sanguine fratrum,
exsilioque domos et dulcia limina mutant,
atque alio patriam quaerunt sub sole iacentem.
Agricola incurvo terram dimovit aratro.[3]

Georgics, ii, 493–513.

59

A countryman, unable to cure his ailing bees, is advised by his mother to consult the sea god Proteus.

"Est in Carpathio Neptuni gurgite vates
caeruleus Proteus, magnum qui piscibus aequor
et iuncto bipedum curru metitur [4] equorum.
Hic nunc Emathiae portus patriamque revisit
Pallenen; hunc et Nymphae veneramur et ipse
grandaevus Nereus; novit namque omnia vates,
quae sint, quae fuerint, quae mox ventura trahantur.
Hic tibi, nate, prius vinclis capiendus, ut omnem
expediat morbi causam, eventusque secundet.
Nam sine vi non ulla dabit praecepta, neque illum
orando flectes; vim duram et vincula capto
tende; doli circum haec demum frangentur inanes.
Ipsa ego te, medios cum sol accenderit aestus,
in secreta senis ducam, quo fessus ab undis
se recipit, facile ut somno adgrediare iacentem."

Georgics, iv, 387–404.

60

The final loss of Eurydice.

Iamque pedem referens casus evaserat omnis,
redditaque Eurydice superas veniebat ad auras,
pone [5] sequens, — namque hanc dederat Proserpina legem —

[1] in open-mouthed wonder. [2] the seats in the theater. [3] plow. [4] traverses.
[5] *pone*, 'behind.'

cum subita incautum dementia cepit amantem,[1]
ignoscenda quidem, scirent si ignoscere Manes:
restitit, Eurydicenque suam, iam luce sub ipsa,
immemor, heu! victusque animi respexit. Ibi omnis
effusus labor, atque immitis [2] rupta tyranni
foedera, terque fragor [3] stagnis auditus Avernis.
Illa "Quis et me" inquit "miseram et te perdidit, Orpheu,
quis tantus furor? En iterum crudelia retro
Fata vocant, conditque natantia lumina somnus.
Iamque vale: feror ingenti circumdata nocte,
invalidasque tibi tendens, heu non tua, palmas!"
Dixit, et ex oculis subito, ceu fumus in auras
commixtus tenuis, fugit diversa, neque illum,
prensantem nequiquam umbras et multa volentem
dicere, praeterea vidit; nec portitor Orci
amplius obiectam passus transire paludem.

Georgics, iv, 485–503.

[1] *amantem*, i.e., Orpheus. [2] *immitis*, 'merciless.' [3] *fragor*, 'peal of thunder.'

HECTOR AND ACHILLES

Achilles, at the left, is engaged in a successful combat against Hector, who is already wounded. Athena, the tutelar goddess of Achilles, encourages and protects him.

CHAPTER XII

WORD FORMATION

PREFIXES

Learn the meaning of each of the following prefixes and use each in two ways: first, to form new Latin verbs from simple verbs; second, to form English derivatives. For example: **dūcō,** *lead* + **ab,** *away* = **abdūcō,** *lead away.* English derivative: **abduct.**

1.	**ā, ab, abs**	*away, from*
2.	**ad**	*to, toward*
3.	**ante**	*before*
4.	**circum**	*around, about*
5.	**con, com, co, col, cor**	*with, together; entirely, thoroughly*
6.	**dē**	*down from, away*
7.	**dis-, dī-**	*apart; not, un-*
8.	**ē, ex**	*out of, from; thoroughly, completely*
9.	**in, im, il, ir**	*in, into*
10.	**in, i, il, im, ir**	*not, un-*
11.	**inter**	*between*
12.	**ob, o, oc, of, op, os**	*against, toward*
13.	**per, pel**	*through; thoroughly, very*
14.	**post**	*after*
15.	**prae**	*before, at the head of; very*
16.	**praeter**	*by, past, beyond*
17.	**prō**	*before, forth, forward*
18.	**re-, red-**	*back, again*
19.	**sē-, sēd-**	*aside, apart*
20.	**sub, suc, suf, sum, sup, sus**	*under, from under, up*
21.	**super**	*over, above*
22.	**trāns, trā**	*across*

Some prefixes change their final consonants to make them like the initial consonants of the words to which they are prefixed. Such a change is called assimilation. For example:

ad + currō = accurrō
ad + ferō = afferō
con + locō = collocō
con + mūniō = commūniō
in + mittō = immittō
in + rīdeō = irrīdeō
ob + ferō = offerō
ob + pōnō = oppōnō
sub + currō = succurrō
sub + portō = supportō

When a Latin verb is compounded with a prefix, short *a* or short *e* in the root of the verb is usually changed to short *i* before a consonant. For example:

in + capiō = incipiō
re + capiō = recipiō
ad + teneō = attineō
re + teneō = retineō

Exercise 1

Divide each of the following compound words into its component parts, and show how the force of the prefix affects the meaning of each:

1. persaepe
2. praeclārus
3. dēligō
4. sēditiō
5. commoveō
6. innumerābilis
7. trāiciō
8. īnfluō
9. succīdō
10. cōgō
11. ēvocō
12. dīripiō
13. attingō
14. sēcūrus
15. occlūdō
16. improbus
17. circumdūcō
18. inimīcitia
19. perfacilis
20. dissimilis
21. trānsmittō
22. sēparō
23. antepōnō
24. redeō
25. obiciō
26. perterreō
27. requīrō
28. innocēns
29. āmēns
30. contineō
31. prōvideō
32. sustineō
33. difficilis
34. abstrahō
35. prōiciō
36. abstineō
37. praetor
38. intercēdō
39. efferō
40. subigō
41. redundō
42. praeparō
43. commūniō
44. suscipiō
45. praeficiō
46. excēdō
47. āmittō
48. dēcidō

49. reddō
50. prohibeō
51. conveniō
52. obtineō
53. rūrsus
54. prōvocō
55. praetereō
56. incertus
57. respiciō
58. abiciō
59. afferō
60. subdūcō
61. repellō
62. oppōnō
63. convocō
64. ēdūcō
65. interpōnō
66. colloquor
67. subeō
68. permultus
69. exclūdō
70. praecēdō
71. anteferō
72. redigō
73. occurrō
74. inīquus
75. trādō
76. adhibeō
77. perficiō
78. antecēdō
79. perfringō
80. dissentiō
81. accurrō
82. circumdō
83. permagnus
84. dīmittō
85. īnfīnītus
86. sēcēdō
87. āvertō
88. dēdūcō
89. cōnferō
90. referō

Prefixes are also used in English to form compounds from simple words; as in Latin, some change their final consonants to make them like the initial consonants of the words to which they are prefixed. For example: **in + legible = illegible.**

Exercise 2

Divide each of the following compound words into its component parts, and show how the force of the prefix affects the meaning of each:

1. translate
2. abstract
3. precede
4. depend
5. subject
6. renovate
7. correct
8. inactive
9. translucent
10. secure
11. postscript
12. include
13. return
14. offer
15. dislocate
16. segregate
17. postpone
18. obstruct
19. suspend
20. acquire
21. separate
22. immigrant
23. propel
24. concur
25. affix
26. dispel
27. illuminate
28. accede
29. depose
30. announce
31. inconsistent
32. distract
33. secede
34. attend
35. proceed
36. subscribe
37. defer
38. circumvent
39. abrupt

40. ignoble
41. differ
42. support
43. educe
44. irruption
45. circumference
46. antecedent
47. avert
48. collect
49. abundance
50. seclude
51. preside
52. disarm
53. recede
54. effect
55. circumscribe
56. suggest
57. perfect
58. abstain
59. deduce
60. avocation
61. egress
62. illegal
63. commotion
64. transfer
65. occur
66. evoke
67. pervade
68. exclude
69. absent
70. deter
71. dishonest
72. impose
73. cohere
74. ascribe
75. oppose

SUFFIXES

A. Suffixes Used to Form Nouns from Verbs

	Suffix	*Meaning*	*Illustration*
1.	**-tor** (**-sor**) M. **-trīx** F.	one who	**ōrā-tor,** *one who speaks,* i.e., a speaker **dēfēn-sor,** *one who defends,* i.e., a defender **vic-trīx,** *she who conquers*
2.	**-a**	one who	**scrīb-a,** *one who writes,* i.e., a clerk
3.	**-or**	activity, condition, state	**am-or,** *love*
4.	**-iō**	action, result of an action	**leg-iō,** *the result of choosing,* i.e., a legion
5.	**-tiō** (**-siō**)	action, result of an action	**dēdi-tiō,** *a surrender* **dēfēn-siō,** *defense*
6.	**-tus** (**-sus**)	action, result of an action	**conven-tus,** *assembly, meeting* **cūr-sus,** *running, course*
7.	**-ēs**	action, result of an action	**caed-ēs,** *slaughter*
8.	**-tūra** (**-sūra**)	action, result of an action	**cul-tūra,** *tilling, cultivation* **tōn-sūra,** *shearing*
9.	**-ium**	action, result of an action	**aedific-ium,** *building*

Suffix	Meaning	Illustration
10. -men	means, place, result of an action	**nō-men**, *means of knowing*, i.e., a name
11. -mentum		**ōrnā-mentum**, *decoration*
12. -bulum		**pā-bulum**, *fodder*
13. -culum		**vehi-culum**, *conveyance*
14. -ulum		**vinc-ulum**, *chain*
15. -crum		**sepul-crum**, *burial-place*
16. -trum		**arā-trum**, *a plow*

B. Suffixes Used to Form Nouns from Nouns

Suffix	Meaning	Illustration
1. -ia	condition, characteristic	**victōr-ia**, *victory*
2. -tās		**cīvi-tās**, *citizenship*
3. -tūs		**servi-tūs**, *slavery*
4. -ātus	office	**cōnsul-ātus**, *consulship*

Diminutives

These are formed from nouns with the suffixes **-lus, -ulus** (***-olus***), **-culus, -ellus,** in any or all genders. They may denote endearment, pity, or contempt.

Examples. — **ātri-olum,** *a little hall* **fīli-ola,** *a little daughter*
lect-ulus, *a little bed* **mulier-cula,** *a little woman*
nāvi-cula, *a little ship*

Patronymics

These are proper names denoting *son of*, *grandson of*, or *daughter of*. The most common suffixes used to form patronymics are: **-īdēs** (M.), **-is** (F).

Examples. — **Tȳd-īdēs,** *son of Tydeus*, i.e., Diomedes
Tyndar-is, *daughter of Tyndareus*, i.e., Helen

C. Suffixes Used to Form Nouns from Adjectives

Suffix	Meaning	Illustration
1. -ia	quality, condition	**audāc-ia**, *boldness*
2. -tia		**trīsti-tia**, *sadness*
3. -tās		**celeri-tās**, *swiftness*
4. -tūdō		**magni-tūdō**, *greatness*

Exercise 3

Define each of the following words according to its etymology:

Model: **ōrātor** = **ōrā** (from **ōrō**, *speak*) + **tor** (*one who*) = *one who speaks*, i.e., a speaker.

1. accūsātiō
2. actiō
3. aditus
4. adventus
5. aegritūdō
6. aerārium
7. agmen
8. agricultūra
9. amīcitia
10. antīquitās
11. armātūra
12. auctor
13. auctoritās
14. audītor
15. beneficium
16. benīgnitās
17. bonitās
18. calor
19. cāsus
20. cēnsor
21. certāmen
22. clāmor
23. claustrum
24. commemorātiō
25. concursus
26. confōrmātiō
27. coniūrātiō
28. cōnsilium
29. cōntiō
30. crūdēlitās
31. cupiditās
32. dēlūbrum
33. difficultās
34. dīligentia
35. discessus
36. documentum
37. ēgressus
38. ēruptiō
39. excursiō
40. exercitus
41. exitus
42. explōrātor
43. expugnātiō
44. exspectātiō
45. fidēs
46. fortitūdō
47. frūctus
48. gaudium
49. hūmānitās
50. iactūra
51. iaculum
52. impedīmentum
53. imperātor
54. imperium
55. incola
56. iūmentum
57. iūstitia
58. lēgātus
59. levitās
60. lībertās
61. longitūdō
62. magistrātus
63. maleficium
64. memoria
65. mēnsūra
66. miseria
67. monumentum
68. mūnīmentum
69. mūnītiō
70. nōbilitās
71. occāsus
72. odium
73. offēnsiō
74. opportūnitās
75. ōrātiō
76. ōrnāmentum
77. perfuga
78. perīculum
79. petītor
80. pīctūra
81. posteritās
82. praetor
83. profectiō
84. prūdentia
85. ratiō
86. reditiō
87. regimen
88. rōstrum
89. scientia
90. scrīptor
91. scrīptūra
92. senātus
93. senectūs

94. sepulcrum	99. timor	104. virtūs
95. sepultūra	100. trāiectus	105. vīsus
96. servitium	101. vehiculum	106. vocābulum
97. solitūdō	102. vēnātrīx	107. vocātiō
98. studium	103. victor	108. volpēcula

Exercise 4

Define each of the following words according to its etymology:

Model: description = **de,** *down* + **scrip** (from **scrībō,** *write*) + **tion** (*act* or *result*) = the act or result of writing down or describing.

1. advent	16. excitement	31. monument
2. agency	17. exposure	32. navigator
3. altitude	18. expulsion	33. opposition
4. avocation	19. fortitude	34. persecutor
5. benefactor	20. inception	35. prediction
6. brevity	21. independence	36. premonition
7. circumlocution	22. injury	37. protection
8. circumnavigation	23. inscription	38. punishment
9. circumspection	24. inspection	39. purity
10. collector	25. inspector	40. recurrence
11. colloquy	26. intention	41. redemption
12. composition	27. intervention	42. servitude
13. disarmament	28. inventor	43. spectator
14. docility	29. magnitude	44. submission
15. elector	30. malediction	45. suspicion

D. Suffixes Used to Form Adjectives from Verbs

Suffix	*Meaning*	*Illustration*
1. **-ilis**	able to be	**fac-ilis,** *able to be done,* i.e., easy
2. **-bilis**	able to be	**mō-bilis,** *able to be moved,* i.e., movable, fickle
3. **-āx**	having the tendency, usually faulty	**aud-āx,** *having a tendency to dare,* i.e., daring
4. **-idus**	being in a condition	**tim-idus,** *being in a condition of fearing,* i.e., timid

E. Suffixes Used to Form Adjectives from Nouns

	Suffix	*Meaning*	*Illustration*
1.	**-ōsus**	full of	**perīcul-ōsus,** *full of danger,* i.e., dangerous
2.	**-lentus**	full of	**opu-lentus,** *wealthy*
3.	**-eus**	made of	**ferr-eus,** *made of iron*
4.	**-ālis**	pertaining to	**nāv-ālis,** *pertaining to a ship,* i.e., naval
5.	**-ānus**	pertaining to	**Rōm-ānus,** *pertaining to Rome,* i.e., Roman
6.	**-āris**	pertaining to	**consul-āris,** *pertaining to a consul,* i.e., consular
7.	**-ārius**	pertaining to	**legiōn-ārius,** *pertaining to a legion,* i.e., legionary
8.	**-ēnsis**	pertaining to	**castr-ēnsis,** *pertaining to a camp*
9.	**-ester**	pertaining to	**equ-ester,** *pertaining to a horseman,* i.e., equestrian
10.	**-icus**	pertaining to	**bell-icus,** *pertaining to war,* i.e., martial
11.	**-īlis**	pertaining to	**serv-īlis,** *pertaining to a slave,* i.e., servile
12.	**-imus**	pertaining to	**marit-imus,** *pertaining to the sea,* i.e., marine
13.	**-īnus**	pertaining to	**Lat-īnus,** *pertaining to Latium,* i.e., Latin
14.	**-īvus**	pertaining to	**aest-īvus,** *pertaining to summer*
15.	**-ius**	pertaining to	**patr-ius,** *pertaining to a father,* i.e., ancestral

Exercise 5

Define each of the following adjectives according to its etymology:

Model 1: urbānus = **urb** (from **urbs,** *city*) + **ānus** (*pertaining to*) = *pertaining to the city,* i.e., of the city.

Model 2: legible = **leg** (from **legō,** *read*) + **ible** (*able to be*) = *able to be read.*

A

1. aliēnus
2. annōsus
3. aureus
4. bellicōsus
5. captīvus
6. cīvīlis
7. cōpiōsus
8. crēdibilis
9. cupidus
10. docilis
11. domesticus
12. edāx
13. extrāneus
14. familiāris
15. fragilis
16. frūmentārius
17. fugitīvus
18. Gallicus
19. Hispāniēnsis
20. hostīlis
21. humilis
22. incrēdibilis
23. laudābilis
24. lēgitimus
25. marīnus
26. marmoreus
27. mīlitāris
28. mīrābilis
29. mūrālis
30. oppidānus
31. ōtiōsus
32. perūtilis
33. puerīlis
34. pūgnāx
35. rēgālis
36. rēgius
37. Rōmānus
38. rusticus
39. studiōsus
40. Sullānus
41. tenāx
42. vīnōsus
43. violentus
44. virīlis
45. vītālis

B

1. American
2. arable
3. civic
4. credible
5. divine
6. domestic
7. feminine
8. fluid
9. inaudible
10. irrevocable
11. laborious
12. legal
13. lunar
14. mental
15. noble
16. ocular
17. permissible
18. servile
19. solar
20. soluble
21. tolerable
22. verbose
23. virile
24. vulgar

Verbs Derived from Verbs

1. Frequentatives, expressing repeated or intensive action, are formed by adding the suffixes: **-tō** (**-itō**), or **-sō** to the stems of other verbs; as,

   clām (from **clāmō**, *shout*) + **itō** (*intensive suffix*) = **clāmitō**, *cry out loudly*

   iac (from **iaciō**, *throw*) + **tō** (*intensive suffix*) = **iactō**, *throw about, toss*

   cur (from **currō**, *run*) + **sō** (*intensive suffix*) = **cursō**, *run about*

2. Inceptives, expressing the beginning of an action, are formed by adding the suffix **-scō** to the stems of other verbs; as,

time (from **timeō,** *be afraid of*) + **scō** (*inceptive suffix*) = **timēscō,** *begin to be afraid of, become afraid of*

ENGLISH DERIVATIVES

Since a very large number of English words has come directly or indirectly from Latin, special attention should be given to the derivation of such words. The following list will be suggestive as a basis for this study. From each of these verbs the pupil should be required to make a list of all the more important English derivatives.

1. servō
2. locō
3. vocō
4. pugnō
5. videō
6. moveō
7. dūcō
8. mittō
9. teneō
10. portō
11. cēdō
12. putō
13. parō
14. nūntiō
15. spectō
16. habeō
17. moneō
18. agō
19. scrībō
20. cōgnōscō
21. pōnō
22. veniō
23. pellō
24. mūniō
25. trahō
26. dīcō
27. sūmō
28. faciō
29. capiō
30. audiō
31. dō
32. doceō
33. premō
34. legō
35. claudō
36. vincō
37. nāvigō
38. sentiō
39. audeō
40. laudō
41. ōrō
42. valeō
43. nāscor
44. tangō
45. quaerō
46. regō
47. currō
48. solvō
49. vereor
50. ūtor
51. mandō
52. arbitror
53. loquor
54. accēdō
55. potior
56. tribuō
57. iungō
58. sequor
59. dēspiciō
60. vertō

With the aid of an unabridged English dictionary study carefully the form and meaning of words like the following and compare with Latin originals:

1. urbane
2. actor
3. trivial
4. tabernacle
5. vespers
6. reporter
7. sinister
8. dexterity
9. salute
10. lunatic
11. bonus
12. miser
13. alumnus
14. virtue
15. superb
16. doctor
17. circus
18. pagan
19. umbrella
20. suburb
21. fraternity
22. capital
23. regalia
24. infinitive
25. gentle
26. fort
27. omnibus
28. ambition
29. faction
30. science
31. insulation
32. temperance
33. governor
34. integer
35. sinecure
36. jovial
37. profound
38. doubt
39. manual
40. gladiolus
41. alibi
42. alias
43. item
44. ensign
45. conjugal
46. responsible
47. patient
48. accident
49. nihilist
50. libretto
51. faculty
52. bounty
53. volume
54. lapidary
55. oriole
56. rapture
57. cordial
58. agent
59. prohibition
60. confectionery
61. ditto
62. congress
63. orient
64. tent
65. album
66. mayor
67. minister
68. adieu
69. exit
70. superior
71. speculator
72. minimum
73. circumvent
74. salary
75. index
76. abductor
77. graduation
78. merchant
79. piano
80. plea
81. hotel
82. automobile
83. motorcycle
84. insult
85. aspirant
86. bankrupt
87. excise
88. expend
89. molasses
90. volcano
91. cupidity
92. stupendous
93. abominable
94. disaster
95. ineffable
96. consider
97. desire
98. estate
99. currency
100. reputation
101. saint
102. soldier
103. hour
104. altar
105. apex
106. feat
107. exact
108. influenza

109. miscreant
110. perspire
111. coroner
112. mob
113. minute
114. czar
115. paper
116. sir
117. desultory
118. quondam
119. tandem
120. duel
121. nocturne
122. adventure
123. examination
124. civility
125. arbitrary
126. fluency
127. October
128. crucible
129. subtle
130. precarious
131. professor
132. frail
133. sure
134. loyal
135. usury
136. neuter
137. journal
138. candle
139. noon
140. chivalry
141. obituary
142. interest
143. apartment
144. dilapidated
145. popularity
146. proclivity
147. redundant
148. insinuate
149. caprice
150. city
151. prove
152. palace
153. cattle
154. exaggerate
155. étude

PARIS AS JUDGE OF BEAUTY

Paris is about to select the most beautiful of the three goddesses. Hera stands before him holding the golden apple, while behind her Athena and Aphrodite are conversing.

CHAPTER XIII

IMPORTANT RULES OF SYNTAX

1. A finite verb agrees with its subject in person and number.
2. A finite verb with two or more subjects is usually in the plural.
3. When two or more singular subjects are connected by the conjunctions **aut . . . aut, nec . . . nec,** the verb is usually singular.
4. A collective noun regularly takes a singular verb, but the plural may be used when the individuals are thought of.
5. In the perfect, pluperfect, and future perfect passive, the participle agrees in gender, number, and case with the subject.
6. A predicate noun or predicate adjective agrees with its subject in case.
7. An appositive agrees in case with the noun which it explains.
8. An adjective, whether attributive or predicate, agrees with the noun or pronoun to which it belongs in gender, number, and case.
9. A relative pronoun agrees with its antecedent in gender and number, but its case is determined by its use in its own clause.
10. The reflexive pronoun may refer to the subject of the clause in which it stands (direct reflexive); or, if it stands in a subordinate clause, it may refer to the subject of the principal clause (indirect reflexive).
11. The possessive pronoun of the third person (**suus, -a, -um**) refers either to the subject of the clause in which it stands, or to the subject of the principal clause.
12. The subject of a finite verb is in the nominative.
13. After the copula **sum, fīō, videor,** and the passive voice of verbs meaning *call, choose, appoint, make,* and the like, a predicate noun or predicate adjective is in the nominative.
14. The name of the person addressed is in the vocative. This case usually follows one or more words of the sentence.

15. The possessive genitive is used with a noun to indicate the possessor.
16. The possessive genitive is used idiomatically with **causā, prīdiē,** and **postrīdiē.** With **causā** the genitive always precedes.
17. The adjectives **cupidus, perītus, imperītus, memor, plēnus,** and others of similar character are followed by the objective genitive.
18. The adjectives **similis, dissimilis,** and **proprius** are usually followed by the genitive of persons.
19. The partitive genitive or genitive of the whole is used with words denoting a part to indicate the whole to which the part belongs.
20. With cardinal numerals (except **mīlia**), **quīdam,** and **paucī,** the ablative with **dē** or **ex** is used, instead of the partitive genitive.
21. The genitive of quality or description is used to describe a person or thing, but only when the noun of quality is modified by an adjective.
22. The genitives **magnī, parvī, tantī, quantī, plūris, minōris** denote indefinite value.
23. The verbs **accūsō, condemnō, damnō,** and **absolvō** take the genitive of the charge or penalty.
24. The following impersonal verbs take the accusative of the person who has the feeling, and the genitive of the object that causes the feeling: **miseret, paenitet, piget, pudet, taedet.**
25. The verbs **meminī** and **oblīvīscor** usually take the genitive.
26. The indirect object of a verb is in the dative. This dative is used especially with verbs of *telling*, *reporting*, and *giving*.
27. The dative of the indirect object is used with the intransitive verbs **cēdō, cōnfīdō, cōnsulō, crēdō, faveō, imperō, minor, minitor, noceō, parcō, pāreō, persuādeō, placeō, resistō, studeō,** and others of like meaning.
28. The verbs enumerated in 27 are used impersonally in the passive. The dative of the indirect object is retained.
29. The dative of the indirect object is used with *some* verbs compounded with **ad, ante, con, dē, in, inter, ob, post, prae, prō, sub,** and **super.**
30. The dative is used with adjectives meaning *near*, *fit*, *friendly*, *pleasing*, *like*, and their opposites.

31. The dative of purpose is used to express the purpose of an action.
32. The possessor may be expressed by the dative with some part of **sum** (dative of the possessor).
33. The dative of agent is used with the passive periphrastic conjugation and sometimes with the compound tenses (the perfect, pluperfect, and future perfect of the passive).
34. The direct object of a transitive verb is in the accusative case.
35. Verbs meaning *name*, *choose*, *call*, and *make* usually take a predicate accusative along with the direct object.
36. The verb **rogō** takes two accusatives, one of the person, the other of the thing.
37. With the verbs **petō** and **quaerō** the person is expressed by the ablative with **ab, dē,** or **ex** (ablative of source) and the thing by the accusative.
38. Duration of time is expressed by the accusative without a preposition.
39. Extent of space is expressed by the accusative without a preposition.
40. The place to which is expressed by the accusative with the prepositions **ad** or **in.**
41. With names of towns, **domus,** and **rūs,** the place to which is expressed by the accusative without a preposition.
42. The subject of the principal clause in an indirect statement is in the accusative.
43. Separation is expressed by the ablative, usually with the prepositions **ā** (**ab**), **dē, ē** (**ex**).
44. The verbs **abdicō mē, careō, dēsistō, līberō,** and **prohibeō** regularly take the ablative of separation without a preposition.
45. The place from which is expressed by the ablative with the prepositions **ā** (**ab**), **dē, ē** (**ex**).
46. With names of towns, **domus,** and **rūs,** the place from which is expressed by the ablative without a preposition.
47. The place in which is expressed by the ablative with the preposition **in.**

48. With **locus,** in the singular and plural, and several other nouns of place modified by **tōtus,** the place in which is expressed by the ablative without a preposition.
49. With names of towns, **domus,** and **rūs,** the place in which is expressed by the locative.
50. Means is expressed by the ablative without a preposition.
51. The deponents **ūtor** and **potior** take the ablative of means.
52. Cause may be expressed by the ablative, usually without a preposition.
53. With a verb in the passive voice, the personal agent is expressed by the ablative with **ā** or **ab.**
54. The manner of an action is expressed by the ablative with **cum;** but **cum** may be omitted if the ablative is modified by an adjective.
55. The degree of difference between two objects or actions is expressed by the ablative without a preposition.
56. The ablative of quality or description (without a preposition) is used to describe a person or thing, but only when the noun of quality is modified by an adjective.
57. The ablative without a preposition is used to denote in what respect something is true (ablative of specification or respect).
58. The adjectives **dignus** and **indignus** take the ablative of specification.
59. Accompaniment is expressed by the ablative with **cum.**
60. A noun or pronoun with a present or perfect participle in agreement may be used in the ablative case to form an ablative absolute.
61. In the ablative absolute construction, an adjective, or a second noun may take the place of the participle.
62. Time when or within which is expressed by the ablative without a preposition.
63. Accordance is expressed by the ablative without a preposition; sometimes with **ex** or **dē.**
64. The adjectives **contentus** and **frētus** are followed by the ablative without a preposition.

65. The way by which is expressed by the ablative without a preposition.
66. After a comparative, if **quam** is expressed, the two things compared are in the same case; but if **quam** is omitted, the second thing compared is put in the ablative without a preposition.
67. A primary tense of the indicative is followed by a primary tense of the subjunctive; a secondary tense of the indicative is followed by a secondary tense of the subjunctive.

    Primary tenses of the indicative: present, future, future perfect.

    Primary tenses of the subjunctive: present (incomplete action), perfect (completed action).

    Secondary tenses of the indicative: imperfect, perfect, pluperfect.

    Secondary tenses of the subjunctive: imperfect (incomplete action), pluperfect (completed action).
68. A purpose clause takes the present or imperfect subjunctive introduced by **ut** or **nē**; the tense of the subjunctive is determined by the rule for the sequence of tenses.
69. The purpose clause is regularly introduced by a relative pronoun if the principal clause contains a definite antecedent.
70. If the purpose clause contains a comparative of either an adjective or adverb, *in order that* is translated by **quō.**
71. The following verbs are followed by substantive clauses of purpose:

cēnseō	**ōrō**
dēcernō	**permittō**
hortor	**persuādeō**
imperō	**petō**
mandō	**postulō**
moneō	**rogō**

72. A result clause takes the subjunctive introduced by **ut** or **ut . . . nōn**; the tense of the subjunctive is determined by the rule for the sequence of tenses.

Note. — After a secondary tense, result clauses very often have the perfect subjunctive, instead of the imperfect.

73. The following verbs are followed by substantive clauses of result: **accidit, fit, faciō,** and **efficiō.**
74. A causal clause introduced by **quod** or **quia** takes the indicative when the writer or speaker gives his own reason; but the subjunctive when the writer or speaker gives another person's reason.
75. A causal clause introduced by **quoniam** takes the indicative.
76. A causal clause introduced by **cum** always takes the subjunctive.
77. A temporal clause introduced by **cum** referring to present time takes the present indicative.
78. A temporal clause introduced by **cum** referring to future time takes the future or future perfect indicative.
79. A temporal clause introduced by **cum** takes some past tense of the indicative if it denotes the time at which the action of the principal verb took place.

NOTE. — The indicative is always used if **cum** is preceded by a noun of time, as **annus, diēs,** or the adverb **tum.**

80. A **cum**-circumstantial clause takes the imperfect or pluperfect subjunctive.
81. A temporal clause introduced by **ut, ubi, postquam,** and **simul atque** takes the indicative, usually the perfect, sometimes the historical present.
82. A temporal clause introduced by **antequam** or **priusquam** takes the indicative when the subordinate verb denotes an actual fact (usually after a negative), but the subjunctive when the subordinate verb denotes an expected event.
83. A temporal clause introduced by **dum,** *until,* takes the indicative when the subordinate verb denotes an actual fact, but the subjunctive when the subordinate verb denotes an expected event.
84. A temporal clause introduced by **dum,** *while,* takes the present indicative, usually translated by the English past progressive.
85. A concessive clause introduced by **cum** takes the subjunctive.
86. A concessive clause introduced by **quamquam** takes the indicative.

87. A relative clause of characteristic or description takes the subjunctive.
88. Verbs of *fearing* are followed by substantive clauses with the subjunctive introduced by **nē,** *that, lest,* or **ut,** *that . . . not.*
89. Verbs of *hindering, preventing,* and *refusing* are followed by substantive clauses with the subjunctive introduced by **nē** or **quōminus** if the principal verb is positive, but by **quīn** if the principal verb is negative.
90. The verb **prohibeō** regularly takes the accusative and the infinitive.
91. Negative and interrogative expressions of *doubting* are followed by substantive clauses with the subjunctive introduced by **quīn.**
92. Simple conditions take the indicative. The tense is the same as that found in the English sentence, except that in a simple condition referring to future time the Latin uses the future or even the future perfect where the English uses the present tense.
93. Future less vivid conditions take the present subjunctive in both clauses.
94. Contrary to fact (unreal) conditions in present time take the imperfect subjunctive in both clauses.
95. Contrary to fact (unreal) conditions in past time take the pluperfect subjunctive in both clauses.
96. Mixed contrary to fact conditions take the pluperfect subjunctive in the condition and the imperfect subjunctive in the conclusion.
97. The verb of a direct question is in the indicative.
98. The verb of an indirect question is in the subjunctive; the tense of the subjunctive is determined by the rule for the sequence of tenses.
99. The verb of a subordinate clause in indirect discourse is in the subjunctive; the tense of the subjunctive is determined by the rule for the sequence of tenses.
100. The verb of a principal clause in indirect discourse is in the present infinitive if its action is contemporaneous with that of the introductory verb.

101. The verb of a principal clause in indirect discourse is in the perfect infinitive if its action occurred before that of the introductory verb.
102. The verb of a principal clause in indirect discourse is in the future infinitive if its action is subsequent to that of the introductory verb.
103. When a verb has no participial stem and the future infinitive active in indirect discourse is required, the expressions **fore ut** or **futūrum esse ut** with the subjunctive are used.
104. Instead of the future infinitive passive in indirect discourse, the expressions **fore ut** or **futūrum esse ut** with the subjunctive are used.
105. The verbs **cōgō, iubeō, patior, sinō,** and **vetō** are followed by the object infinitive and subject accusative.
106. The following verbs are followed by the complementary infinitive:

audeō	**dubitō** (*hesitate*)
coepī	**incipiō**
cōnor	**mātūrō**
cōnstituō	**possum**
cōnsuēscō	**soleō**
contendō	**statuō**
dēbeō	**videor**

107. The genitive of the gerund or gerundive followed by **causā,** *for the sake of*, expresses purpose.
108. The accusative of the gerund or gerundive with **ad** expresses purpose.
109. The future active participle is used with the forms of **sum** to express a future or intended action.
110. The future passive participle is used with the forms of **sum** to express necessity or obligation.
111. The supine in **-um** is used with verbs of motion to express purpose.
112. The supine in **-ū** is used with certain adjectives as an ablative of specification.

113. An exhortation or command in the first or third person is expressed by the present subjunctive. The negative is **nē.**

114. A command in the second person is expressed by the imperative.

115. A negative command in the second person is expressed by **nōlī** (singular) or **nōlīte** (plural) with the infinitive.

116. A wish which is possible of fulfillment is expressed by the present subjunctive. The negative is **nē.**

117. A wish which is impossible of fulfillment in present time is expressed by the imperfect subjunctive, regularly introduced by **utinam.** The negative is **nē.**

118. A wish which is impossible of fulfillment in past time is expressed by the pluperfect subjunctive, regularly introduced by **utinam.** The negative is **nē.**

119. In a question implying doubt or indignation the verb is either in the present subjunctive (referring to present time) or in the imperfect subjunctive (referring to past time). The negative is **nōn.**

120. **Dum, dummodo, modo,** *provided that, if only*, take the subjunctive.

121. Future conditions in indirect discourse:
    (*a*) The verb of the condition is always in the subjunctive (the tense of the subjunctive is determined by the rule for the sequence of tenses).
    (*b*) The present subjunctive in the conclusion of a future less vivid condition becomes a future infinitive.
    (*c*) The future or future perfect indicative in the conclusion of a future more vivid condition becomes a future infinitive.

122. Contrary to fact conditions in indirect discourse:
    (*a*) The condition always remains *unchanged.*
    (*b*) If the conclusion of either a present or past contrary to fact condition is in the active voice, the verb becomes an infinitive in **-ūrum fuisse.**
    (*c*) If the verb of the conclusion is passive or has no participial stem, it takes the form **futūrum fuisse ut** and the imperfect subjunctive.

123. A subordinate clause takes the subjunctive when it expresses the thought of some person other than the writer or speaker.

124. With **iam diū, iam prīdem, iam dūdum** the present is regularly used to denote an action begun in the past and continuing in the present.

125. With **iam diū, iam prīdem, iam dūdum** the imperfect is regularly used to denote an action continuing in the past but begun at some previous time.

THE DEPARTURE OF HECTOR

Hector stands before his mother, Hecuba, who is about to pour a libation for him, while his father, Priam, muses sadly over the dangers Hector must face in battle.

CHAPTER XIV

PASSAGES FOR TRANSLATION INTO LATIN

NOTE. — *Numbers within parentheses refer to Important Rules of Syntax, pp. 91–100.*

1

When the Senator from Indiana was speaking (*80*) of this dreadful war, he declared that we should be worthy (*6*) of scorn (*58*) if we were to disregard (*99*) what the war had taught. "For," said he, "the times are changed, and our policies must be changed (*110*) in accordance with the times. Don't you realize that during these years, owing to the scarcity of our ships, not even our wealthiest cities (*42*) have been safe? We are like the foolish bird (*30*) which, to avoid (*68*) danger, hides its head in the sand. Let (*113*) us, therefore, my friends, urge the American people to take (*71*) the necessary action. For I myself have no doubt that (*91*), now the matter has been clearly stated, you all think as I do."

2

The Commissioners chosen by Turkey and by the several Balkan states to conclude (*108*) peace assembled in London (*41*) a few years ago. Greece also sent Commissioners to participate in the conference, although she had refused (*85; 86*) to join the armistice. Day after day the Turks, according to their custom (*63*), prolonged the conferences and delayed the business of the commission. This they did because they hoped (*74*) to obtain (*102*) better terms by delay, or even to secure intervention by the Great Powers. The one condition laid down by the Balkan Commissioners, without which there could be no peace, was that Turkey should surrender (*68*) the ancient city of Adrianople. This the Turkish envoys said they (*10*) never would do.

3

Let (*liceat 113*) me ask the distinguished Senator what he would have done had he been (*95*) President of the United States when Francesco Villa led his troop of bandits within our boundaries and raided several towns in Arizona. Would he have addressed a note to Carranza, calling upon him for satisfaction? Would he not rather have ordered the General (*105*) of our army to pursue the bandit leader until he captured (*83*) or killed him? The American people really bear no grudge against either the Mexicans or against the First Chief personally. This Carranza well knows; and he knows also that the American people wish the Mexicans to be peaceful (*6*) and prosperous. If, however, the First Chief's own troops should attack (*93*) the American soldiers, then and then only could war be made on the Mexicans (*29*).

4

Some Roman writers tell us (*26*) that Pompey was undeservedly praised for having wrested Mithridates' kingdom from him. We cannot, therefore, doubt that (*91*) these men believed Pompey's personal enemies (*27*), who pointed out that Lucullus had almost broken (*101*) the power of Mithridates before Pompey was put in command of this war (*29*). Furthermore, they are convinced that, if the king's son had not rebelled (*95*) against his father, Pompey would have been defeated (*122, c*) by the Asiatic king.

There are others also who, eager to criticize Pompey, quote (*87*) these words of Cato: "The whole Mithridatic war," he said, "was waged against women." To this Cicero himself makes reply that Sulla could not crush this king; and furthermore that Mithridates, after taking several years to strengthen (*108*) his resources for war, became so powerful that he planned (*72*) to join the Ocean with the Pontus, and the forces of Sertorius in Spain with his own.

5

You, Soldiers of the National Army, are undertaking a great duty. Do not doubt (*115*) that (*91*) the heart of the whole country is with you. Everything that you do will be watched with the deepest solicitude (*54*), not only by those (*53*) who are near and dear to you (*30*), but by the whole nation besides. For this great war draws us all together, makes us all comrades (*35*) and brothers, as all true Americans felt themselves to be when we made good our national independence. Let it be (*113*) your pride, therefore, to show all men (*26*) everywhere, not only what good soldiers you are (*98*), but also what good men you are. My affectionate confidence goes with you in every battle and in every test. God keep (*116*) and guide you.

6

In Cicero's opinion (*63*), if a state possesses a citizen of extraordinary ability (*21; 56*), it should keep him always employed in promoting its interests. But let us imagine (*113*) what would happen were we to follow strictly this reasoning. Suppose there were a state which thought it possessed a king endowed with such superhuman skill in governing that he ought (*72*) to rule the world. Would this state hesitate, though unprovoked, to attack other states that this man's talent might become (*68*) useful to his country? Once a Roman congratulated his countrymen in these words (*50*): "We ought to be (*106*) most grateful to the gods, that (*74*) Africanus was born in our country. For there is no doubt that (*91*) the rule of the world must be where he lives." May we not suspect that certain Germans have made their emperor believe (*73*) that he is a second Scipio?

7

In saying (*80*) that the enemy (*33*) must no longer destroy towns and murder their inhabitants our leader spoke for us all. For until the enemy is willing to spare the lives (*27*) of women and children there is no doubt that (*91*) the people of this country will be unwilling to spare the enemy. Let (*113*) us not be afraid, then, that our soldiers will (*88*) not fight for many years (*38*), if necessary, in order to punish those who are unworthy of the name (*58*) of men. For there is no one who trusts (*87*) them (*27*), even when they come to seek (*68; 107; 108*) peace. If they had not made (*95*) war upon the Belgians with great cruelty and committed many other crimes, they (*27; 28*) might have been pardoned. But after they had done (*81*) these things all good men became their enemies (*13*).

8

I believe that when Cicero said that honor should be sought more than all other things in life he (*42*) spoke words worthy of a great orator (*58*). For in all the best men of our own time there seems to be a certain moral worth which urges them to forget (*71*) all other rewards (*25*) of labor and hardship. The brave soldiers who are fighting our battles in other lands while we are safe at home (*49*) would ask for nothing more. If Cicero were (*94*) now living he would have realized from the example of these men of surpassing courage (*21*) that he was wise in speaking as he did. Let (*113*) us too seek honor always, even if it should be necessary to give our lives to gain (*68*) it.

9

After peace (*60*) had been made, many believed that we (*33*) ought to urge all citizens to think (*71*) very carefully regarding domestic difficulties; these had long been causing (*125*) men to fear (*73*) that (*88*) our country would forget its former glory (*25*). The difficulties were of many kinds, and there was need of great effort if we wished to overcome them. Would that we had realized (*118*) that they were so numerous, for then it would have been easier to ask all good men (*36*) for aid (*36*). If they had given (*95*) us (*26*) this aid there is no doubt that (*91*) we should now be enjoying better fortune (*51*). We waited, however, until evil men showed (*83*) that they were unworthy of our confidence (*58*), before we attempted to punish them, and they had already injured the republic (*27*).

10

There was no one of our senators last year (*62*) who did not think (*87*) that this country ought to lead all other nations toward a lasting peace. And yet there were some who saw (*87*) dangers to be avoided if we should attempt to do this. It therefore happened that many of the senators felt (*73*) that we (*27; 28*) ought not to be persuaded to adopt (*71*) any plan which seemed to increase these dangers. While the matter was being discussed (*84*) some asked whether it was (*98*) wise to do anything contrary to the customs of our ancestors. Others said that if we had always followed these customs we should not now have (*122, b*) the power which has been ours for many years (*38*). Finally the senate regretted its long delay and decided that it would do what the people wished.

11

In the first Punic war Regulus, a Roman consul, had the misfortune to be captured by the Carthaginians. They, thinking that they (*10*) could use him (*51*) for their own purpose, sent him to Rome (*41*) to persuade the senate (*27*) to surrender (*71*) certain noble Carthaginians whom the Romans were holding. He was under oath to return himself if he could not accomplish this. But after he entered (*81*) the senate, he refused to vote on the matter, saying that he was not worthy (*6*) to be (*87*) a senator since he was bound (*76*) by an oath to a public enemy, and urged that the captives should not be returned (*71*). So it turned out. He was noble enough to consider (*72*) his life of less value (*22*) than the good of his country, and went back to Africa to die.

12

Who can doubt that (*91*) the second Punic war was one of (*20*) the greatest ever waged? We know now that the gods finally favored the Romans (*27*), but for a long time no one could tell what the end would be (*98*). After the battle of Cannae it seemed that all was lost, and there was need of the true Roman spirit to save the Roman cause. Though the senate knew (*85; 86*) that eight thousand men (*19*) whom Hannibal held prisoners could be ransomed at small cost, it refused to bring them home (*41*), because they had not been captured fighting, but in camp. It was thus shown that a man was not worthy to be (*87*) a soldier, if he allowed himself to be taken alive — that the soldier (*33*) must conquer or die.

13

Who will deny that Julius Caesar was one (*6*) of (*20*) the most famous Romans? Although he was sprung (*85; 86*) from noble ancestry, he always favored the common people (*27*). Sulla, consequently, hated and feared him. He used to say that he saw in Caesar many Mariuses, and that some day this young man would overthrow (*102*) the aristocracy. After this Caesar (*33*) had to flee for his life; he went to Asia Minor, and waited there for Sulla to die (*83*). Several years (*55*) later he gained control of Gaul (*51*), and then, by defeating Pompey (*60*), he became all-powerful. Still he used his power (*51*) wisely. Would Brutus have slain (*95*) such a great man, if he had realized what he was doing (*98*)?

14

In Cicero's consulship (61) the government appeared to be in very grave danger; for Catiline thought that he (*10*) could obtain (*100*) control of affairs by a bold conspiracy. For several months (*38*) he made preparations, and persuaded many other nobles (*27*) to join (*71*) him. But one day when Catiline came into the senate, Cicero, who knew what had been going on (*98*), accused him with such violence that he immediately left (*72*) the city, and took up arms against his country. Before his plans could (*82*) be carried out, however, the consul captured the conspirators without any bloodshed. And so we cannot doubt that (*91*) the state was saved from destruction (*44*) by Cicero's courage (*52*) and foresight.

15

Vergil was born near Mantua in the consulship (*61*) of Pompey and Crassus. He was still living as a boy in the distant valley of the Po at the time when Catiline began (*79*) to plot against the government at Rome. It is said that there were at the same time (*62*) some disturbances in Cisalpine Gaul. Rumor travels fast, and we may imagine what anxiety was felt (*98; 67*) even there while it was uncertain where Catiline would go (*109; 98*). Many feared that (*88*) even if his route should not bring him to Mantua (*41*), he would still pass through the territory in trying to escape into Gaul. Can we doubt, therefore, that (*91*) the news of this nefarious conspiracy reached (*67*) the ears of the young Vergil, then a lad of seven years (*21*)?

16

The letters of Cicero are of great value because they show more truly than his speeches (*66*) what sort of man he was (*98*). For example, in a letter sent to Lucceius, a well-known writer (*7*), although he knew (*85; 86*) that he was transgressing the bounds of modesty, he said boldly that he (*10*) hoped Lucceius (*42*) would glorify (*102*) the events of his consulship. "Alexander," he wrote, "asked the great Apelles to paint (*71*) him because he was (*123*) so famous that he ought (*72*) not to have a bad picture; do not wonder (*115*), then, if I ask you to write about me." No one will doubt that (*91*) Cicero tried (*67*) to serve his country. To many, however, he would seem (*96*) a greater man (*13*) if he had said (*96*) less about his own deeds.

17

Pompey seems to have been a soldier (*13*) of unusual training (*21*) and of unusual success. He (*32*) had all the qualities which Cicero said a general ought to have. He controlled himself and his army so well that foreign nations preferred (*72*) to be subject (*106*) to him rather than to command others (*27*). We know how quickly and well he carried on (*98*) all his campaigns. Therefore we can see why Cicero felt (*67*) that he ought to be put in command (*106; 110*) of the Mithridatic war (*29*). At that time there was no doubt that (*91*) the people loved him, and that the senate feared him. If he had been (*95*) equally worthy of being (*87*) at the head of the state (*29*), he would have escaped such a death as (*9*) many years (*55*) later befell him.

18

There were many Romans who believed (*87*) that Caesar was hoping to be (*102*) king (*6*) and who feared that (*88*) he would destroy their liberty if they did not kill (*123*) him. While he was going (*84*) to the meeting of the senate on the last day (*62*) of his life, friends warned him not to enter (*71*) the senate-house. His wife had already tried to persuade (*106*) him (*27*) to stay (*71*) at home (*49*). But believing that the time of danger was past, he asked them if they still thought (*98*) he was going to die (*102*) on the Ides (*62*) of March, and hastened on to his death. Many think that if he had obeyed (*122, a; 95*) the warnings (*27*), he would have been (*122, b*) unharmed. But a sudden and swift death was what he once said he hoped for.

19

When the Greeks gathered, before starting (*82*) for Troy (*41*), there were two men absent. The mother of one, knowing that her son was (*100*) mortal and would die (*102*) in the war, tried to keep him from going (*90*). So she persuaded him (*27*), clad as a girl, to hide (*71*) among the daughters of a king. But when a trader came to sell (*68*) pretty things, among which had been placed some arms, he forgot who he was supposed to be, and was discovered because he picked out a shield. The other man was happy at home with his wife and son. By acting as if he were insane, he hoped to escape (*102*). But when the ambassadors sent for him and proved that he (*42*) was sane, he (*33; 110*) too had to go to war.

20

The senate had ordered Caesar, who was in Gaul, to give up (*71; 105*) his command or to be declared an enemy. As soon as the report reached (*81*) him, he called his soldiers together to tell (*68*) them (*26*) what the senate had done (*98*). "For nine years (*38*)," he said, "I have served (*124*) my country loyally. If the senate had thanked (*95*) me, it would have acted only justly. I was willing none the less to obey the senate (*27*) if Pompey also was willing (*92*), and yet he is not even asked to disband (*71*) his army." This and much more he said, until he so aroused (*83*) his soldiers that they all promised (*72*) to follow (*102*) him. In a short time (*62*) they made the senate understand (*73*) that Caesar (*42*) was the ruler (*6*).

21

After Troy was captured (*81; 60*) and burned, Aeneas set out to find (*68*) a new home for himself and his companions. But at the very first place (*48*) he reached he was warned to flee (*71*). So when he again landed, he consulted the oracle of Apollo to learn (*68*) where he was to go (*110; 98*), and was bidden to seek his ancient mother, which his father Anchises said was (*100*) surely Crete. But arriving (*80*) there, he again had to leave (*110*), for the gods informed him that not Crete but Italy was the ancient mother. And so after this, although he delayed (*85; 86*) in many places (*48*) where he would have been willing to stay, he believed the oracle (*27*) and proceeded on until he should reach (*83*) Italy.

22

We wonder why Cicero thought (*98*) that the character of Catiline could ever be altered. He had always been one to fear (*87*) neither God nor man. If he had gone into exile, he would not have done (*95*) so to escape (*68*) from the law and to free the state, but to make plans for bringing impious war upon his fatherland (*29*). Cicero knew that he had already sent (*101*) to the camp of Manlius that standard which the army of Marius was said (*99*) to have borne. He certainly must have sent it for Manlius to use (*68*) when he was ready to fight. As for his forces, not a good man could be seen among them, but all were like him (*30*) and worthy to follow (*87*) such an infamous leader.

23

While desperate fighting was going on (*84*) not far from Lake Regillus, the general was afraid that (*88*) without the help of the gods his own men might be overpowered by the enemy. So he promised to build (*102*) a temple at Rome (*49*) in honor of Castor and his brother, if they would come (*99*) to his (*10*) assistance. Soon afterwards there appeared in the ranks two horsemen of superhuman beauty, who fought with such vigor (*54*) that the whole army was amazed and the enemy routed (*72* Note). That night (*62*), the story goes, these same horsemen rode into the Forum and stopped near a certain spring to allow their tired horses (*105*) to drink. They informed the citizens who they were (*98*), and said that the foe had been prevented from invading (*90*) the city. On this very spot (*48*) a few years (*55*) later a splendid temple was erected to the two gods.

24

As Phaeton wished (*76*) to prove that he was really the child (*6*) of the Sun, he made his way to the palace where his father was about to drive (*109*) his famous horses through the sky.

"Let (*113*, *liceat*, etc.) me, dear father, drive the chariot today," said Phaeton.

But his father answered, "Do not ask (*115*) me (*36*) such a favor! No mortal is sufficiently strong or worthy to restrain (*87*) these sacred animals."

"That is just the reason why I beg you," cried Phaeton. "If I should be able (*93*) to drive them from sea to sea, no one would hereafter doubt that (*91*) I too am immortal."

With such words, Phaeton, unconscious of his fate, persuaded his father (*27*) to grant (*71*) his request.

25

Can we doubt that the Greeks greatly admired (*67*) their poets and even called them holy (*35*)? It is said that one of (*20*) the bards of olden time sang so sweetly that rivers stood still, and animals forgot (*72*) their prey to listen (*68*) to his voice. Furthermore, if Alexander the Great, when he made (*80*) his expedition into Asia, had not taken (*96*) with him writers of great ability, we should not know (*96*) what he accomplished (*98*). Some years (*55*) later, before Greece became (*82*) a Roman province (*13*), libraries were built in Pergamum (*49*) and at Alexandria, for the sake of preserving (*107*) those very books (*107*) which all the best educated persons read to this day.

26

At Syracuse (*49*), not far from the harbor, is an extremely beautiful fountain of great size. A Roman poet tells us (*26*) why it is called Arethusa (*13*). The story is that a certain nymph (*42*), Arethusa by name (*57*), who lived (*99*) on the other shore of the Adriatic, tried to escape from the river god, Alpheus, who was pursuing her. Fearing that (*88*) he would overtake her (*10*), she prayed to Diana to help (*71*) her. So, before the god could seize (*82*) her, the goddess changed her into a stream of water which flowed under the sea toward Sicily and emerged on an island near Syracuse. The ancients believed that if anything should be thrown into the river Alpheus, it (*42*) would later appear in this fountain.

27

After the defeat of Antiochus, Hannibal, fearing that (*88*) he would be handed over to the Romans, fled to Crete before he could be seized (*82*). There this shrewd man saw in what danger he would be (*109; 98*) if he did not take some precautions against the greed of the inhabitants. So, to keep (*68*) them from getting (*90*) possession of his money (*51*), he filled many jars with stones (*50*) and covered them with gold. Then he openly placed these in the temple of Diana. The money itself he put in the small statues that he used to carry with him (*59; 10*), and then threw them aside in his house. Without doubt he would have lost (*95*) his wealth if he had not taken these measures.

28

Not long (*55*) after this, it was reported to the senate (*26*) at Rome that Hannibal was living in Bithynia, and since no one doubted (*76*) that (*91*) the state would always be (*109*) in danger so long as he lived, ambassadors were sent to request (*69*) the king to surrender (*71*) him at once. The latter replied that he would not do what was (*99*) contrary to the rights of hospitality, but that they might arrest him if they could find him. Hannibal, however, fearing that (*88*), if they caught him, they would take him (*10*) to Rome (*41*), did not hesitate to kill (*106*) himself.

29

While King Pyrrhus was carrying on (*84*) war with the Roman people, an intimate friend of his went to the camp of Fabricius to promise (*69*) that, if given a reward, he would kill (*102*) the king secretly. Although the consul wished (*85*) to defeat his enemy, he had (*curo* with the gerundive) the fellow handed over to the king, not only because he did not wish (*74*) to win the war by such means, but also because he feared that (*88*) the neighboring states would think that the king had been murdered at his instigation (*60*). Pyrrhus was so pleased that he thanked (*72* Note) the consul and sent back to the Romans all the prisoners he had. In your opinion, which deserved the more credit, the king or the consul?

30

Once Hannibal wished to arrange for an exchange of captives. He therefore sent ten Roman nobles to the senate at Rome (*41*) after he had made them promise (*73*) to return (*102*) to him (*40*). Nine kept their word, but the tenth, who at the beginning of their journey had returned as if he had forgotten something, remained at Rome (*49*); for he believed that he had been freed from his oath (*44*) by his return to the camp. The senate, however, not only sent him back, but decreed that the eight thousand men (*19*) who had been left in the camp by the consul should not be ransomed (*71*), since Roman soldiers were accustomed either to conquer or to die (*106*).

PRIAM PETITIONS ACHILLES

Priam kneels before the victorious Achilles and begs him for the corpse of Hector. Achilles' friend, Automedon (at the left), and his aged tutor, Phoenix (in center), urge Achilles to grant Priam's petition. Hermes, who stands behind Phoenix, guided the Trojan king secretly through the Greek camp.

CHAPTER XV

LATIN-ENGLISH VOCABULARY

A

accendō, -ere, -cendi, -cēnsus *kindle.*
acuō, -ere, -uī, -ūtus *sharpen.*
aēneus (**aēnus**), **-a, -um,** adj. *of copper, brazen.*
aequō, -āre, -āvī, -ātus *make equal.*
aequor, -oris, n. *sea.*
āēr, āeris, m. *air.*
aethēr, -eris, m. *upper air, sky.*
aevum, -ī, n. *lifetime, age.*
agitō, -āre, -āvī, -ātus *drive, pursue.*
āgnōscō, -ere, -gnōvī, -gnitus *recognize.*
āla, -ae, f. *wing.*
albus, -a, -um, adj. *white.*
āles, -itis, adj. *winged;* as a noun, *bird.*
almus, -a, -um, adj. *nourishing, kindly.*
altāria, -ium, n. *altar.*
alternus, -a, -um, adj. *alternating, by turns.*
ambō, -ae, -ō, num. adj. *both.*
āmēns, -entis, adj. *without mind, mad.*
amictus, -ūs, m. *cloak.*
amnis, -is, m. *river.*
amplector, -ī, -plexus *embrace.*
anguis, -is, m. and f. *snake.*
anima, -ae, f. *breath, life, soul.*
antequam, adv. and conj. (*sooner than*) *before.*
antrum, -ī, n. *cave, grotto*
appāreō, -ēre, -uī, -itūrus *appear.*
aptō, -āre, -āvī, -ātus *fit to.*
āra, -ae, f. *altar.*
arceō, -ēre, -uī *confine, keep off.*

arcus, -ūs, m.	*bow, arch.*
arduus, -a, -um, adj.	*high, steep.*
armentum, -ī, n.	*cattle, herd.*
arō, -āre, -āvī, -ātus	*plough.*
arrigō, -ere, -rēxī, -rēctus	*raise up.*
artus, -ūs, m.	*joint, limb.*
arvum, -ī, n.	*field.*
arx, arcis, f.	*citadel.*
asper, -era, -erum, adj.	*rough, harsh.*
astō, -āre, -stitī	*stand near.*
astrum, -ī, n.	*star.*
āter, -tra, -trum, adj.	*black.*
attonitus, -a, -um, adj.	*thunderstruck.*
attonō, -āre, -tonuī, -tonitus	*thunder at, strike with thunder.*
auferō, -ferre, abstulī, ablātus	*bear off.*
augurium, -ī, n.	*knowledge of augury.*
aura, -ae, f.	*air, breeze.*
aureus, -a, -um, adj.	*golden.*
aurōra, -ae, f.	*dawn.*
aurum, -ī, n.	*gold.*
avis, -is, f.	*bird.*
axis, -is, m.	*axle, axis.*

B

bibō, -ere, bibī	*drink.*
bōs, bovis, m. and f.	*ox, cow.*
bracchium, -ī, n.	*arm (of body).*

C

caecus, -a, -um, adj.	*blind, dark, hidden.*
caeruleus, -a, -um, adj.	*dark blue, green.*
caleō, -ēre, -uī	*be warm, glow.*
candeō, -ēre, -uī	*be white, glow.*
canis, -is, m. and f.	*dog.*
canō, -ere, cecinī	*sing.*
cānus, -a, -um, adj.	*white, hoary.*

capillus, -ī, m.	*hair.*
carīna, -ae, f.	*keel.*
carmen, -inis, n.	*song.*
carpō, -ere, -psī, -ptus	*pluck.*
castus, -a, -um, adj.	*pure.*
caterva, -ae, f.	*crowd.*
cavus, -a, -um, adj.	*hollow.*
celerō, -āre, -āvī, -ātus	*hasten.*
celsus, -a, -um, adj.	*high.*
certāmen, -inis, n.	*contest.*
cervīx, -īcis, f.	*neck, head.*
cervus, -ī, m.	*stag.*
cessō, -āre, -āvī, -ātus	*delay.*
ceu, adv.	*as, as if.*
chorus, -ī, m.	*dance, troop.*
cieō, -ēre, cīvī, citus	*move, stir up.*
cingō, -ere, cīnxī, cīnctus	*gird, surround.*
cinis, -eris, m.	*ashes.*
citus, -a, -um, adj.	*swift.*
clipeus, -ī, m.	*shield.*
cognōmen, -inis, n.	*surname.*
collum, -ī, n.	*neck.*
coma, -ae, f.	*hair, foliage.*
comitor, -ārī, -ātus	*accompany.*
compellō, -āre, -āvī, -ātus	*hail, address.*
complector, -ī, -plexus	*embrace.*
compōnō, -ere, -posuī, -positus	*put together, put to rest.*
concutiō, -ere, -cussī, -cussus	*shake up, shatter.*
coniugium, -ī, n.	*wedlock.*
cōnscius, -a, -um, adj.	*conscious.*
cōnūbium, -ī, n.	*marriage.*
cor, cordis, n.	*heart.*
corōna, -ae, f.	*wreath.*
corripiō, -ere, -ripuī, -reptus	*snatch up, press on.*
coruscus, -a, -um, adj.	*waving, flashing.*
crātēr, -ēris, m. (acc. sing. **-ēra**)	*mixing bowl.*

crepō, -āre, -uī, -itum	*creak.*
crīmen, -inis, n.	*decision, charge.*
crīnis, -is, m.	*hair.*
crista, -ae, f.	*crest.*
cruentus, -a, -um, adj.	*bloodstained.*
cruor, -ōris, m.	*gore.*
crūs, crūris, n.	*thigh, leg, shin.*
culmen, -inis, n.	*top.*
cūnctor, -ārī, -ātus	*delay.*
cupīdō, -inis, f.	*desire.*
currus, -ūs, m.	*chariot.*
curvus, -a, -um, adj.	*bent.*
cuspis, -idis, f.	*spear point.*

D

daps, dapis, f.	*feast, banquet.*
decōrus, -a, -um, adj.	*becoming.*
decus, -oris, n.	*beauty, ornament, glory.*
dēmittō, -ere, -mīsī, -missus	*let go down, depress.*
dēmum, adv.	*at last.*
dēns, dentis, m.	*tooth.*
dēnsus, -a, -um, adj.	*thick.*
digitus, -ī, m.	*finger, toe.*
dignor, -ārī, -ātus	*deem worthy.*
dīrus, -a, -um, adj.	*fearful, cursed.*
dīves, dīvitis, adj.	*rich.*
dīvus, -a, -um, adj.	*godlike;* as a noun, *god.*
doleō, -ēre, -uī, -itūrus	*grieve.*
dolus, -ī, m.	*deceit, trickery.*
dominor, -ārī, -ātus	*be master.*
domō, -āre, -uī, -itus	*vanquish, subdue.*
dōnec, conj.	*until.*
dōnum, -ī, n.	*gift.*
dūdum, adv.	*lately, for a long time.*
duplex, -icis, adj.	*twofold.*
dūrus, -a, -um, adj.	*hard, harsh.*

E

ebur, -oris, n.	*ivory.*
ecce, interj.	*lo!*
edō, -ere, ēdī, ēsus	*eat.*
ēn, interj.	*lo!*
ēnsis, -is, m.	*sword.*
epulae, -ārum, f.	*banquet.*
equidem, adv.	*indeed.*
ērigō, -ere, -rēxī, -rēctus	*raise up.*
ēruō, -ere, ēruī, ērutus	*cast out, overthrow.*
ēvādō, -ere, -vāsī, -vāsus	*go out, escape.*
exanimus, -a, -um, adj.	*breathless, lifeless.*
excutiō, -ere, -cussī, -cussus	*shake out.*
exsequor, -ī, -secūtus	*follow out, perform.*
exsultō, -āre, -āvī, -ātum	*leap, exult.*
extemplō, adv.	*forthwith.*
exuō, -ere, -uī, -ūtus	*put off, lay aside.*
exuviae, -ārum, f.	*garment, armor, spoils.*

F

faciēs, -ēī, f.	*form, appearance, face.*
famulus, -ī, m.	*servant.*
fās, indecl. n.	*divine right, law.*
fātālis, -e, adj.	*deathdealing, destined.*
fatīgō, -āre, -āvī, -ātus	*wear out, tire.*
faux, faucis, f.	*throat, jaws, mouth.*
fēlix, -īcis, adj.	*lucky.*
fēmina, -ae, f.	*woman.*
feriō, -īre	*strike.*
ferōx, -ōcis, adj.	*wild, fierce.*
ferreus, -a, -um, adj.	*of iron.*
ferveō, -ēre, -buī	*boil, glow.*
fessus, -a, -um, adj.	*tired out.*
fīdus, -a, -um, adj.	*faithful.*
fīgō, -ere, fīxī, fīxus	*fasten.*
flāvus, -a, -um, adj.	*yellow.*

flectō, -ere, flexī, flexus	*bend, turn.*
fleō, -ēre, flēvī, flētus	*weep.*
flētus, -ūs, m.	*weeping.*
flō, flāre, flāvī, flātus	*blow.*
flōs, flōris, m.	*flower, bloom.*
flūctus, -ūs, m.	*flood, billow.*
fluō, -ere, flūxī, flūxum	*flow.*
fluvius, -ī, m.	*river.*
fodiō, -ere, fōdī, fossus	*dig.*
foedus, -a, -um, adj.	*foul.*
folium, -ī, n.	*leaf.*
fōns, fontis, m.	*spring.*
for, fārī, fātus	*speak.*
foris, -is, f.	*door.*
fōrma, -ae, f.	*shape, beauty.*
foveō, -ēre, fōvī, fōtus	*warm, cherish.*
frangō, -ere, frēgī, frāctus	*break.*
fraus, fraudis, f.	*fraud, deceit.*
fremō, -ere, -uī, -itum	*mutter.*
frēnum, -ī, n.	*bit, bridle.*
fretum, -ī, n.	*strait.*
frōns, frondis, f.	*leaf, foliage.*
fulgeō, -ere, fulsī	*gleam flash.*
fulmen, -inis, n.	*lightning, thunderbolt.*
fulvus, -a, -um, adj.	*tawny.*
fūmus, -ī, m.	*smoke.*
fundō, -ere, fūdī, fūsus	*pour out.*
fūnis, -is, m.	*rope.*
fūnus, -eris, n.	*funeral, death.*
furia, -ae, f.	*rage, madness;* pl. *rage.*

G

galea, -ae, f.	*helmet.*
gaudeō, -ēre, gāvīsus	*rejoice.*
gaudium, -ī, n.	*joy.*

gelidus, -a, -um, adj.	*ice cold.*
geminus, -a, -um, adj.	*twin.*
gemitus, -ūs, m.	*groan.*
gemō, -ere, -uī, -itum	*groan, lament.*
gener, -erī, m.	*son-in-law.*
genitor, -ōris, m.	*begetter, parent.*
genū, -ūs, n.	*knee.*
germānus, -ī, m.	*own brother.*
gignō, -ere, genuī, genitus	*beget.*
glomerō, -āre, -āvī, -ātus	*collect.*
gradior, -ī, gressus	*step, walk.*
grāmen, -inis, n.	*grass.*
grātus, -a, -um, adj.	*pleasing, grateful.*
gremium, -ī, n.	*lap, bosom.*
gressus, -ūs, m.	*step, walk.*
gurges, -itis, m.	*whirlpool.*

H

habēna, -ae, f.	*rein.*
haereō, -ēre, haesī, haesum	*stick.*
harēna, -ae, f.	*sand.*
harundō, -inis, f.	*reed, arrow.*
hasta, -ae, f.	*spear.*
haud, adv.	*not.*
hauriō, -īre, hausī, haustus	*drink, drain.*
herba, -ae, f.	*herb, grass.*
hērōs, -ōis, m.	*hero.*
heu, interj.	*alas!*
hiō, -āre, -āvī, -ātum	*yawn, gape.*
horreō, -ēre, horruī	*bristle, shudder.*
horridus, -a, -um, adj.	*bristling, terrible.*
hospes, -itis, m.	*guest, stranger.*
hospitium, -ī, n.	*guest friendship, shelter.*
humus, -ī, f.	*ground.*
hymenaeus, -ī, m.	*wedding song.*

I

iaculum, -ī, n. *javelin.*
ictus, -ūs, m. *blow.*
ignārus, -a, -um, adj. *not knowing.*
ignōtus, -a, -um, adj. *unknown.*
īlex, -icis, f. *oak.*
imber, -bris, m. *rainstorm.*
immānis, -e, adj. *huge.*
immēnsus, -a, -um, adj. *unmeasured.*
immineō, -ēre *threaten.*
immittō, -ere, -mīsī, -missus *send at, let go.*
implicō, -āre, -āvī (-uī), -ātus (-itus) *enfold.*
inānis, -e, adj. *empty.*
incēdō, -ere, -cessī, -cessum *walk on.*
incumbō, -ere, -cubuī, -cubitum *lean on, bend to.*
induō, -ere, -uī, -ūtus *put on.*
īnferī, -ōrum, m. *the dead.*
ingeminō, -āre, -āvī, -ātus *redouble.*
ingēns, -tis, adj. *huge.*
īnscius, -a, -um, adj. *not knowing.*
īnsignis, -e, adj. *marked, distinguished.*
intendō, -ere, -tendī, -tentus *stretch, strain.*
intrō, -āre, -āvī, -ātus *enter.*
intus, adv. *inside.*
invādō, -ere, -vāsī, -vāsus *attack.*
īra, -ae, f. *wrath.*
iuvencus, -ī, m. *bullock.*
iuvenis, -e, adj. *young;* as a noun, *young man.*
iuventa, -ae, f. *youth.*
iuventūs, -ūtis, f. *youth.*
iūxtā, adv. *close by.*

L

lābor, -ī, lāpsus *glide, slip.*
lacertus, -ī, m. *upper arm.*

lacrimō, -āre, -āvī, -ātum	*shed tears.*
lacus, -ūs, m.	*lake.*
laedō, -ere, laesī, laesus	*hurt, injure.*
laetus, -a, -um, adj.	*joyful.*
laevus, -a, -um, adj.	*left.*
latebra, -ae, f.	*hiding place.*
lateō, -ēre, -uī	*be hidden.*
laurus, -ī (-ūs), f.	*laurel.*
laxō, -āre, -āvī, -ātus	*loosen.*
lentus, -a, -um, adj.	*slow, pliant.*
leō, -ōnis, m.	*lion.*
lētum, -ī, n.	*death.*
lēvis, -e, adj.	*smooth.*
lībō, -āre, -āvī, -ātus	*taste, sip, offer a libation.*
līmen, -inis, n.	*threshold.*
lingua, -ae, f.	*tongue, language.*
linquo, -ere, līquī	*leave.*
liquidus, -a, -um, adj.	*liquid, clear.*
locō, -āre, -āvī, -ātus	*place.*
longaevus, -a, -um, adj.	*longlived.*
lōrīca, -ae, f.	*corselet.*
lūceō, -ēre, lūxī	*gleam, shine.*
luctor, -ārī, -ātus	*struggle, wrestle.*
lūctus, -ūs, m.	*grief, mourning.*
lūcus, -ī, m.	*grove.*
lūdō, -ere, lūsī, lūsus	*play.*
lūgeō, -ēre, lūxī, lūctus	*mourn.*
lūna, -ae, f.	*moon.*
lupus, -ī, m.	*wolf.*
lūstrō, -āre, -āvī, -ātus	*purify, illumine.*

M

mactō, -āre, -āvī, -ātus	*magnify, honor, sacrifice.*
macula, -ae, f.	*spot, stain, disgrace.*
madeō, -ēre, -uī	*be dripping.*
maestus, -a, -um, adj.	*sad.*

magnanimus, -a, -um, adj. *high-spirited.*
mānēs, -ium, m. *shades.*
marmor, -oris, n. *marble.*
membrum, -ī, n. *limb.*
memor, -oris, adj. *mindful, remembering.*
memorō, -āre, -āvī, -ātus *recall, recount.*
mēnsa, -ae, f. *table, dish.*
mergō, -ere, mersī, mersus *immerse, sink.*
mēta, -ae, f. *boundary mark, limit, goal.*
mētior, -īrī, mēnsus *measure out, distribute.*
micō, -āre, -uī *dart, flash, gleam.*
minae, -ārum, f. *threats.*
minor, -ārī, -ātus *threaten.*
mīrābilis, -e, adj. *wonderful.*
misereor, -ērī, -itus *pity.*
miseror, -ārī, -ātus *pity.*
mītis, -e, adj. *kind.*
mōlēs, -is, f. *mass, pile, dike.*
mollis, -e, adj. *soft, kind.*
mōnstrō, -āre, -āvī, -ātus *point out.*
mōnstrum, -ī, n. *warning, portent.*
morsus, -ūs, m. *bite, fluke* (of anchor).
mox, adv. *presently.*
mūcrō, -ōnis, m. *sword point.*
mūgiō, -īre, -īvī (-iī), **-ītum** *low, bellow.*
mulceō, -ēre, mulsī, mulsus *stroke, soothe.*

N

namque, conj. *for indeed, for.*
nectō, -ere, nexuī (**nexī**), **nexus** *bind.*
nefandus, -a, -um, adj. *unutterable, accursed.*
nefās, n., indecl. noun *impiety.*
nemus, -oris, n. *forest.*
nepōs, -ōtis, m. *grandson, descendant.*
nēquīquam, adv. *in vain.*
nervus, -ī, m. *sinew, nerve.*

nī, conj. — *if not.*
niger, -gra, -grum, adj. — *black.*
nimbus, -ī, m. — *storm-cloud.*
niteō, -ere, -uī — *gleam.*
nītor, -ī, nīsus (**nīxus**) — *strive.*
nix, nivis, f. — *snow.*
nō, -āre, -āvī, -ātum — *swim.*
nōdus, -ī, m. — *knot.*
nūbēs, -is, f. — *cloud.*
nūbila, -ōrum, n. — *clouds.*
nūbilus, -a, -um, adj. — *cloudy.*
nūmen, -inis, n. — *nod, divine will.*
nūsquam, adv. — *nowhere.*
nympha, -ae, f. — *nymph.*

O

obruō, -ere, -ruī, -rutus — *overwhelm.*
obstipēscō, -ere, -stipuī — *be amazed.*
obvius, -a, -um, adj. — *in the way of.*
ōcior, -ius, adj. — *swifter.*
ōcius, adv. — *more swiftly.*
ōlim, adv. — *formerly.*
ōmen, -inis, n. — *omen.*
opācus, -a, -um, adj. — *shaded, dark.*
ōrdior, -īrī, ōrsus — *begin.*
orīgō, -inis, f. — *origin, source.*
os, ossis, n. — *bone.*
ōsculum, -ī, n. — *kiss.*
ostentō, -āre, -āvī, -ātus — *display.*
ovō, -āre, -āvī, -ātum — *rejoice.*

P

pallēns, -entis, f. — *pale.*
palleō, -ēre, -uī — *be pale.*
palma, -ae, f. — *palm* (tree and hand).

pandō, -ere, pandī, pānsus (passus)	*spread out.*
parcō, -ere, pepercī (parsī), parsūrus	*spare.*
pāscō, -ere, pāvī, pāstus	*feed.*
passim, adv.	*here and there.*
pāstor, -ōris, m.	*herdsman.*
patera, -ae, f.	*bowl.*
paveō, -ēre	*tremble with fear.*
pectus, -oris, n.	*breast.*
pecus, -udis, f.	*cattle.*
pelagus, -ī, n.	*sea.*
pellis, -is, f.	*skin, hide.*
pendeō, -ēre, pependī	*hang, be suspended.*
penetrālis, -e, adj.	*innermost.*
penna, -ae, f.	*feather.*
peragō, -ere, -ēgī, -āctus	*drive through, accomplish.*
pergō, -ere, -rēxī, -rēctum	*continue.*
pharetra, -ae, f.	*quiver.*
pietās, -ātis, f.	*devotion.*
pignus, -oris, n.	*pledge, token.*
pingō, -ere, pīnxī, pictus	*paint.*
pinguis, -e, adj.	*fat, rich.*
pinna, -ae, f.	*feather.*
pīnus, -ūs (-ī), *f.*	*pine tree.*
pius, -a, -um, adj.	*dutiful, devoted.*
placidus, -a, -um, adj.	*quiet, serene.*
plausus, -ūs, m.	*applause.*
polus, -ī, m.	*pole, sky.*
pondus, -eris, n.	*weight.*
pontus, -i, m.	*sea.*
porrigō, -ere, -rēxī, -rēctus	*reach forth, extend.*
postis, -is, m.	*doorpost.*
praeceps, -cipitis, adj.	*headlong.*
precor, -ārī, -ātus	*pray.*
prehendō, -ere, -hendī, -hēnsus	*seize.*

prīncipium, -ī, n.	*beginning.*
prōcumbō, -ere, -cubuī, -cubitum	*fall forward, lie down.*
prōgeniēs, -ēī, f.	*lineage, offspring.*
prōlēs, -is, f.	*offspring.*
prōmittō, -ere, -mīsī, -missus	*promise.*
prōnus, -a, -um, adj.	*stretched out.*
properō, -āre, -āvī, -ātus	*hasten.*
prōra, -ae, f.	*prow.*
prōtinus, adv.	*at once.*
pūbēs, -is, f.	*youth.*
pulsō, -āre, -āvī, -ātus	*beat.*
pulvis, -eris, m.	*dust.*
puppis, -is, f.	*poop, stern.*
purpura, -ae, f.	*purple.*

Q

quatiō, -ere, —, quassus	*shake.*

R

rabiēs, (-ēī), f.	*madness, frenzy.*
radius, -ī, m.	*staff, ray.*
rādīx, -īcis, f.	*root.*
rāmus, -ī, m.	*bough.*
rapidus, -a, -um, adj.	*swift.*
rapiō, -ere, rapuī, raptus	*seize.*
ratis, -is, f.	*raft, ship.*
raucus, -a, -um, adj.	*roaring.*
rēgīna, -ae, f.	*queen.*
reliquiae, -ārum, f.	*remnant.*
rēmus, -ī, m.	*oar.*
reor, rērī, ratus	*think.*
resīdō, -ere, -sēdī	*settle back.*
resolvō, -ere, -solvī, -solūtus	*untie.*
respiciō, -ere, -spexī, -spectus	*look back, regard.*
retrō, adv.	*back, again.*
rīdeō, -ēre, rīsī, rīsum	*laugh.*

rigeō, -ēre, riguī *be stiff.*
rīte, adv. *duly.*
rōstrum, ī, n. *beak.*
rota, -ae, f. *wheel.*
rubeō, -ēre, -uī *be red.*
ruīna, -ae, f. *downfall, destruction.*
rumpō, -ere, rūpī, ruptus *break.*
ruō, -ere, ruī, rutus *rush, dig.*
rūpēs, -is, f. *rock, cliff.*

S

sacer, sacra, sacrum, adj. *set apart, holy, cursed.*
sacerdōs, -ōtis, m. and f. *priest, priestess.*
sacrō, -āre, -āvī, -ātus *make holy.*
saeculum, -ī, n. *generation, century, time.*
saeviō, -īre, -iī, -ītum *rage.*
saevus, -a, -um, adj. *fierce, savage.*
sāl, salis, m. and n. *salt, sea.*
saliō, -īre, -uī *leap.*
saucius, -a, -um, adj. *wounded.*
scēptrum, -ī, n. *staff.*
scindō, -ere, scidī, scissus *split, tear down.*
scopulus, -ī, m. *crag.*
secō, -āre, secuī, sectus *cut.*
secūris, -is, f. *axe.*
secus, adv. *otherwise.*
sēgnis, -e, adj. *sluggish.*
sepulcrum, -ī, n. *tomb.*
serēnus, -a, -um, adj. *bright, clear, peaceful.*
serō, -ere, sēvī, satus *sow.*
serpō, -ere, serpsī, serptum *creep.*
sertum, -ī, n. *wreath.*
sērus, -a, -um, adj. *late, tardy.*
siccus, -a, -um, adj. *dry.*
sīdō, -ere, sīdī (sēdī) *settle.*
sīdus, -eris, n. *star, constellation.*

signō, -āre, -āvī, -ātus	*seal, mark.*
sileō, -ēre, -uī	*be silent.*
simulācrum, -ī, n.	*image, statue.*
sinus, -ūs, m.	*bosom, bay, fold.*
sistō, -ere, stitī, status	*make stand, stand still.*
socer, -erī, m.	*father-in-law.*
solidus, -a, -um, adj.	*whole, solid.*
sōlor, -ārī, -ātus	*comfort.*
solum, -ī, n.	*soil, ground.*
sonitus, -ūs, m.	*sound.*
sonō, -āre, -uī, -itum	*make a sound.*
sopor, -ōris, m.	*slumber.*
spargō, -ere, sparsī, sparsus	*spatter, sprinkle.*
spēlunca, -ae, f.	*cave.*
spernō, -ere, sprēvī, sprētus	*reject.*
spīculum, -ī, n.	*javelin.*
spīrō, -āre, -āvī, -ātum	*breathe.*
spolium, -ī, n.	*spoil.*
spūma, -ae, f.	*foam.*
stabulum, -ī, n.	*stall, stable.*
stāgnum, -ī, n.	*pool.*
stella, -ae, f.	*star.*
sternō, -ere, strāvī, strātus	*spread, lay low.*
stimulus, -ī, m.	*goad, spur.*
stirps, stirpis, f.	*root, trunk.*
strīdeō, -ēre, strīdī	*shrill, hiss.*
stringō, -ere, strīnxī, strictus	*draw, bind.*
struō, -ere, strūxī, strūctus	*pile up, build, plan.*
stupeō, -ēre, -uī	*be dazed.*
subitus, -a, -um, adj.	*sudden.*
sublīmis, -e, adj.	*lofty.*
succurrō, -ere, -currī, -cursum	*run up, assist.*
suēscō, -ere, suēvī, suētus	*become accustomed.*
sulcus, -ī, m.	*furrow, track.*
super, adv. and prep.	*over, above.*
superbus, -a, -um, adj.	*overbearing.*

superī, -ōrum, m.	*those above, the gods.*
surgō, -ere, surrēxī, surrēctum	*rise up.*
suspendō, -ere, -pendī, -pēnsus	*hang.*
suspiciō, -ere, -spexī, -spectus	*look from below, suspect.*

T

taeda, -ae, f.	*torch.*
taurus, -ī, m.	*bull.*
tellūs, -ūris, f.	*earth.*
tendō, -ere, tetendī, tentus (tēnsus)	*stretch.*
tepeō, -ere, -uī	*be warm.*
ter, num. adv.	*thrice.*
terreō, -ēre, -uī, -itus	*frighten.*
testor, -ārī, -ātus	*call to witness.*
texō, -ere, texuī, textus	*weave, construct.*
thalamus, -ī, m.	*bridal chamber.*
tingō, -ere, tīnxī, tīnctus	*wet, dip.*
tondeō, -ēre, totondī, tōnsus	*shear.*
tonō, -āre, -uī	*thunder.*
torqueō, -ēre, torsī, tortus	*twist, turn.*
torreō, -ēre, -uī, tostus	*roast.*
torus, -ī, m.	*couch.*
torvus, -a, -um, adj.	*grim.*
trabs, trabis, f.	*beam.*
tremō, -ere, -uī	*tremble.*
trepidus, -a, -um, adj.	*trembling.*
trīstis, -e, adj.	*sad.*
truncus, -ī, m.	*stock, trunk.*
tumeō, -ēre, -uī	*swell.*
tumidus, -a, -um, adj.	*swelling, swollen.*
tundō, -ere, tutudī, tūnsus	*lash, assail.*
turba, -ae, f.	*crowd.*
turbidus, -a, -um, adj.	*disturbed, turbulent.*
turbō, -inis, m.	*whirlwind.*
turbō, -āre, -āvī, -ātus	*disturb.*

U

ūber, -eris, n.	*udder, fertility.*
ultor, -ōris, m.	*avenger.*
ululō, -āre, -āvī, -ātum	*yell.*
umbra, -ae, f.	*shade.*
umerus, -ī, m.	*shoulder.*
ūmidus, -a, -um, adj.	*moist.*
uncus, -a, -um, adj.	*crooked, curved.*
unda, -ae, f.	*wave.*
unguis, -is, m.	*nail, claw.*
urgeō, -ēre, ursī	*press on, urge.*
ūrō, -ere, ussī, ustus	*burn.*
usquam, adv.	*anywhere.*

V

vādō, -ere	*walk, go.*
validus, -a, -um, adj.	*strong.*
vānus, -a, -um, adj.	*vain.*
vāstus, -a, -um, adj.	*huge, vast.*
vātēs, -is, m. and f.	*seer, prophet, prophetess*
-ve, enclitic conj.	*or.*
vehō, -ere, vexī, vectus	*carry.*
vellō, -ere, vellī, vulsus (volsus)	*pluck.*
vēlō, -āre, -āvī, -ātus	*veil, cover.*
vēlōx, -ōcis, adj.	*swift.*
vēlum, -ī, n.	*veil, sail.*
velut, adv.	*just as.*
veneror, -ārī, -ātus	*revere.*
vēnor, -ārī, -ātus	*hunt.*
verber, -eris, n.	*lash, stripes.*
vertex, -icis, m.	*top, whirl.*
vestis, -is, f.	*cloth, garment.*
vetō, -āre, -uī, -itus	*forbid.*
vicis (gen.), f.	*turn.*
vīctus, -ūs, m.	*livelihood, food.*
vinciō, -īre, vīnxī, vīnctus	*bind.*

virga, -ae, f. — *twig, wand.*
viridis, -e, adj. — *green.*
vīscus, -eris, n. — *inner part of the body;* pl. **vīscera, -um**, *entrails, vitals.*
vīsō, -ere, vīsī, vīsus — *look at, visit.*
vīsus, -ūs, m. — *sight.*
vitta, -ae, f. — *ribbon, fillet.*
volō, -āre, -āvī, -ātum — *fly.*
volucer, -cris, -cre, adj. — *winged.*
volvō, -ere, volvī, volūtus — *roll.*
voveō, -ēre, vōvī, vōtus — *vow.*

ACHILLES AND BRISEIS

Achilles bids farewell to his slave, Briseis, who is about to pour a libation for him

CHAPTER XVI

ENGLISH–LATIN VOCABULARY

A

ability	*ingenium, -ī*, n.
about	*dē* (prep. with abl.).
absent (be)	*absum, -esse, āfuī, āfutūrus.*
accomplish	*cōnficiō, -ere, -fēcī, -fectus; perficiō, -ere, -fēcī, -fectus; gerō, -ere, gessī, gestus; cōnsequor, -ī, -secūtus.*
accordance (in acc. with)	*prō* (prep. with abl.).
according to	expressed by abl. with or without *prō, dē*, or *ex.*
accuse	*accūsō, -āre, -āvī, -ātus.*
accustomed (be)	*soleō, -ēre, solitus.*
act (behave)	*mē gerō, -ere, gessī, gestus.*
address (a note)	*per epistulam aliquem adeō, -īre, -iī, -itus.*
admire	*admīror, -ārī, -ātus.*
adopt (a plan)	*capiō, -ere, cēpī, captus; ineō, -īre, -iī, -itus.*
Adrianople	*Hadrianopolis, -is*, f.
Adriatic	*sinus Adriāticus, -ūs Adriāticī; Mare Superum, -is Superī.*
Aeneas	*Aenēās, -ae*, m.
affair	*rēs, reī*, f.
affectionate confidence	translate by "love and confidence."
afraid (be)	*timeō, -ēre, -uī; vereor, -ērī, -itus; metuō, -ere, -uī.*
Africa	*Āfrica, -ae*, f.

Africanus	*Āfricānus, -ī,* m.
after (prep.)	*post* (with acc.).
after (conj.)	*postquam.*
again	*rūrsus; iterum.*
against	*ad; in; contrā* (preps. with acc.).
ago	*abhinc* (adv. with acc.).
aid	*auxilium, -ī,* n.; *opera, -ae,* f.; *subsidium, -ī,* n.
Alexander	*Alexander, -drī,* m.
Alexandria	*Alexandrīa, -ae,* f.
alive	*vīvus, -a, -um.*
all	*omnis, -e.*
allow	*patior, -ī, passus; sinō, -ere, sīvī, situs.*
all-powerful	*omnipotēns, -potentis.*
almost	*paene; ferē.*
Alpheus	*Alpheus, -ī,* m.
already	*iam.*
also	*etiam; quoque.*
alter	*mūtō, -āre, -āvī, -ātus.*
although	*cum; quamquam.*
always	*semper.*
amazed (be)	*stupeō, -ere, stupuī; obstupēscō, -ere, -puī.*
ambassador	*lēgātus, -ī,* m.
American (adj.)	*Americānus, -a, -um.*
American (noun)	*Americānus, -ī,* m.
among	*apud; inter* (preps. with acc.).
ancestors	*maiōrēs, -um,* m.
ancestry (of distinguished ancestry)	*amplissimō genere nātus.*
Anchises	*Anchīsēs, -ae,* m.
ancient	*vetus, -eris; antīquus, -a, -um.*
and	*et; -que; atque; ac.*
and so	*itaque; igitur.*
animal	*animal, -ālis,* n.

answer	*respondeō, -ēre, -spondī, -spōnsus.*
Antiochus	*Antiochus, -ī,* m.
anxiety	*cūra, -ae,* f.; *sollicitūdō, -dinis,* f.
any (after negat.)	*quisquam, quidquam; ūllus, -a, -um.*
(after *sī, nisi, nē, num*)	*quis, qua, quid.*
any one, anything	*aliquis, aliquid.*
any one, anything (after *sī, nisi, nē, num*)	*quis, quid.*
Apelles	*Apellēs, -is,* m.
Apollo	*Apollō, -inis,* m.
appear	*videor, -ērī, vīsus.*
Arethusa	*Arethūsa, -ae,* f.
aristocracy	*optimātēs, -ium,* m.
Arizona	*Arizōna, -ae,* f.
armistice	*indūtiae, -ārum,* f.
arms	*arma, -ōrum,* n.
army	*exercitus, -ūs,* m.
arouse	*commoveō, -ere, -mōvī, -mōtus; excitō, -āre, -āvī, -ātus; incitō, -āre, -āvī, -ātus.*
arrange	*cūrō, -āre, -āvī, -ātus* with gerundive.
arrest	*comprehendō, -ere, -hendī, -hēnsus.*
arrive	*perveniō, -īre, -vēnī, -ventūrus* (*ad* with acc.).
as (rel. pron.)	*quī, quae, quod.*
as (since)	*cum.*
as (when)	*cum.*
as	*ut; quem ad modum.*
as for, as regards	*dē* (prep. with abl.).
as if	*velut sī; tamquam sī.*
as soon as	*simul atque* (*ac*); *cum* (*ut*) *prīmum.*
Asia Minor	*Asia, -ae,* f.
Asiatic	*Asiāticus, -a, -um.*

ask	*rogō, -āre, -āvī, -ātus; petō, -ere, -īvī, -ītus; quaerō, -ere, -sīvī, -sītus.*
assemble (**come together**)	*conveniō, -īre, -vēnī, -ventūrus.*
(**bring together**)	*condūcō, -ere, -dūxī, -ductus; comparō, -āre, -āvī, -ātus.*
assistance (**come to the assistance of**)	*subveniō, -īre, -vēnī, -ventūrus* (with dat.).
attack	*oppugnō, -āre, -āvī, -ātus; aggredior, -ī, -gressus; adorior, -īrī, -ortus; impetum faciō, -ere, fēcī, factus.*
attempt	*cōnor, -ārī, ātus; temptō, -āre, -āvī, -ātus.*
avoid	*vītō, -āre, -āvī, -ātus.*

B

bad	*malus, -a, -um.*
Balkan	*Balcānus, -a, -um.*
bandit	*latrō, -ōnis,* m.; *praedō, -ōnis,* m.
bard	*poēta, -ae,* m.; *vātēs, -is,* m.
battle	*proelium, -ī,* n.; *pugna, -ae,* f.
be	*sum, esse, fuī, futūrus.*
be at the head of	*praesum, -esse, -fuī, -futūrus* (with dat.).
be subject to	*serviō, -īre, -īvī, -ītum.*
bear	*ferō, ferre, tulī, lātus.*
bear a grudge	*suscēnseō, -ēre, -suī; invideō, -ēre, -vīdī, -vīsus.*
beautiful	*pulcher, -chra, -chrum.*
beauty	*pulchritūdō, -dinis,* f.
because	*quod; quoniam; quia.*
become	*fīō, fierī, factus.*
befall	*accidō, -ere, -cidī.*
before (adv.)	*ante; anteā.*
before (conj.)	*priusquam; antequam.*

before (prep.)	*ante* (with acc.); *prō* (with abl.).
beg	*ōrō, -āre, -āvī, -ātus; rogō, -āre, -āvī, -ātus; obsecrō, -āre, -āvī, -ātus.*
began	*coepī, coepisse, coeptus.*
begin	*incipiō, -ere, -cēpī, -ceptus.*
beginning (the)	*initium, -ī,* n.
Belgians	*Belgae, -ārum,* m.
believe	*crēdō, -ere, crēdidī, crēditus.*
besides	*praetereā.*
bid (order)	*iubeō, -ēre, iussī, iussus.*
bind (by oath)	*ad iūs iūrandum adigō, -ere, -ēgī, -āctus.*
bird	*avis, is,* f.
Bithynia	*Bīthȳnia, -ae,* f.
bloodshed	*caedēs, -is,* f.
bold	*audāx, -ācis; fortis, -e.*
boldly	*audācter.*
born (be)	*nāscor, -ī, nātus.*
boundary	*fīnis, -is,* m.
bounds	*modus, -ī,* m.
boy	*puer, puerī,* m.
brave	*fortis, -e.*
break	*frangō, -ere, frēgī, frāctus.*
bring	*dūcō, -ere, dūxī, ductus.*
bring back	*redūcō, -ere, -dūxī, -ductus; reportō, -āre, -āvī, -ātus.*
bring war upon	*bellum īnferō, -ferre, -tulī, illātus.*
brother	*frāter, -tris,* m.
Brutus	*Brūtus, -ī,* m.
build	*aedificō, -āre, -āvī, -ātus.*
burn	*incendō, -ere, -cendī, -cēnsus.*
business	*negōtium, -ī,* n.; *rēs, reī,* f.
but	*sed; autem.*
but also	*sed (vērum) etiam.*
by (of a person)	*ā* or *ab* (prep. with abl.).

C

Caesar	*Caesar, -aris,* m.
call	*vocō, -āre, -āvī, -ātus; appellō, -are, -āvī, -ātus.*
call together	*convocō, -āre, -āvī, -ātus.*
call upon for satisfaction	*rēs repetō, -ere, -petīvī, -petītus.*
camp	*castra, -ōrum,* n.
campaign	*bellum, -ī,* n.
can	*possum, posse, potuī.*
Cannae (of)	*Cannēnsis, -e.*
captive	*captīvus, -ī,* m.
capture	*capiō, -ere, cēpī, captus; expugnō, -āre, -āvī, -ātus.*
carefully	*dīligenter.*
carry	*portō, -āre, -āvī, -ātus; ferrō, ferre, tulī, lātus.*
carry on	*gerō, -ere, gessī, gestus.*
carry out (a plan)	*cōnficiō, -ere, -fēcī, -fectus; exsequor, -ī, -secūtus.*
Carthaginians	*Carthāginiēnses, -ium,* m.
Catiline	*Catilīna, -ae,* m.
Cato	*Catō, -ōnis,* m.
cause (noun)	*causa, -ae,* f.
cause (verb)	*faciō, -ere, fēcī, factus; efficiō, -ere, -fēcī, -fectus.*
certain	*quīdam, quaedam, quoddam (quiddam); certus, -a, -um.*
certainly	*certē; certō; profectō.*
change	*mūtō, -āre, -āvī, -ātus; vertō, -ere, vertī, versus.*
character	*ingenium, -ī,* n.
chief	*prīnceps, -cipis,* m.
children	*līberī, -ōrum,* m.; *puerī, -ōrum,* m.
choose	*dēligō, -ere, -lēgī, -lēctus.*
Cicero	*Cicerō, -ōnis,* m.
Cisalpine	*Cisalpīnus, -a, -um.*

citizen	*cīvis, -is*, m. and f.
city	*urbs, urbis*, f.
clad	*vestītus, -a, -um.*
clearly	*clārē; manifēstē; manifēstō.*
come	*veniō, -īre, vēnī, ventūrus.*
come to the assistance of	*subveniō, -īre, -vēnī, -ventūrus* (with dat.).
command (verb)	*imperō, -āre, -āvī, -ātus.*
command (noun)	*imperium, -ī*, n.
command (put in command of)	*praeficiō, -ere, -fēcī, -fectus; praepōnō, -ere, -posuī, -positus.*
commission	*lēgātiō, -ōnis*, f.
commissioner	*lēgātus, -ī*, m.
commit	*committō, -ere, -mīsī, -missus.*
common people	*plēbs, plēbis*, f.; *multitūdō, -dinis*, f.
companion	*socius, -ī*, m.; *comes, -itis*, m.
comrade	*socius, -ī*, m.; *comes, -itis*, m.
conclude	*cōnfīrmō, -āre, -āvī, -ātus.*
condition	*condiciō, -ōnis*, f.
conference	*colloquium, -ī*, n.; *concilium, -ī*, n.
confidence	*fidēs, -eī*, f.
congratulate	*grātulor, -ārī, -ātus.*
conquer	*superō, -āre, -āvī, -ātus; vincō, -ere, vīcī, victus.*
consequently	*igitur; itaque.*
consider	*habeō, -ēre, habuī, habitus; iūdicō, -āre, -āvī, -ātus; dūcō, -ere, dūxī, ductus.*
conspiracy	*coniūrātiō, -ōnis*, f.
conspirator	*coniūrātus, -ī*, m.
consul	*cōnsul, -ulis*, m.
consulship	*cōnsulātus, -ūs*, m.
consult	*cōnsulō, -ere, -suluī, -sultus.*
contrary to	*contrā* (prep. with acc.).
control (gain control)	*potior, -īrī, potītus.*

control	*contineō, -ēre, -tinuī, -tentus; coerceō, -ēre, -uī, -itus.*
convince	*persuādeō, -ēre, -suāsī, -suāsum.*
cost (at small cost)	*parvī.*
country (native land)	*patria, -ae,* f.
countrymen	*cīvēs, -ium,* m.
courage	*virtūs, -tūtis,* f.
cover	*operiō, -īre, -eruī, -ertus.*
Crassus	*Crassus, -ī,* m.
credit	*laus, laudis,* f.; *honor, -ōris,* m.
Crete	*Crēta, -ae,* f.
crime	*scelus, -eris,* n.; *facinus, -oris,* n.
criticize	*reprehendō, -ere, -endī, -ēnsus.*
cruelty	*crūdēlitās, -tātis,* f.
crush	*opprimō, -ere, -pressī, -pressus.*
cry	*conclāmō, -āre, -āvī, -ātus; exclāmō, -āre, -āvī, -ātus.*
custom	*mōs, mōris,* m.; *cōnsuētūdō, -dinis,* f.

D

danger	*perīculum, -ī,* n.
daughter	*fīlia, -ae,* f.
day after day	*in diēs; diem dē diē.*
day, one day	*ōlim; quondam.*
dear	*cārus, -a, -um.*
death	*mors, mortis,* f.
decide	*cōnstituō, -ere, -stituī, -stitūtus; statuō, -ere, statuī, statūtus.*
declare	*cōnfīrmō, -āre, -āvī, -ātus; dēclārō, -āre, -āvī, -ātus; dīcō, -ere, dīxī, dictus.*
declare (war)	*bellum indīcō, -ere, -dīxī, -dictus.*
decree	*dēcernō, -ere, -crēvī, -crētus.*
deed	*factum, -ī,* n.
deep	*altus, -a, -um; gravis, -e.*

defeat (noun)	*clādēs, -is,* f.
defeat (verb)	*vincō, -ere, vīcī, victus; superō, -āre, -āvī, -ātus.*
delay (noun)	*mora, -ae,* f.; **without delay,** *cōnfēstim.*
delay (verb)	*moror, -ārī, -ātus; cūnctor, -ārī, -ātus.*
deny	*negō, -āre, -āvī, -ātus.*
deserve	*mereō, -ēre, -uī; mereor, -ērī, meritus.*
desperate	*atrōx, -ōcis.*
destroy	*dēleō, -ēre, -ēvī, -ētus; interficiō, -ere, -fēcī, -fectus; exscindō, -ere, -scidī, -scissus.*
destruction	*perniciēs, -ēī,* f.; *exitium, -ī,* n.; *interitus, -ūs,* m.
Diana	*Diāna, -ae,* f.
die	*morior, -ī, mortuus.*
difficulty	*difficultās, -ātis,* f.
disband	*dīmittō, -ere, -mīsī, -missus.*
discover	*comperiō, -īre, -perī, -pertus; reperiō, -īre, -pperī, -pertus.*
discuss	*agō, -ere, ēgī, āctus.*
disregard	*neglegō, -ere, -lēxī, -lēctus.*
distant	*longinquus, -a, -um.*
distant (be)	*absum, -esse, āfuī, āfutūrus.*
distinguished	*īnsīgnis, -e; praeclārus, -a, -um.*
disturbance	*tumultus, -ūs,* m.; *mōtus, -ūs,* m.
do	*faciō, -ere, fēcī, factus; agō, -ere, ēgī, āctus.*
domestic	*domesticus, -a, -um.*
doubt (noun)	*dubium, -ī,* n.
doubt (verb)	*dubitō, -āre, -āvī, -ātum.*
draw together	*contrahō, -ere, -trāxī, -tractus; colligō, -ere, -lēgī, -lēctus.*
dreadful	*horribilis, -e; atrōx, -ōcis.*

drink	*bibō, -ere, bibī; pōtō, -āre, -āvī, -ātus (pōtus).*
drive	*agō, -ere, ēgī, āctus; agitō, -āre, -āvī, -ātus.*
duty	*officium, -ī,* n.; *mūnus, -eris,* n.; do one's duty, *officiō fungor, -ī, fūnctus.*

E

eager	*cupidus, -a, -um; appetēns, -entis.*
ear	*auris, -is,* f.
easily	*facile.*
easy	*facilis, -e.*
educated	*ērudītus, -a, -um.*
effort	*labor, -ōris,* m.; *studium, -ī,* n.
eight	*octō.*
either	*aut; vel.*
either . . . or	*aut . . . aut; vel . . . vel.*
emerge	*ēmergō, -ere, -mersī, -mersus.*
emperor	*imperātor, -ōris,* m.
employ	*ūtor, -ī, ūsus; adhibeō, -ēre, -hibuī, -hibitus; negōtium dō, dare, dedī, datus.*
end	*fīnis, -is,* m.
endowed	*praeditus, -a, -um.*
enemy (public)	*hostis, -is,* m.; *hostēs, -ium,* m.
enemy (private)	*inimīcus, -ī,* m.
enjoy	*fruor, -ī, frūctus; ūtor, -ī, ūsus.*
enough	*satis.*
enter	*ineō, -īre, -iī, -itus; intrō, -āre, -āvī, -ātus; veniō, -īre, vēnī, ventūrus* (with *in*).
envoy	*lēgātus, -ī,* m.
equally	*aequē.*
erect	*aedificō, -āre, -āvī, -ātus.*
escape	*effugiō, -ere, -fūgī, -fugitūrus.*

even — *etiam; quoque; vel;* **not . . . even,** *nē . . . quidem.*
event — *rēs, reī,* f.
ever — *semper;* (with negat.) *umquam.*
every — *omnis, -e; quisque, quaeque, quidque (quodque).*
everything — *omnia, -ium,* n.
everywhere — *ubīque; ubivīs; omnibus locīs.*
evil — *malus, -a, -um.*
example — *exemplum, -ī,* n.; **for example,** *verbī causā.*
exchange — *inter sē dare, dedī, datus.*
exile — *exsilium, -ī,* n.
expedition — *expedītiō, -ōnis,* f.; *iter, itineris,* n.
extraordinary — *singulāris, -e; īnsīgnis, -e.*
extremely — use superlative of adjective.

F

Fabricius — *Fabricius, -ī,* m.
famous — *clārus, -a, -um; praeclārus, -a, -um.*
far — *longē; multō; procul.*
fast — *celeriter.*
fate — *fātum, -ī,* n.
father — *pater, patris,* m.
fatherland — *patria, -ae,* f.
favor (noun) — *beneficium, -ī,* n.
favor (verb) — *faveō, -ēre, fāvī, fautum.*
fear (noun) — *metus, -ūs,* m.; *timor, -ōris,* m.
fear (verb) — *timeō, -ēre, -uī; metuō, -ere, -uī; vereor, -ērī, veritus.*
feel — *sentiō, -īre, sēnsī, sēnsus.*
fellow — *socius, -ī,* m.; *homō, hominis,* m.
few — *paucī, -ae, -a.*
fight (noun) — *pugna, -ae,* f.; *proelium, -ī,* n.

fight (verb) *pugnō, -āre, -āvī, -ātus; dīmicō, -āre, -āvī, -ātus; contendō, -ere, -tendī, -tentus.*
fill *compleō, -ēre, -plēvī, -plētus.*
finally *tandem; dēnique; dēmum; postrēmō.*
find *reperiō, -īre, repperī, repertus; inveniō, -īre, -vēnī, -ventus.*
first *prīmus, -a, -um;* **at first,** *prīmō.*
flee *fugiō, -ere, fūgī, fugitūrus.*
flow *fluō, -ere, flūxī.*
follow *sequor, -ī, secūtus.*
foolish *stultus, -a, -um; īnsipiēns, -entis.*
for (conj.) *nam; enim.*
for (in behalf of) *prō* (prep. with abl.).
forces *cōpiae, -ārum,* f.
foreign *exterus, -a, -um.*
foresight *prūdentia, -ae,* f.; *cōnsilium, -ī,* n.
forget *oblīvīscor, -ī, oblītus.*
former *prīstinus, -a, -um; prior, -ōris; superior, -ōris.*
fortune *fortūna, -ae,* f.
fortune (property) *rēs, rērum,* f.
Forum *Forum, -ī,* n.
fountain *fōns, fontis,* m.
free (adj.) *līber, -era, -erum.*
free (verb) *līberō, -āre, -āvī, -ātus.*
freedom *lībertās, -ātis,* f.
friend *amīcus, -ī,* m.
from *ā; ab* (preps. with abl.).
furthermore *praetereā; quīn etiam.*

G

gain *adsequor, -ī, -secūtus; consequor, -ī, -secūtus.*
gain control *potior, -īrī, potītus.*

gather (come together)	*conveniō, -īre, -vēnī, -ventum.*
gather (bring together)	*cōgō, -ere, coēgī, coāctus; comparō, -āre, -āvī, -ātus; colligō, -ere, -lēgī, -lēctus.*
Gaul	*Gallia, -ae,* f.
general	*imperātor, -ōris,* m.
German	*Germānus, -ī,* m.
get possession	*potior, -īrī, potītus.*
girl	*puella, -ae,* f.
give	*dō, dare, dedī, datus.*
give up	*trādō, -ere, -didī, -ditus.*
glorify	*illūstrō, -āre, -āvī, -ātus; celebrō, -āre, -āvī, -ātus.*
glory	*glōria, -ae,* f.; *fāma, -ae,* f.; *laus, laudis,* f.
go	*eō, īre, iī, itūrus.*
go back	*redeō, -īre, -iī, -itūrus; revertor, -ī, revertī.*
go on (be done)	*geror, -ī, gestus; agor, -ī, āctus.*
god	*deus, -ī,* m.
goddess	*dea, -ae,* f.
good	*bonus, -a, -um.*
govern	*regō, -ere, rēxī, rēctus; praesum, -esse, -fuī, -futūrus.*
government	*rēs pūblica, reī pūblicae,* f.
grant	*concēdō, -ere, -cessī, -cessus.*
grateful, feel grateful	*grātiam habeō, -ēre, -uī, -itus.*
grave	*gravis, -e.*
great	*magnus, -a, -um; ingēns, -entis.*
greatly	*magnopere; vehementer.*
Greece	*Graecia, -ae,* f.
greed	*avāritia, -ae,* f.; *cupiditās, -ātis,* f.
Greeks	*Graecī, -ōrum,* m.
grudge, bear grudge	*suscēnseō, -ēre, -uī; invideō, -ēre, -vīdī, -vīsus.*

guide (noun)	*dux, ducis,* m.
guide (verb)	*dūcō, -ere, dūxī, ductus.*

H

hand over	*trādō, -ere, -didī, -ditus.*
Hannibal	*Hannibal, -alis,* m.
happen (it happens)	*accidit, -ere, accidit; fit, fierī, factum est.*
happy	*beātus, -a, -um.*
harbor	*portus, -ūs,* m.
hardship	*labor, -ōris,* m.; *incommodum, -ī,* n.
hasten	*properō, -āre, -āvī, -ātum; mātūrō, -āre, -āvī, -ātum; contendō, -ere, -tendī, -tentum.*
hate	*ōdī, ōdisse, ōsūrus.*
have doubt	*dubitō, -āre, -āvī, -ātus.*
he	*is; ille.*
head	*caput, -itis,* n.
head (be at the head of)	*praesum, -esse, -fuī, -futūrus.*
heart (affections)	*animus, -ī,* m.
(disposition)	*ingenium, -ī,* n.
help	*auxilium, -ī,* n.
hereafter	*posteā; posthāc.*
hesitate	*dubitō, -āre, -āvī, -ātus.*
hide	*occultō, -āre, -āvī, -ātus; cēlō, -āre, -āvī, -ātus.*
himself (intensive)	*ipse, -a, -um.*
his	*ēius; illīus; suus, -a, -um.*
hold (have)	*teneō, -ēre, -uī; habeō, -ēre, -uī, -itus; obtineō, -ēre, -tinuī, -tentus.*
hold (think)	*dūcō, -ere, dūxī, ductus; habeō, -ēre, -uī, -itus.*
holy	*sānctus, -a, -um.*
home (towards)	*domum.*

home (at home) *domī.*
honor (good faith) *fidēs, -eī,* f.
honor (distinction) *honor, -ōris,* m.
hope (noun) *spēs, -eī,* f.
hope (verb) *spērō, -āre, -āvī, -ātus.*
horse *equus, -ī,* m.
horseman *eques, -itis,* m.
hospitality (rights of) *iūs hospitī.*
however *autem; tamen.*

I

I *ego.*
Ides *Īdūs, -uum,* f.
if *sī.*
imagine *animō concipiō, -ere, -cēpī, -ceptus; putō, -āre, -āvī, -ātus; animō fingō, -ere, fīnxī, fictus.*
immediately *statim.*
immortal *immortālis, -e.*
impious *impius, -a, -um.*
in *in* (prep. with abl.).
increase *augeō, -ēre, auxī, auctus.*
independence *lībertās, -tātis,* f.
Indiana *Indiāna, -ae,* f.
infamous *īnfāmis, -e; turpis, -e.*
inform *certiōrem (-ēs) faciō, -ere, fēcī, factus.*
inhabitant *incola, -ae,* m.
injure *noceō, -ēre, nocuī, nocitūrus.*
insane *īnsānus, -a, -um.*
instigation use *auctor* or *suādeō* or *moneō* with the person in the abl. absolute.
interests *rēs, rērum,* f.
intervention *interventus, -ūs,* m.
intimate *familiāris, -e.*

invade	*bellum īnferō, -ferre, -tulī, illātus* (*in* with acc.).
island	*īnsula, -ae,* f.
Italy	*Ītalia, -ae,* f.

J

jar	*amphora, -ae,* f.
join	*coniungō, -ere, -iūnxī, -iūnctus.*
join (armistice)	*indūtiās faciō, -ere, fēcī, factus.*
journey	*iter, itineris,* n.
Julius	*Iūlius, -ī,* m.
just (adv.)	*ipse, -a, -um.*
justly	*iūre.*

K

keep	*servō, -āre, -āvī, -ātus; cōnservō, -āre, -āvī, -ātus.*
keep away, keep from	*prohibeō, -ēre, -hibuī, -hibitus; arceō, -ēre, -uī; interclūdō, -ere, -clūsī, -clūsus.*
keep (one's word)	*fidem servō, -āre, -āvī, -ātus.*
kill	*interficiō, -ere, -fēcī, -fectus; occīdō, -ere, -cīdī, -cīsus.*
kind	*genus, generis,* n.; *modus, -ī,* m.
king	*rēx, rēgis,* m.
kingdom	*rēgnum, -ī,* n.
know	*sciō, -īre, scīvī, scītus.*

L

labor	*labor, -ōris,* m.
lad	*puer, puerī,* m.
lake	*lacus, -ūs,* m.
land (noun)	*ager, agrī,* m.; *fīnēs, -ium,* m.
land (verb)	*expōnō, -ere, -posuī, -positus; ēgredior, -ī, ēgressus.*

last — *proximus, -a, -um; ultimus, -a, -um.*
lasting — *diūturnus, -a, -um.*
later — *posteā; post.*
latter (the latter) — *hīc, hae, hōc.*
law — *lēx, lēgis*, f.
lay down — *prōpōnō, -ere, -posuī, -positus; abiciō, -ere, -iēcī, -iectus.*
lead — *dūcō, -ere, dūxī, ductus.*
leader — *dux, ducis*, m.
learn (find out) — *cōgnōscō, -ere, -gnōvī, -gnitus; reperiō, -īre, repperī, repertus; certior (-ēs) fierī.*
leave (go out of) — *exeō, -īre, -iī, -itus; excēdō, -ere, -cessī, -cessum; ēgredior, -ī, ēgressus.*
less (adj.) — *minor, minus.*
less (adv.) — *minus.*
letter — *litterae, -ārum*, f.; *epistula, -ae*, f.
liberty — *lībertās, -tātis*, f.
library — *bibliothēca, -ae*, f.
life — *vīta, -ae*, f.
like — *similis, -e.*
listen to — *audiō, -īre, -īvī, -ītus.*
live — *vīvō, -ere, vīxī, vīctus; habitō, -āre, -āvī, -ātus; incolō, -ere, -coluī.*
London — *Londinium, -ī*, n.
long (adj.) — *longus, -a, -um.*
long (adv.) — *diū.*
long after — *multō post.*
lose — *āmittō, -ere, -mīsī, -missus.*
love (noun) — *amor, -ōris*, m.
love (verb) — *amō, -āre, -āvī, -ātus; dīligō, -ere, -lēxī, -lēctus.*
loyally — *fidēliter.*

Lucceius	*Lucceius, -ī,* m.
Lucullus	*Lūcullus, -ī,* m.

M

make	*faciō, -ere, fēcī, factus; efficiō, -ere, -fēcī, -fectus.*
make (expedition)	*iter faciō, -ere, fēcī, factus; expedītiōnem suscipiō, -ere, -cēpī, -ceptus.*
make (peace)	*cōnfīrmō, -āre, -āvī, -ātus.*
make good	*cōnfīrmō, -āre, -āvī, -ātus.*
make preparations	*parō, -āre, -āvī, -ātus.*
make a reply	*respondeō, -ēre, -spondī, -spōnsus.*
make war	*bellum īnferō, -ferre, -tulī, illātus.*
man	*homō, hominis,* m. and f.; *vir, virī,* m.
Manlius (of)	*Mānliānus, -a, -um.*
Mantua	*Mantua, -ae,* f.
many	*multī, -ae, -a; complūrēs, -a (-ia).*
March (of)	*Mārtius, -a, -um.*
Marius	*Marius, -ī,* m.
matter	*rēs, reī,* f.
means (by such means)	*tālī (hāc) ratiōne; hōc modō.*
measures (take)	*cōnsulō, -ere, -suluī, -sultus; prōvideō, -ere, -vīdī, -vīsus.*
meeting	*conventus, -ūs,* m.; *concilium, -ī,* n.
Mexican	*Mexicānus, -i,* m.
misfortune (have)	translate by "be so unfortunate that."
Mithridates	*Mithridātēs, -is,* m.
Mithridatic	*Mithridāticus, -a, -um.*
modesty	*verēcundia, -ae,* f.; *pudor, -ōris,* m.
money	*pecūnia, -ae,* f.
month	*mēnsis, -is,* m.
moral worth	*virtūs, -tūtis,* f.

more (noun)	*plūs, plūris,* n.
more (adj.)	*plūres, plūra.*
more (adv.)	*magis; plūs; amplius.*
more (with compar.)	*multō.*
mortal	*mortālis, -e.*
mother	*māter, -tris,* f.
murder (noun)	*caedēs, -is,* f.
murder (verb)	*interficiō, -ere, -fēcī, -fectus; occīdō, -ere, -cīdī, -cīsus; necō, -āre, -āvī, -ātus.*
my	*meus, -a, -um.*

N

name	*nōmen, -inis,* n.
nation	*gēns, gentis,* f.; *nātiō, -ōnis,* f.
near (adv. and prep.)	*prope.*
near (adj.)	*propinquus, -a, -um.*
necessary (it is)	*necesse est.*
need (there is need)	*opus est.*
nefarious	*nefārius, -a, -um.*
neighboring	*fīnitimus, -a, -um.*
neither . . . nor	*neque (nec) . . . neque (nec).*
never	*numquam.*
news	*nūntius, -ī,* m.
night	*nox, noctis,* f.
nine	*novem.*
no (adj.)	*nūllus, -a, -um.*
noble	*nōbilis, -e.*
no longer	*nōn iam.*
none the less	*nihilō minus.*
no one	*nēmō.*
not	*nōn.*
not even	*nē . . . quidem.*
nothing	*nihil.*
not only	*nōn sōlum (modo).*
now	*nunc; iam.*

numerous — *crēber, -bra, -brum; multī, -ae, -a.*
nymph — *nympha, -ae,* f.

O

oath — *iūs iūrandum, iūris iūrandī,* n.
obey — *pāreō, -ēre, -uī; obtemperō, -āre, -āvī, -ātum.*
obtain — *consequor, -ī, -secūtus; impetrō, -āre, -āvī, -ātus; potior, -īrī, potītus.*
Ōcean — *Ōceanus, -ī,* m.
of (concerning) — *dē* (prep. with abl.).
olden — *prīscus, -a, -um.*
olden time — *vetustās, -tātis,* f.
once — *ōlim.*
once (at once) — *statim.*
one — *ūnus, -a, -um.*
one day — *quondam; ōlim.*
only (adj.) — *sōlus, -a, -um.*
only (adv.) — *tantum; sōlum; modo.*
only (then only) — *tum dēmum.*
openly — *apertē; palam.*
opinion — *sententia, -ae,* f.; *opīniō, -ōnis,* f.
or — *aut; vel.*
oracle — *ōrāculum, -ī,* n.
orator — *ōrātor, -ōris,* m.
order — *iubeō, -ēre, iussī, iussus; imperō, -āre, -āvī, -ātum; mandō, -āre, -āvī, -ātus.*
other (another) — *alius, -a, -ud.*
other (the other) — *alter, -a, -um.*
other (the others) — *cēterī, -ae, -a; reliquī, -ae, -a.*
ought — *dēbeō, -ēre, -uī, -itus; oportet, -ēre, oportuit.*
our — *noster, -tra, -trum.*

overcome — *superō, -āre, -āvī, -ātus; vincō, -ere, vīcī, victus.*
overpower — *opprimō, -ere, -pressī, -pressus; superō, -āre, -āvī, -ātus.*
overtake — *cōnsequor, -ī, -secūtus.*
overthrow — *ēvertō, -ere, -vertī, -versus.*
owing to — *propter* (prep. with acc.).

P

paint — *pingō, -ere, pīnxī, pictus.*
palace — *rēgia, -ae,* f.
pardon — *īgnōscō, -ere, -gnōvī, -gnōtus.*
participate in — *particeps sum (fīō).*
pass through — *trānseō, -īre, -iī, -itus.*
past — *praeteritus, -a, -um.*
peace — *pāx, pācis,* f.
peaceful — *pācātus, -a, -um.*
people — *populus, -ī,* m.; *hominēs, -um,* m.
Pergamum — *Pergamum, -ī,* n.
personal enemy — *inimīcus, -ī,* m.
personally — *ipse, -a, -um.*
persuade — *persuādeō, -ēre, -suāsī, -suāsum.*
Phaeton — *Phaetōn, -ontis,* m.
pick out — *ēligō, -ere, -lēgī, -lēctus.*
picture — *pictūra, -ae,* f.
place — *pōnō, -ere, posuī, positus; locō, -āre, -āvī, -ātus; collocō, -āre, -āvī, -ātus.*
plan (noun) — *cōnsilium, -ī,* n.; *ratiō, -ōnis,* f.
plan (verb) — *cōgitō, -āre, -āvī, -ātus; mōlior, -īrī, mōlītus.*
please — *placeō, -ēre, -uī, -itum; dēlectō, -āre, -āvī, -ātus.*
plot — *mōlior, -īrī, mōlītus; coniūrō, -āre, -āvī, -ātus; cōgitō, -āre, -āvī, -ātus.*

Po	*Padus*, -*ī*, m.
poet	*poēta*, -*ae*, m.
point out	*dēmōnstrō*, -*āre*, -*āvī*, -*ātus*; *ostendō*, -*ere*, -*dī*, -*tus*.
policy	*cōnsilia*, -*ōrum*, n.; *ratiō*, -*ōnis*, f.
Pompey	*Pompēius*, -*ī*, m.
Pontus	*Pontus*, -*ī*, m.
possess	*habeō*, -*ēre*, -*uī*, -*itus*.
power (ability)	*facultās*, -*tātis*, f.
power (might)	*potentia*, -*ae*, f.
power (military)	*imperium*, -*ī*, n.
powerful	*potēns*, -*entis*.
powerful (be)	*possum*, *posse*, *potuī*; *valeō*, -*ēre*, -*uī*, -*itūrus*.
praise (noun)	*laus*, *laudis*, f.
praise (verb)	*laudō*, -*āre*, *āvī*, -*ātus*.
pray	*precor*, -*ārī*, -*ātus*.
precaution (take)	*prōvideō et praecaveō*, -*ēre*, -*cāvī*, -*cautus*.
prefer	*mālō*, *mālle*, *māluī*.
preparations (make)	*parō*, -*āre*, -*āvī*, -*ātus*; *comparō*, -*āre*, -*āvī*, -*ātus*.
preserve	*servō*, -*āre*, -*āvī*, -*ātus*; *cōnservō*, -*āre*, -*āvī*, -*ātus*.
President	*praeses*, -*idis*, m.; *praefectus*, -*ī*, m.
pretty	*pulcher*, -*chra*, -*chrum*.
prevent	*prohibeō*, -*ēre*, -*uī*, -*itus*; *impediō*, -*īre*, -*īvī*, -*ītus*; *dēterreō*, -*ēre*, -*terruī*, -*territus*.
prey	*praeda*, -*ae*, f.
pride	*decus*, -*oris*, n.; *superbia*, -*ae*, f.
prisoner	*captīvus*, -*ī*, m.
proceed	*pergō*, -*ere*, *perrēxī*, *perrēctus*; *prōgredior*, -*ī*, *prōgressus*.
prolong	*prōdūcō*, -*ere*, -*dūxī*, -*ductus*.

promise (noun)	*prōmissum, -ī,* n.
promise (verb)	*polliceor, -ērī, pollicitus.*
promote interests of	*ūtilitātem tueor, -ērī, tuitus; amplificō, -āre, -āvī, -ātus.*
prosperous	*secundus, -a, -um.*
prove (show)	*doceō, -ēre, docuī, doctus.*
province	*prōvincia, -ae,* f.
public enemy	*hostis, -is,* m.; *hostēs, -ium,* m.
Punic	*Pūnicus, -a, -um.*
punish	*pūniō, -īre, -īvī, -ītus; ulcīscor, -ī, ultus; poenās sūmō (dē), -ere, sūmpsī, sūmptus.*
punished (am)	*poenās dō, dare, dedī, datus.*
purpose (for the purpose of)	*causā (grātiā)* with gen. or poss. adj.
pursue	*sequor, -ī, secūtus; subsequor, -ī, -secūtus.*
put	*pōnō, -ere, posuī, positus; locō, -āre, -āvī, -ātus.*
put in command	*praeficiō, -ere, -fēcī, -fectus; praepōnō, -ere, -posuī, -positus.*
Pyrrhus	*Pyrrhus, -i,* m.

Q

quality	*virtūs, -tūtis,* f.
quickly	*celeriter.*
quote	*memorō, -āre, -āvī, -ātus; proferō, -ferre, -tulī, -lātus; ūtor, -ī, ūsus.*

R

raid (make)	*incursiōnem faciō, -ere, fēcī, factus* (*in* with acc.).
rank	*ōrdō, -inis,* m.
ransom	*redimō, -ere, -ēmī, -ēmptus.*
rather	*potius.*

read	*legō, -ere, lēgī, lēctus.*
ready	*parātus, -a, -um.*
reach	*perveniō, -īre, -vēnī, -ventum.*
realize	*sentiō, -īre, sēnsī, sēnsus; animō (mente) concipiō, -ere, -cēpī, -ceptus.*
really	*rē; rē vērā; rē ipsā.*
reason	*causa, -ae,* f.
reasoning	*ratiō, -ōnis,* f.
rebel	*ā rē pūblicā dēficiō, -ere, -fēcī, -fectus.*
refuse	*recūsō, -āre, -āvī, -ātus; nōlō, nōlle, nōluī.*
regarding	*dē* (prep. with abl.).
regret	*paenitet, -ēre, paenituit.*
Regulus	*Rēgulus, -ī,* m.
reply (noun)	*respōnsum, -ī,* n.
reply (verb)	*respondeō, -ēre, -spondī, -spōnsus.*
report (noun)	*nūntius, -ī,* m.
report (verb)	*nūntiō, -āre, -āvī, -ātus; renūntiō, -āre, -āvī, -ātus.*
republic	*rēs pūblica, reī pūblicae,* f.
request	*petō, -ere, -īvī, -ītus; pōscō, -ere, popōscī.*
request (grant)	*petentī satisfaciō, -ere, -fēcī, -factus.*
resources	*opēs, -um,* f.; *subsidia, -ōrum,* n.
restrain	*coerceō, -ēre, -cuī, -citus; prohibeō, -ēre, -uī, -itus.*
return (noun)	*reditus, -ūs,* m.
return (go back)	*redeō, -īre, -iī, -itūrus; revertor, -ī, revertī.*
return (give back)	*reddō, -ere, -didī, -ditus.*
reward	*praemium, -ī,* n.
ride	*vehor, -ī, vectus; equitō, -āre, -āvī, -ātum.*

rights of hospitality *iūs hospitī.*
river *flūmen, -inis,* n.; *fluvius, -ī,* m.
Roman (adj.) *Rōmānus, -a, -um.*
Roman (noun) *Rōmānus, -ī,* m.
Rome *Rōma, -ae,* f.
rout *fundō, -ere, fūdī, fūsus.*
route *iter, itineris,* n.
rule (noun) *imperium, -ī,* n.
rule (verb) *regō, -ere, rēxī, rēctus; imperō, -āre, -āvī, -ātum.*
ruler *rēx, rēgis,* m.; *praeses, -idis,* m.
rumor *rūmor, -ōris,* m.

S

sacred *sānctus, -a, -um; sacer, -cra, -crum.*
safe *tūtus, -a, -um; incolumis, -e.*
sake (for the sake of) *causā (grātiā)* preceded by gen.
same *īdem, eadem, idem.*
sand *arēna, -ae,* f.
sane *sānus, -a, -um.*
satisfaction (render) *satisfaciō, -ere, -fēcī, -factus.*
save *servō, -āre, -āvī, -ātus; cōnservō, -āre, -āvī, -ātus; ēripiō, -ere, -ripuī, -reptus.*
say *inquam, inquit; dīcō, -ere, dīxī, dictus.*
scarcity *inopia, -ae,* f.; *paucitās, -tātis,* f.
Scipio *Scīpiō, -ōnis,* m.
scorn (noun) *contemptiō, -ōnis,* f.
scorn (verb) *contemnō, -ere, -tempsī, -temptus.*
sea *mare, -is,* n.
second *secundus, -a, -um; alter, -a, -um.*
secretly *sēcrētō; fūrtim; clam.*
secure *adsequor, -ī, -secūtus; nancīscor, -ī, nactus.*

see	*videō, -ēre, vīdī, vīsus.*
seek	*petō, -ere, -īvī, -ītus.*
seem	*videor, -ērī, vīsus.*
sell	*vēndō, -ere, -didī, -ditus.*
senate	*senātus, -ūs*, m.
senate-house	*cūria, -ae*, f.
senator	*senātor, -ōris*, m.
send	*mittō, -ere, mīsī, missus.*
send back	*remittō, -ere, -mīsī, -missus.*
send for	*arcessō, -ere, -īvī, -ītus.*
Sertorius	*Sertōrius, -ī*, m.
serve	*serviō, -īre, -īvī, -ītum.*
set out	*proficīscor, -ī, profectus.*
seven	*septem.*
several	*complūrēs, -a (-ia); aliquot.*
shield	*scūtum, -ī*, n.
ship	*nāvis, -is*, f.
shore	*lītus, -oris*, n.
short	*brevis, -e.*
show	*doceō, -ēre, docuī, doctus; dēmōnstrō, -āre, -āvī, -ātus; ostendō, -ere, -dī, -tus.*
shrewd	*acūtus, -a, -um; callidus, -a, -um.*
Sicily	*Sicilia, -ae*, f.
since	*cum; quoniam.*
sing	*canō, -ere, cecinī.*
size	*magnitūdō, -inis*, f.
skill	*ars, artis*, f.; *scientia, -ae*, f.
sky	*caelum, -ī*, n.
slay	*occīdō, -ere, -cīdī, -cīsus.*
small	*parvus, -a -um.*
small (at small cost)	*parvī.*
so (with verbs)	*ita; sīc.*
so (with adjs. and advs.)	*tam.*
so (accordingly)	*itaque.*
soldier	*mīles, -itis*, m.

solicitude	*cūra, -ae,* f.; *sollicitūdō, -inis,* f.
some	*aliquī, -a, -od; nōnnūllī, -ae, -a.*
some day	*aliquandō.*
son	*fīlius, -ī,* m.
soon	*mox.*
soon afterwards	*paulō post.*
soon (as soon as)	*simul atque; cum prīmum.*
sort (what sort of)	*quālis, -e.*
Spain	*Hispānia, -ae,* f.
Spanish	*Hispāniēnsis, -e; Hispānus, -a, -um.*
spare	*parcō, -ere, pepercī, parsūrus.*
speak	*loquor, -ī, locūtus; dīcō, -ere, dīxī, dictus.*
speech	*ōrātiō, -ōnis,* f.
spirit	*animus, -ī,* m.
splendid	*amplus, -a, -um.*
spot	*locus, -ī,* m.; plu. *loca, -ōrum,* n.
spring (season)	*vēr, vēris,* n.
spring (fountain)	*fōns, fontis,* m.
sprung from	*ortus, -a, -um.*
stand still	*cōnsistō, -ere, -stitī.*
standard	*sīgnum, -ī,* n.
start	*proficīscor, -ī, -fectus.*
state (noun)	*cīvitās, -tātis,* f.
state (verb)	*dīcō, -ere, dīxī, dictus; cōnfīrmō, -āre, -āvī, -ātus.*
statue	*statua, -ae,* f.
stay	*maneō, -ēre, mānsī, mānsūrus; remaneō, -ēre, -mānsī, -mānsūrus.*
still	*nunc; etiam.*
still (nevertheless)	*tamen.*
stone	*lapis, -idis,* m.
stop	*sistō, -ere, stitī (stetī), statūrus.*
story (the story goes)	*ferunt.*

stream	*rīvus, -ī,* m.
strengthen	*cōnfīrmō, -āre, -āvī, -ātus.*
strictly	*dīligenter.*
strong	*fīrmus, -a, -um; validus, -a, -um.*
subject (be subject to)	*serviō, -īre, -īvī, -ītum.*
success	*fēlīcitās, -tātis,* f.; *rēs secundae, rērum secundārum,* f.
such (of such a character)	*tālis, -e; ēius modī.*
such (so great)	*tantus, -a, -um.*
sudden	*subitus, -a, -um; repentīnus, -a, -um.*
sufficiently	*satis.*
Sulla	*Sulla, -ae,* m.
sun	*sōl, sōlis,* m.
superhuman	*dīvīnus, -a, -um.*
suppose	*crēdō, -ere, -didī, -ditus; putō, -āre, -āvī, -ātus; exīstimō, -āre, -āvī, -ātus.*
surely	*certē; certō; profectō.*
surpassing	*excellēns, -entis.*
surrender (noun)	*dēditiō, -ōnis,* f.
surrender (verb)	*dēdō, -ere, -didī, -ditus; trādō, -ere, -didī, -ditus.*
suspect	*suspicor, -ārī, -ātus; suspiciō, -ere, -spēxi, -spectus.*
sweetly	*dulce.*
swift	*celer, -eris, -ere.*
Syracuse	*Syrācūsae, -ārum,* f.

T

take	*capiō, -ere, cēpī, captus; dūcō, -ere, dūxī, ductus.*
take (measures)	*cōnsulō, -ere, -suluī, -sultus; prōvideō, -ēre, -vīdī, -vīsus.*
take (precautions)	*prōvideō et praecaveō, -ēre, -cāvī, -cautus.*

take up (**arms**) *suscipiō, -ere, -cēpī, -ceptus.*
talent *ingenium, -ī,* n.
teach *doceō, -ēre, docuī, doctus.*
tell *dīcō, -ere, dīxī, dictus.*
temple *templum, -ī,* n.
tenth *decimus, -a, -um.*
terms *condiciō, -ōnis,* f.
territory *fīnēs, -ium,* m.
test *perīculum, -ī,* n.
thank *grātiās agō, -ere, ēgī, āctus.*
that (dem. pron.) *ille, -a, -ud; is, ea, id.*
that (rel. pron.) *quī, quae, quod.*
that (conj.) *ut; quō* (with comparatives); *nē* (with verbs of fearing); *quīn* (with negative expressions of doubt).
their (reflexive) *suus, -a, -um.*
their (not reflexive) *eōrum; eārum.*
then *tum; eō tempore.*
then and then only *tum dēmum.*
then (therefore) *igitur; itaque.*
there *ibi.*
there (**to that place**) *eō; illūc.*
therefore *itaque; igitur.*
thing *rēs, reī,* f.
think *putō, -āre, -āvī, -ātus; arbitror, -ārī, -ātus; exīstimō, -are, -āvī, -ātus.*
this *hīc, haec, hōc; is, ea, id.*
though *cum; quamquam.*
thousand *mīlle.*
thousands *mīlia, -ium,* n.
through *per* (prep. with acc.).
throw *iaciō, -ere, iēcī, iactus; coniciō, -ere, -iēcī, -iectus.*
thus *ita; sīc.*

time	*tempus, -oris,* n.
time (at the time when)	*tum (eō tempore) cum.*
tired	*dēfessus, -a, -um.*
to	*ad* (prep. with acc.).
to-day	*hodiē.*
too (also)	*etiam; quoque.*
toward	*ad; in* (preps. with acc.).
town	*oppidum, -ī,* n.
trader	*mercātor, -ōris,* m.
training	*disciplīna, -ae,* f.; *exercitātiō, -ōnis,* f.
transgress	*trānseō, -īre, -iī, -itus.*
travel	*iter faciō, -ere, fēcī, factus; eō, īre, iī, itūrūs.*
troop	*cohors, -tis,* f.
troops	*cōpiae, -ārum,* f.
Troy	*Trōia, -ae,* f.
true	*vērus, -a, -um; bonus, -a, -um; optimus, -a, -um.*
truly	*vērō; certē; bene.*
trust	*cōnfīdō, -ere, cōnfīsus.*
try	*cōnor, -ārī, -ātus; temptō, -āre, -āvī, -ātus.*
Turkey	*Turcia, -ae,* f.
Turkish	*Turcicus, -a, -um.*
Turks	*Turcae, -ārum,* m.
turn out	*ēveniō, -īre, -vēnī, -ventum.*
two	*duo, duae, duo.*

U

uncertain	*incertus, -a, -um.*
unconscious	*īgnārus, -a, -um; īnscius, -a, -um.*
under	*sub* (prep. with acc. and abl.).
understand	*intellegō, -ere, -lēxī, -lēctus.*
undertake	*suscipiō, -ere, -cēpī, -ceptus.*
undeservedly	*immeritō.*

unfortunate	*īnfēlīx, -īcis; miser, -era, -erum.*
unharmed	*incolumis, -e.*
United States	*Cīvitātēs Cōnsociātae, -ium -ārum,* f.
unprovoked	*inlacessītus, -a, -um; ultrō.*
until (prep.)	*ad* (prep. with acc.).
until (conj.)	*dum; dōnec; quoad.*
unusual	*novus, -a, -um; inūsitātus, -a, -um; singulāris, -e.*
unwilling (be)	*nōlō, nōlle, nōluī.*
unworthy	*indīgnus, -a, -um.*
urge	*hortor, -ārī, -ātus; cohortor, -ārī, -ātus.*
use	*ūtor, -ī, ūsus.*
use (be wont)	*soleō, -ēre, solitus.*
useful	*ūtilis, -e.*

V

valley	*vāllēs, -is,* f.
value (of great value)	*magnī.*
value (of less value)	*minōris.*
Vergil	*Vergilius, -ī,* m.
very	*ipse, -a, -um.*
vigor (spirit)	*ferōcia, -ae,* f.
vigor (force)	*vīs, vim, vī,* f.
violence	*vīs, vim, vī,* f.
voice	*vōx, vōcis,* f.
vote	*sententiam dō, dare, dedī, datus; sententiam ferō, ferre, tulī, lātus.*

W

wage	*gerō, -ere, gessī, gestus.*
wait	*exspectō, -āre, -āvī, -ātus; moror, -ārī, -ātus.*
war	*bellum, -ī,* n.
warn	*moneō, -ēre, -uī, -itus.*

warning — *monitus, -ūs*, m.
watch — *cūstōdiō, -īre, -īvī, -ītus; vigilō, -āre, -āvī, -ātum.*
way — *iter, itineris*, n.
wealth — *dīvitiae, -ārum*, f.
wealthy — *opulentus, -a, -um; dīves, -itis.*
well — *bene.*
well known — *nōtus, -a, -um.*
what (inter. adj.) — *quī, quae, quod.*
what (inter. pron.) — *quid.*
when — *cum; ubi; quandō.*
where — *ubi.*
whether — *num; sī; utrum.*
which — *quī, quae, quod.*
while — *dum.*
whole — *tōtus, -a, -um; cūnctus, -a, -um.*
why — *cūr; quid; quā rē; quam ob rem.*
wife — *uxor, -ōris*, f.; *coniūnx, -iugis*, f.
willing (be) — *volō, velle, voluī.*
win — *vincō, -ere, vīcī, victus.*
wise — *sapiēns, -entis.*
wisely — *sapienter; prūdenter.*
wish — *volō, velle, voluī; cupiō, -ere, -īvī, -ītus.*
with — *cum* (prep. with abl.).
within — *intrā* (prep. with acc.).
without — *sine* (prep. with abl.).
woman — *mulier, -eris*, f.
wonder — *mīror, -ārī, -ātus.*
word — *verbum, -ī*, n.
word (keep one's word) — *fidem praestō, -āre, -stitī, -statūrus.*
world — *orbis terrārum, -is*, m.
worth — *virtūs, -tūtis*, f.
worthy — *dīgnus, -a, -um.*
would that — *utinam.*
wrest — *ēripiō, -ere, -ripuī, -reptus.*

write — *scrībo, -ere, scrīpsī, scrīptus.*
writer — *scrīptor, -ōris,* m.

Y

year — *annus, -ī,* m.
yet — *tamen; autem.*
you — *tū; vōs.*
young — *iuvenis, -is.*
young man — *adulēscēns, -entis,* m.; *iuvenis, -is,* m.

HECTOR AND DIOMEDES

Hector fights with Diomedes, one of the most distinguished Greek warriors at the siege of Troy.

CHAPTER XVII

PASSAGES FOR SIGHT COMPREHENSION

1

Atalanta's race

Forsitan audieris aliquam certamine cursus
veloces superasse viros. Non fabula rumor
ille fuit (superabat enim), nec dicere posses,
laude pedum formaene bono praestantior esset.
Scitanti [1] deus huic de coniuge, "Coniuge," dixit,
"nil opus est, Atalanta, tibi. Fuge coniugis [2] usum.[2]
Nec tamen effugies, teque ipsa viva carebis."
Territa sorte dei per opacas innuba [3] silvas
vivit, et instantem turbam violenta procorum [4]
condicione fugat, "Nec sum potienda, nisi," inquit,
"victa prius cursu. Pedibus contendite mecum.
Praemia veloci coniunx thalamique dabuntur,
mors pretium tardis. Ea lex certaminis esto." [5]

OVID, *Metamorphoses*, X, 560–572.

[1] when she was inquiring.
[2] the marriage bond.
[3] unmarried.
[4] suitors.
[5] shall be.

1. In what two respects did Atalanta excel?
2. What advice did the god give Atalanta? Will Atalanta succeed in carrying out this advice?
3. How was she affected by the god's oracle? Where did she live? Was she left in peace there?
4. With what terms did she try to repel her suitors?
5. What will be the reward of the victor, what the reward of the loser?

2

Pyramus and Thisbe

Pyramus et Thisbe, iuvenum pulcherrimus alter,
altera, quas oriens habuit, praelata puellis,
contiguas tenuere domos, ubi dicitur altam
coctilibus[1] muris cinxisse Semiramis urbem.
Notitiam primosque gradus vicinia fecit;
tempore crevit amor. Taedae[2] quoque iure[2] coissent,[2]
sed vetuere patres: quod non potuere vetare,
ex[3] aequo[3] captis[4] ardebant mentibus[4] ambo.
Conscius omnis abest: nutu signisque loquuntur;
quoque magis tegitur, tectus magis aestuat ignis.
Fissus erat tenui rima, quam duxerat olim
cum fieret, paries domui communis utrique.
Id vitium nulli per saecula longa notatum—
quid non sentit amor?—primi vidistis amantes,
et vocis facistis iter; tutaeque per illud
murmure blanditiae[5] minimo transire solebant.

Ovid, *Metamorphoses,* IV, 55–70.

[1] made of brick.
[2] they would have been joined in marriage.
[3] equally.
[4] in their passionate hearts.
[5] soft words.

1. Which words in the passage tell you that Pyramus and Thisbe were neighbors?
2. Did their acquaintance ripen into love? How do you know?
3. How did they manage to communicate with each other at first? How later on?
4. What words in the passage tell you that love knows everything?
5. What English poet presents this story in dramatic form, and in which one of his plays is it found?

3

Perseus seeks aid from his own enemy.

Verum ubi virtutem turbae [1] succumbere vidit,
"Auxilium," Perseus, "quoniam sic cogitis ipsi,"
dixit, "ab hoste petam: vultus avertite vestros,
si quis amicus adest!" Et Gorgonis extulit ora.
"Quaere alium, tua quem moveant miracula," dixit
Thescelus; utque manu iaculum fatale parabat
mittere, in hoc haesit signum de marmore gestu.
Proximus huic Ampyx animi plenissima magni
pectora Lyncidae [2] gladio petit: inque petendo
dextera deriguit [3] nec citra mota nec ultra est.
At Nileus, qui se genitum septemplice [4] Nilo
ementitus [5] erat,[5] clipeo quoque flumina septem
argento partim, partim caelaverat [6] auro,
"Adspice," ait, "Perseu, nostrae primordia [7] gentis:
magna feres tacitas solacia mortis ad umbras,
a tanto cecidisse viro." Pars ultima vocis
in medio suppressa sono est, adapertaque [8] velle
ora loqui credas, nec sunt ea pervia [9] verbis.

OVID, *Metamorphoses,* V, 177–194.

[1] dative case.
[2] Perseus.
[3] stiffened.
[4] sevenfold.
[5] had pretended.
[6] had engraved.
[7] origin.
[8] open.
[9] passable.

1. What was Perseus forced to do?
2. What warning did he give to his friends? Why?
3. What did Thescelus say? What did he do? What happened to him then?
4. Did Ampyx fare any better? What happened to him?
5. Whose son did Nileus claim to be? How did he represent his origin?
6. What did Nileus say to Perseus? What happened to him?

4

Orpheus and Eurydice

Talia dicentem nervosque[1] ad verba moventem
exsangues flebant animae; nec Tantalus undam
captavit[2] refugam, stupuitque Ixionis orbis.
Tunc primum lacrimis victarum carmine fama est
Eumenidum maduisse[3] genas.[4] Nec regia coniunx
sustinet oranti, nec qui regit ima, negare;
Eurydicen vocant. Umbras erat illa recentes
inter, et incessit passu de vulnere tardo.
Hanc simul et legem Rhodopeius[5] accipit Orpheus,
ne flectat retro sua lumina, donec Avernas
exierit valles: aut irrita[6] dona futura.
Carpitur[7] adclivis per muta silentia trames,[8]
arduus, obscurus, caligine densus opaca.
Nec procul afuerunt telluris margine summae:
hic, ne deficeret metuens, avidusque videndi,
flexit amans oculos—et protinus illa relapsa est.

Ovid, *Metamorphoses,* X, 40–57.

[1] the strings.
[2] tried to catch.
[3] were wet.
[4] cheeks.
[5] Thracian.
[6] useless, in vain.
[7] is traversed.
[8] path.

1. What was the punishment of Tantalus in Hades? Which words in the passage suggest the answer to this question?
2. How did the Eumenides react to Orpheus's words?
3. Who is meant by *regia coniunx?* What was the effect of Orpheus's plea on her?
4. Why did Eurydice come with halting steps?
5. On what condition did Orpheus receive his wife? What was to happen if he did not carry out his part of the bargain?
6. The poet Milton applies the adjective "half-regained" to Eurydice. What in this passage gives you the clue to his use of this adjective?

5

The disappearance of Silenus

Hunc adsueta cohors, Satyri Bacchaeque, frequentant,
at Silenus abest. Titubantem [1] annisque meroque
ruricolae cepere Phryges, vinctumque coronis
ad regem duxere Midan, cui Thracius Orpheus
orgia tradiderat cum Cecropio Eumolpo.
Qui simul agnovit socium comitemque sacrorum,[2]
hospitis adventu festum genialiter [3] egit
per bis quinque dies et iunctas ordine noctes.
Et iam stellarum sublime coegerat agmen
Lucifer undecimus, Lydos [4] cum laetus in agros
rex venit, et iuveni Silenum reddit alumno.[5]
Huic deus optandi gratum, sed inutile, fecit
muneris arbitrium,[6] gaudens altore [7] recepto.
Ille, male usurus donis, ait, "Effice quidquid
corpore contigero fulvum vertatur in aurum."

Ovid, *Metamorphoses,* XI, 89–103.

[1] stumbling.
[2] sacred rites.
[3] merrily.
[4] Lydian.
[5] foster son, *i. e.,* Bacchus.
[6] choice.
[7] foster father.

1. Who were the usual attendants of Bacchus?
2. How does Ovid characterize Silenus?
3. What befell Silenus?
4. Was Silenus a stranger to the king of Phrygia? Which Latin words contain the answer to this question?
5. How was the coming of the guest celebrated?
6. In return for what kind deed did Bacchus grant Midas the privilege of choosing a gift?
7. What gift did Midas choose? Was it a wise choice?

6

A sacrifice enables the Greek fleet to sail from Aulis.

Permanet Aoniis Nereus violentus in undis
bellaque non transfert; et sunt qui parcere Troiae
Neptunum credant, quia moenia fecerat urbi;
at non Thestorides:[1] nec enim nescitve tacetve
sanguine virgineo placandam virginis iram
esse deae. Postquam pietatem publica causa
rexque patrem vicit, castumque datura cruorem
flentibus ante aram stetit Iphigenia ministris,
victa dea est nubemque oculis obiecit, et inter
officium turbamque sacri vocesque precantum
supposita fertur mutasse Mycenida[2] cerva.[3]
Ergo ubi, qua decuit, lenita[4] est[4] caede Diana,
et pariter Phoebes, pariter maris ira recessit,
accipiunt ventos a tergo mille carinae,
multaque perpessae[5] Phrygia potiuntur harena.

OVID, *Metamorphoses,* XII, 24–38.

[1] the son of Thestor, *i. e.,* Calchas.
[2] Iphigenia.
[3] a hind.
[4] was appeased.
[5] *perpessae* = *per* + *patior.*

1. Who, in the opinion of some of the Greeks gathered at Aulis, was opposed to the destruction of Troy? Why?
2. What did Calchas urge the Greeks to do?
3. Explain just what the poet means by *rex patrem vicit,* remembering that *rex* and *pater* refer to Agamemnon, the father of Iphigenia.
4. What happened amidst the confusion of the sacrifice and the cries of the suppliants?
5. Would you infer from what followed that Diana was appeased? Explain.
6. Where else in your Latin course have you read this story?

7

The death of Achilles

Delius indulgens nebula[1] velatus in agmen
pervenit Iliacum mediaque in caede virorum
rara per ignotos pargentem cernit Achivos
tela Parin; fassusque deum, "Quid spicula perdis
sanguine plebis?" ait. "Sique est tibi cura tuorum,
vertere in Aeaciden caesosque ulciscere fratres!"
Dixit et ostendens sternentem Troica ferro
corpora Peliden, arcus obvertit in illum
certaque letifera[2] direxit spicula dextra.
Quod Priamus gaudere senex post Hectora posset,
hoc fuit; ille igitur tantorum victor, Achille,
victus es a timido Graiae raptore maritae![3]
At si femineo fuerat tibi Marte cadendum,
Thermodontiaca[4] malles cecidisse bipenni.[5]

OVID, *Metamorphoses*, XII, 598–611.

[1] cloud.
[2] fatal, deadly.
[3] wife.
[4] of an Amazon.
[5] double battle-ax.

1. What was Paris doing when Apollo came to the Trojan lines?
2. Did the god disclose his identity to Paris? What did he urge Paris to do in order to avenge the death of his brothers?
3. What was Achilles doing?
4. Did Apollo remain passive after giving his advice to Paris?
5. How was Priam affected by what followed?
6. Who, according to the poet, was the conqueror of Achilles?
7. If Achilles had had his choice, whom would he have preferred as his conqueror?

8

Ajax pleads his cause.

Consedere duces, et vulgi stante corona [1]
surgit ad hos clipei dominus septemplicis [2] Aiax;
utque erat impatiens irae, Sigeia torvo
litora respexit classemque in litore vultu,
intendensque manus "Agimus, pro Iuppiter!" inquit,
"ante rates causam, et mecum confertur Ulixes!
At non Hectoreis dubitavit cedere flammis,
quas ego sustinui, quas hac a classe fugavi.
Tutius est igitur fictis contendere verbis,
quam pugnare manu. Sed nec mihi dicere promptum,[3]
nec facere est isti; quantumque ego Marte feroci
inque acie valeo, tantum valet iste loquendo.
Nec memoranda tamen vobis mea facta, Pelasgi,
esse reor; vidistis enim. Sua narret Ulixes,
quae sine teste gerit, quorum nox conscia sola est!"

Ovid, *Metamorphoses,* XIII, 1–15.

[1] assembly, crowd.
[2] sevenfold.
[3] easy.

1. To whom is Ajax addressing himself?
2. How does the poet describe Ajax's feelings?
3. Who is Ajax's rival?
4. Which of the two showed himself superior before Troy?
5. In what respect is Ulysses superior to Ajax?
6. In what respect is Ajax superior to Ulysses? Write out the Latin words that contain the answer to this question.
7. Why is it not necessary for Ajax to recount his deeds? Why is it necessary for Ulysses to recount his?

9

Ulysses's services to the Greeks

"Mittor et Iliacas audax orator ad arces,
visaque et intrata est altae mihi curia Troiae,
plenaque adhuc erat illa viris. Interritus egi
quam mihi mandarat communis Graecia causam,
accusoque Parin praedamque Helenamque reposco,
et moveo Priamum Priamoque Antenora iunctum.
At Paris et fratres et qui rapuere sub illo
vix tenuere manus (scis hoc, Menelae) nefandas,
primaque lux nostri tecum fuit illa pericli.
Longa referre mora est quae consilioque manuque
utiliter feci spatiosi tempore belli.
Post acies primas urbis se moenibus hostes
continuere diu, nec aperti copia Martis
ulla fuit; decimo demum pugnavimus anno.
Nam si mea facta requiris,
hostibus insidior, fossa munimina[1] cingo,
consolor socios, ut longi taedia[2] belli
mente ferant placida."

OVID, *Metamorphoses*, XIII, 196–214.

[1] fortifications. [2] weariness.

1. On what mission was Ulysses sent by the Greeks?
2. Did Ulysses show any signs of fear when he entered the senate-house of Troy?
3. What was the substance of his demand? Was that demand successful?
4. What almost happened to Ulysses at the hands of some of the Trojans? Was Menelaus aware of that?
5. Why did the Greeks find it difficult to meet the Trojans in open battle during the first nine years of the war?
6. Can you mention the chief snare laid by Ulysses for the enemy?
7. Mention three other services of Ulysses to the Greeks.

10

The captive Trojan women bid a sad farewell to their country.

Ilion ardebat, neque adhuc consederat ignis;
exiguumque [1] senis Priami Iovis ara cruorem
combiberat. Tractata [2] comis antistita [3] Phoebi
non [4] profecturas [4] tendebat ad aethera palmas.
Dardanidas matres patriorum signa [5] deorum,
dum licet, amplexas succensaque templa tenentes
invidiosa trahunt victores praemia Grai.
Mittitur [6] Astyanax illis de turribus, unde
pugnantem pro se proavitaque [7] regna tuentem
saepe videre patrem monstratum a matre solebat.
Iamque viam suadet Boreas, flatuque [8] secundo
carbasa [9] mota sonant. Iubet uti navita ventis.
"Troia, vale! Rapimur" clamant, dant oscula terrae
Troades, et patriae fumantia tecta relinquunt.
Ultima conscendit classem, miserabile visu,
in mediis Hecuba natorum inventa sepulcris.

OVID, *Metamorphoses*, XIII, 408–423.

[1] scanty.
[2] dragged.
[3] priestess.
[4] unavailing.
[5] the images.
[6] is hurled.
[7] ancestral.
[8] breeze.
[9] =*vela*.

1. Mention the exact spot where Priam died.
2. What was the lot of the priestess of Apollo? What does the poet wish us to infer from his use of the words *non profecturas?*
3. What were the Trojan women doing when the Greeks came upon them?
4. What was the lot of Astyanax? Tell in your own words what Astyanax's mother used to point out to him from the lofty tower.
5. How do the Trojan women take leave of their native land?
6. Who is the last to go on board? Where had she been all this time?

11

The sacrifice of Polyxena

Litore Threicio classem religarat[1] Atrides,
dum mare pacatum, dum ventus amicior esset.
Hic subito, quantus, cum viveret, esse solebat,
exit humo late rupta, similisque minanti
temporis illius vultum referebat Achilles,
quo ferus iniusto petiit Agamemnona ferro:
"Immemores" que "mei disceditis," inquit, "Achivi?
Obrutaque est mecum virtutis gratia nostrae?
Ne facite! Utque meum non sit sine honore sepulcrum,
placet Achilleos mactata Polyxena manes."
Dixit, et immiti sociis parentibus umbrae,
rapta sinu matris, quam iam prope sola fovebat,
fortis et infelix et plus quam femina virgo
ducitur ad tumulum, diroque fit hostia[2] busto.[3]
Utque Neoptolemum stantem ferrumque tenentem
inque suo vidit figentem lumina vultu,
"Utere iam dudum generoso[4] sanguine", dixit,
"nulla mora est, aut tu iugulo[5] vel pectore telum
conde meo."

Ovid, *Metamorphoses,* XIII, 439–459.

[1] had anchored.
[2] victim.
[3] mound, tomb.
[4] noble.
[5] throat.

1. Why had Atrides moored his fleet on the Thracian coast?
2. How does Achilles look when he rises from the earth?
3. Why does he reproach the Greeks?
4. What honor does he demand of them?
5. Did the Greeks carry out his wish?
6. Did Polyxena show any womanish fears? Which Latin words contain the answer to this question?
7. What did she say to Neoptolemus?

12

King Anius describes the wonderful power which Bacchus gave to his daughters.

Tum pius Anchises: "O Phoebi lecte sacerdos,
fallor, an et natum, cum primum haec moenia vidi,
bisque duas natas, quantum reminiscor,[1] habebas?"
Huic Anius niveis circumdata tempora vittis
concutiens et tristis ait: "Non falleris, heros
maxime; vidisti natorum quinque parentem,
quem nunc (tanta homines rerum inconstantia versat)
paene vides orbum.[2] Quod enim mihi filius absens
auxilium, quem dicta suo de nomine tellus
Andros[3] habet, pro patre locumque et regna tenentem?
Delius augurium dedit huic; dedit altera Liber[4]
femineae stirpi voto maiora fideque
munera. Nam tactu natarum cuncta mearum
in segetem[5] laticemque meri canaeque Minervae
transformabantur, divesque erat usus[6] in illis.

OVID, *Metamorphoses,* XIII, 640–654.

[1] recall.
[2] bereft, childless.
[3] name of an island.
[4] =Bacchus.
[5] corn, grain.
[6] gain, profit.

1. Is this the first meeting between Anchises and Anius? Which Latin words contain the answer to this question?
2. What other office does Anius hold besides that of king? Upon what two facts do you base your answer to this question?
3. How many daughters does Anius have? Are they with their father?
4. Where is Anius's son? What power did Apollo bestow upon him?
5. What wonderful power did Bacchus give to Anius's daughters?

13

Some scenes represented on Hannibal's shield

Condebat primae Dido Carthaginis arces,
instabatque operi subducta classe iuventus.
Molibus hi claudunt portus, his tecta domosque
partiris,[1] iustae Bitia venerande senectae.
Ostentant caput effosa tellure repertum
bellatoris equi atque omen clamore salutant.
Has inter species orbatum[2] classe suisque
Aenean pulsum pelago dextraque precantem
cernere erat. Fronte hunc avide regina serena
infelix ac iam vultu spectabat amico.
Hinc et speluncam furtivaque foedera amantum
Callaicae[3] fecere manus; it clamor ad auras
latratusque[4] canum, subitoque exterrita nimbo
occultant alae venantum corpora silvis.
Nec procul Aeneadum vacuo iam litore classis
aequora nequiquam revocante petebat Elissa.

SILIUS ITALICUS, *Punica*, II, 406–431.

[1] you divide, you distribute.
[2] bereft.
[3] Spanish.
[4] barking.

1. What is Dido represented as doing?
2. What is Bitias engaged in doing? How is he characterized?
3. What favorable omen did the builders of Carthage find? Where?
4. Name the three definite facts we are given about Aeneas.
5. Is Dido represented as kindly disposed toward Aeneas? On what specific words do you base your answer?
6. Where else in Latin literature have you read of the cave mentioned in this selection?
7. Who is Elissa? How is she affected by the departure of the Trojan fleet?

14

Aeneas and Pallas set out for the Tuscan camp.

Iamque adeo exierat portis equitatus apertis,
Aeneas inter primos et fidus Achates,
inde alii Troiae proceres,[1] ipse agmine Pallas
in medio, chlamyde [2] et pictis conspectus in armis:
qualis ubi Oceani perfusus Lucifer unda,
quem Venus ante alios astrorum diligit ignes,
extulit os sacrum caelo tenebrasque resolvit.
Stant pavidae in muris matres oculisque sequuntur
pulveream nubem et fulgentes aere catervas.
Olli per dumos,[3] qua proxima meta viarum,
armati tendunt; it clamor, et agmine facto
quadrupedante [4] putrem [5] sonitu quatit ungula [6] campum.
Est ingens gelidum lucus prope Caeritis amnem,
religione patrum late sacer; undique colles
inclusere cavi et nigra nemus abiete cingunt.

Aeneid, VIII, 585–599.

[1] chieftains.
[2] cloak.
[3] thickets.
[4] galloping.
[5] crumbling.
[6] hoof.

1. What distinguishes Pallas from the rest of the princes?
2. What does the poet tell us about the star to whom he compares Pallas?
3. What are the feelings of the women who watch the departing throng? What is their vantage point?
4. What striking peculiarity do you notice in line 596?
5. Locate the vast grove the poet speaks of, describe its surroundings, and tell its religious significance.

15

Nisus and Euryalus offer themselves as messengers to Aeneas.

Cetera per terras omnes animalia somno
laxabant curas et corda oblita laborum;
ductores Teucrum primi, delecta iuventus,
consilium summis regni de rebus habebant,
quid facerent quisve Aeneae iam nuntius esset.
Stant longis adnixi hastis et scuta tenentes
castrorum et campi medio. Tum Nisus et una
Euryalus confestim [1] alacres admittier [2] orant:
rem magnam pretiumque morae fore. Primus Iulus
accepit trepidos ac Nisum dicere iussit.
Tum sic Hyrtacides: [3] "Audite o mentibus aequis,
Aeneadae, neve haec nostris spectentur ab annis,
quae ferimus. Rutuli somno vinoque soluti
conticuere; locum insidiis conspeximus ipsi.
Si fortuna permittitis uti,
quaesitum Aenean et moenia Pallantea,
mox hic cum spoliis, ingenti caede peracta,
adfore cernetis."

Aeneid, IX, 224–243.

[1] immediately, without delay.
[2] =*admitti*.
[3] =Nisus.

1. At what time of the day do the events of this selection take place? How do you know?
2. What are the Teucrian captains deliberating? Where does the conference take place?
3. Why do Nisus and Euryalus ask for a speedy audience?
4. Is their request granted? How do you know?
5. What information do they bring about the Rutulians? How did they obtain this?
6. What do they promise to accomplish if given permission to seek the walls of Pallanteum?

16

Nisus offers himself in behalf of his friend Euryalus.

Tum vero exterritus, amens,
conclamat Nisus nec se celare tenebris
amplius aut tantum potuit perferre dolorem:
"Me, me, adsum qui feci, in me convertite ferrum,
O Rutuli! Mea fraus omnis; nihil iste nec ausus
nec potuit; caelum hoc et conscia sidera testor;
tantum infelicem nimium dilexit amicum."
Talia dicta dabat, sed viribus ensis adactus[1]
transabiit costas[2] et candida pectora rumpit.
Volvitur Euryalus leto, pulchrosque per artus
it cruor inque umeros cervix conlapsa recumbit.
At Nisus ruit in medios solumque per omnes
Volcentem petit, in solo Volcente moratur.
Quem circum glomerati hostes hinc comminus atque hinc
proturbant. Instat non setius ac rotat[3] ensem
fulmineum, donec Rutuli clamantis in ore
condidit adverso et moriens animam abstulit hosti.
Tum super exanimum sese proiecit amicum
confossus,[4] placidaque ibi demum morte quievit.

Aeneid, IX, 424–445.

[1] driven.
[2] ribs.
[3] whirls.
[4] pierced through.

1. What request does Nisus make of the Rutulians?
2. Whom does he call to witness that the guilt is all his?
3. What is the fate of Euryalus?
4. Does Nisus find it easy to reach Volcens? Which Latin words contain the answer to this question?
5. Does Nisus finally succeed in avenging his friend's death? How do you know?
6. What happens to Nisus?

17

The funeral rites of Pallas

Haec ubi deflevit, tolli miserabile corpus
imperat, et toto lectos ex agmine mittit
mille viros, qui supremum comitentur honorem
intersintque patris lacrimis, solacia[1] luctus
exigua ingentis, misero sed debita patri.
Hic iuvenem agresti sublimem stramine[2] ponunt.
Tum geminas vestes auroque ostroque[3] rigentes
extulit Aeneas, quas illi laeta laborum
ipsa suis quondam manibus Sidonia Dido
fecerat et tenui telas[4] discreverat[5] auro.
Harum unam iuveni supremum maestus honorem
induit.
Addit equos et tela, quibus spoliaverat hostem.
Ducitur infelix aevo confectus Acoetes.
Ducunt et Rutulo perfusos sanguine currus.
Post bellator equus, positis insignibus, Aethon
it lacrimans guttisque[6] umectat grandibus ora.
Hastam alii galeamque ferunt; nam cetera Turnus
victor habet.

Aeneid, XI, 59–92 (adapted)

[1] solace.
[2] bed, bier.
[3] purple.
[4] web.
[5] had interwoven.
[6] drops.

1. On what errand are the men sent by Aeneas?
2. Describe the robes which Dido presented to Aeneas. For what purpose does Aeneas use one of these now?
3. Where did Aeneas procure the horses and arms that he adds?
4. Is there any indication in the passage that even brute beasts shared the grief of men?
5. Of the arms of Pallas only the spear and the helmet are mentioned. What has become of the rest?

18

Juno addresses Juturna.

Extemplo Turni sic est adfata sororem,
diva deam, stagnis quae fluminibusque sonoris
praesidet:
"Disce tuum, ne me incuses, Iuturna, dolorem.
Qua visa est Fortuna pati Parcaeque sinebant
cedere[1] res Latio, Turnum et tua moenia texi;
nunc iuvenem imparibus video concurrere fatis,
Parcarumque dies et vis inimica propinquat.
Non pugnam aspicere hanc oculis, non foedera possum.
Tu pro germano si quid praesentius audes,
perge; decet. Forsan miseros meliora sequentur."
Vix ea, cum lacrimas oculis Iuturna profudit
terque quaterque manu pectus percussit honestum.
"Non lacrimis hoc tempus" ait Saturnia Iuno;
"Accelera et fratrem, si quis modus, eripe morti;
aut tu bella cie conceptumque excute foedus.
Auctor ego audendi."

Aeneid, XII, 138–159 (adapted)

[1] to prosper.

1. Who is Juturna?
2. To whom do *diva* and *deam* in line 139 refer?
3. What sad information does the goddess impart to Juturna?
4. Why is Juno no longer able to protect Turnus?
5. What does she urge Juturna to do?
6. How did Juturna react to Juno's words?
7. Paraphrase the last three words of this selection.

19

Aeneas makes a vow.

Tum pius Aeneas stricto sic ense precatur:
"Esto nunc Sol testis et haec mihi Terra precanti,
quam propter tantos potui perferre labores,
et Pater omnipotens et tu Saturnia coniunx,
iam melior, iam, diva, precor; tuque inclute[1] Mavors,
cuncta tuo qui bella, Pater, sub numine torques;
Fontesque Fluviosque voco, quaeque aetheris alti
religio et quae caeruleo sunt numina ponto:
cesserit Ausonio si fors[2] Victoria Turno,
convenit[3] Evandri victos discedere ad urbem,
cedet Iulus agris, nec post arma ulla rebelles[4]
Aeneadae referent ferrove haec regna lacessent.
Sin nostrum adnuerit[5] nobis Victoria Martem
(ut potius reor et potius di numine firment),
non ego nec Teucris Italos parere iubebo
nec mihi regna peto."

Aeneid, XII, 175–190

[1] famous.
[2] perchance, perhaps.
[3] it is agreed.
[4] renewing the war.
[5] shall grant.

1. To what deities does Aeneas pray?
2. Why does he pray to Terra?
3. Who is *Saturnia coniunx?* How is she characterized?
4. What power does Aeneas ascribe to Mars?
5. What will the vanquished do if victory falls to Turnus? What will Iulus do? What will the followers of Aeneas do?
6. What will be the lot of the Italians if victory falls to the Trojans?

20

The combat between Aeneas and Turnus

At pater Aeneas, audito nomine Turni,
deserit et muros et summas arces
praecipitatque [1] moras omnes, opera omnia rumpit,
laetitia exsultans, horrendumque intonat armis.
Iam vero et Rutuli certatim [2] et Troes et omnes
convertere oculos Itali, quique alta tenebant
moenia quique imos pulsabant ariete muros,
armaque deposuere umeris. Stupet ipse Latinus
ingentes, genitos diversis partibus orbis,
inter se coiisse viros et cernere ferro.
Atque illi, ut vacuo patuerunt aequore campi,
procursu rapido, coniectis eminus [3] hastis,
invadunt Martem clipeis atque aere sonoro.
Dat gemitum tellus; tum crebros ensibus ictus [4]
congeminant; [4] fors et virtus miscentur in unum.

Aeneid, XII, 697–714.

[1] flings aside.
[2] in rivalry, emulously.
[3] from a distance.
[4] shower blow on blow.

1. What feelings does Aeneas experience when he hears Turnus's name? What does he then do?
2. In what two activities were the Italians engaged just before the two leaders met?
3. Does the poet indicate the birthplace of the leaders? Explain.
4. Tell in detail the successive events which followed as soon as the lists were clear on the open plain.

VERGIL

June, 1934

Answer three questions.

1. Translate the following passages into English:

[The Trojans, seeing the enemy approach, prepare to defend their encampment. In the absence of Aeneas, who had forbidden any offensive move, Caicus acts as leader.]

1 Hic subitam nigro glomerari pulvere nubem
2 prospiciunt Teucri ac tenebras insurgere campis.
3 Primus ab adversa conclamat mole Caicus:
4 "Quis globus, o cives, caligine volvitur atra?
5 Ferte citi ferrum, date tela, ascendite muros.
6 Hostis adest, heia!" Ingenti clamore per omnes
7 condunt se Teucri portas et moenia complent.
8 Namque ita discedens praeceperat optimus armis
9 Aeneas: si qua interea fortuna fuisset,
10 neu struere auderent aciem, neu credere campo;
11 castra modo et tutos servarent aggere muros.
12 Ergo, etsi conferre manum pudor iraque monstrat,
13 obiciunt portas tamen et praecepta facessunt
14 armatique cavis exspectant turribus hostem.

—*Aeneid,* IX, 33-46 [35]

insurgere (verse 2) = rises over, (is) rising over
mole (verse 3) = rampart
globus (verse 4) = mass (literally, ball)
caligine (verse 4) = from *caligo, caliginis,* mist
heia (verse 6) = ho!
condunt se (verse 7) = take shelter
fortuna fuisset (verse 9) = change should occur
auderent (verse 10) and *servarent* (verse 11) — Use "should" in translating
conferre manum (verse 12) — Translate "to give battle"
obiciunt (verse 13) = bar

[After his arrival at the Tiber, Aeneas had received an omen for which he is now offering a prayer of gratitude to various gods; he receives a new omen in answer to his prayer.]

15 Sic deinde effatus frondenti tempora ramo
16 implicat et Geniumque loci primamque deorum
17 Tellurem Nymphasque et adhuc ignota precatur
18 flumina; tum Noctem Noctisque orientia signa
19 Idaeumque Iovem Phrygiamque ex ordine Matrem
20 invocat et duplices Caeloque Ereboque parentes.
21 Hic pater omnipotens ter caelo clarus ab alto
22 intonuit radiisque ardentem lucis et auro
23 ipse manu quatiens ostendit ab aethere nubem.
24 Diditur hic subito Troiana per agmina rumor
25 advenisse diem, quo debita moenia condant.
26 Certatim instaurant epulas atque omine magno
27 crateras laeti statuunt et vina coronant.

—*Aeneid,* VII, 135-147 [33]

tempora (verse 15) = temples (of the head)
Genium (verse 16) = guardian spirit
primam deorum (verse 16) — in apposition with the name *Tellurem*
Idaeum (verse 19) = from Mount Ida (adjective)
duplices (verse 20) = his two
Erebo (verse 20) — Erebus is a name for the lower world
manu quatiens ostendit (verse 23) = with his hand shook forth to view
Diditur (verse 24) = spreads
Certatim (verse 26) = eagerly
instaurant (verse 26) — from *instaurare,* to renew

2. Answer *all* of the following:
   a. Give the syntax of *pulvere* (verse 1), *turribus* (verse 14). [2]
   b. From what verb is the frequentative *facessunt* (verse 13) derived? [1]
   c. Scan verses 4 and 5, indicating the quantity of syllables and the division into feet. [4]
   d. In what way does the meter of verse 5 correspond with the meaning? [1]
   e. Who is meant by *Phrygia Mater* (verse 19)? [1]

f. Who are meant by *duplices parentes* (verse 20) [1]? Why are they thus separated (*Caeloque Ereboque*) [2]?

g. What religious significance is there in the expression *ter intonuit* (verses 21 and 22)? [1]

h. Quote from memory the *four* verses immediately following the quotation below. [4]

Excudent alii spirantia mollius aera . . .

i. Explain each of *four* of the following terms: hendiadys, prolepsis, personification, tmesis, diminutives. [4]

j. In verse 8 Aeneas is called *optimus armis.* What even more outstanding quality or epithet does Vergil use to describe Aeneas? [1]

3. Answer *each* of the following:

a. In what *two* ways does the Sibyl help Aeneas in the sixth book of the *Aeneid*? [2]

b. Give the reasons why each of *four* of the following is either friendly or hostile to Aeneas: Aeolus, Juno, Venus, Apollo, Turnus, Iarbas. [4]

c. Give *four* essential characteristics of an epic [2]. Show briefly how the *Aeneid* satisfies *each* of these essentials [2].

4. Answer *each* of the following:

a. Locate each of *two* of the following: Alba Longa, Numidia, Ithaca. [2]

b. Name an earlier Latin epic that influenced Vergil. [1]

c. What do we learn from the following lines about the character of Vergil? [4]

(1) *Non ignara mali miseris succurrere disco.*

(2) *Omnis in Ascanio cari stat cura parentis.*

(3) *Sunt lacrimae rerum et mentem mortalia tangunt.*

(4) *At sperate deos memores fandi atque nefandi.*

d. For what *three* purposes does Vergil make Aeneas descend into the lower world? [3]

VERGIL

January, 1935

Answer three questions.

1. Translate the following passages into English:

[Encouraged by Mars, the Latins storm the gate to the Trojan camp; Pandarus shuts it, but inadvertently has admitted Turnus.]

1 Hic Mars armipotens animum viresque Latinis
2 addidit et stimulos acres sub pectore vertit;
3 immisitque Fugam Teucris atrumque Timorem.
4 Undique conveniunt, quoniam data copia pugnae,
5 bellatorque animo deus incidit.
6 Pandarus, ut fuso germanum corpore cernit,
7 et quo sit fortuna loco, qui casus agat res,
8 portam vi magna converso cardine torquet,
9 obnixus latis umeris, multosque suorum
10 moenibus exclusos duro in certamine linquit;
11 ast alios secum includit recipitque ruentes,
12 demens! qui Rutulum in medio non agmine regem
13 viderit inrumpentem, ultroque incluserit urbi,
14 immanem veluti pecora inter inertia tigrim.

—*Aeneid,* IX, 717-730 [35]

bellator (verse 5) = warrior
cardine (verse 8) = hinge
obnixus (verse 9) = pushing against
ast (verse 11) = *at*
ultro (verse 13) = inadvertently
inertia (verse 14) — from *iners,* helpless
tigrim (verse 14) = tiger

[In view of the impending conflict with the Rutuli, Venus implores her husband, Vulcan, to make armor for Aeneas as he has done for others.]

15 Dum bello Argolici vastabant Pergama reges
16 debita casurasque inimicis ignibus arces,
17 non ullum auxilium miseris, non arma rogavi
18 artis opisque tuae; nec te, carissime coniunx,
19 incassumve tuos volui exercere labores,
20 quamvis et Priami deberem plurima natis
21 et durum Aeneae flevissem saepe laborem.
22 Nunc Iovis imperiis Rutulorum constitit oris:
23 ergo eadem supplex venio et, sanctum mihi numen,
24 arma rogo, genetrix nato. Te filia Nerei,
25 te potuit lacrimis Tithonia flectere coniunx.
26 Aspice, qui coeant populi, quae moenia clausis

27 ferrum acuant portis in me excidiumque meorum.

—*Aeneid,* VIII, 374-386 [33]

debita (verse 16) = doomed
incassum (verse 19) = in vain
exercere (verse 19) = to tax
eadem (verse 23) — nominative feminine
genetrix (verse 24) = mother
Nerei (verse 24) = of Nereus
coeant (verse 26) — from *co-ire*
excidium (verse 27) = destruction

2. Answer *all* of the following:
   a. Give the syntax of *viderit* (verse 13), *miseris* (verse 17), *oris* (verse 22). [3]
   b. Scan verses 8 and 17, indicating the quantity of syllables and the division into feet [4]. Show the relation of meter to content in verse 8 *or* point out and name the metrical peculiarity in verse 24 [1].
   c. Show by derivation the appropriateness of *armipotens* (verse 1). [1]
   d. Name *one* of the *Argolici reges* (verse 15) [1]. What other Latin name for *Pergama* (verse 15) do you know [1]? Why did Venus owe much to one of Priam's sons [1]?
   e. Quote from memory any *five* consecutive lines from Vergil's description of Fama *or* complete with the next *five* lines the quotation beginning
      Nox erat et placidum carpebant fessa soporem............[5]
   f. Explain each of *three* of the following terms: metaphor, simile, onomatopoeia, patronymic, alliteration. [3]
   g. What figure of speech is indicated by the capitalization of *Fugam* and *Timorem* (verse 3)? [1]

Answer EITHER question 3 OR question 4.

3. Answer *each* of the following:
   a. Tell briefly why you consider Sinon's acts in book II either justified or wrong. [2]
   b. Give a function and an attribute of each of *five* of the following: Bacchus, Diana, Hercules, Iris, Mercury, Janus. [*Example*: Jupiter—king of heaven and earth—the thunderbolt] [5]
   c. Name *two* characteristics of the *Aeneid* that substantiate its claim to be a national epic. [2]
   d. In praising Vergil's gentleness and human sympathy, Horace calls him a "white soul." Point out *two* instances in the *Aeneid* that bear out this judgment. [2]

4. Answer *each* of the following:
   a. Locate *two* of the following: Cumae, Tenedos, Styx. [2]
   b. In the *Aeneid* what role is played by or what interest attaches to each of *four* of the following: Andromache, Daedalus, Lavinia, Minos, Laocoon, the Sibyl? [4]

c. For what different purposes do both Venus and Juno favor Dido's falling in love with Aeneas? [2]
d. Name an incident in the *Aeneid* that justifies the epithet *pius* as applied to Aeneas. [1]
e. Name and characterize briefly the content of *one* of the works of Vergil that preceded the *Aeneid.* [2]

VERGIL

June 18, 1935

Answer three questions.

1. Translate the following passages into English:

[King Evander recalls the time in his boyhood when Anchises with other Trojans visited his father in Arcadia. Therefore with his son Pallas he welcomes Aeneas and promises to aid him.]

1 Mirabarque duces Teucros, mirabar et ipsum
2 *Laomedontiaden;* sed *cunctis* altior ibat
3 Anchises. Mihi mens iuvenali ardebat amore
4 compellare virum et dextrae coniungere dextram;
5 accessi et cupidus Phenei sub moenia duxi.
6 Ille mihi insignem pharetram Lyciasque sagittas
7 discedens chlamydemque auro dedit intertextam,
8 frenaque bina, meus quae nunc habet, aurea, Pallas.
9 Ergo et quam petitis iuncta est mihi foedere dextra
10 et, lux cum primum terris se crastina reddet,
11 auxilio laetos dimittam opibusque iuvabo.
12 Interea sacra haec, quando huc venistis amici,
13 annua, quae differre nefas, celebrate faventes
14 nobiscum et iam nunc sociorum adsuescite mensis.

—*Aeneid,* VIII, 161–174 [35]

iuvenali (verse 3) = youthful
Phenei (verse 5) = of Pheneus
Lycias (verse 6) = Lycian
chlamydem (verse 7) = cloak
intertextam (verse 7) = interwoven
quam (verse 9) — the antecedent is *dextra* (nominative)
mihi (verse 9) — Translate as a dative of agency
crastina (verse 10) = tomorrow's
sacra . . . annua (verses 12–13) = yearly rites (object of *celebrate*)
differre (verse 13) = to postpone

[By Juno's command, the Fury Alecto appears to Turnus to incite him against Aeneas.]

15 Turne, tot incassum fusos *patiere* labores,
16 et tua Dardaniis transcribi sceptra colonis?
17 Rex tibi coniugium et quaesitas sanguine dotes

18 abnegat externusque in regnum quaeritur heres
19 I nunc, ingratis offer te, *inrise, periclis;*
20 Tyrrhenas, i, sterne acies; tege pace Latinos.
21 Haec adeo tibi me, placida cum nocte iaceres,
22 ipsa palam fari omnipotens Saturnia iussit.
23 Quare age et armari pubem portisque moveri
24 laetus in arma para, et Phrygios, qui *flumine* pulchro
25 *consedere,* duces pictasque exure carinas.
26 Caelestum vis magna iubet. Rex ipse Latinus,
27 ni dare coniugium et dicto parere fatetur,
28 *sentiat,* et tandem Turnum experiatur in armis.

—*Aeneid,* VII, 421–434 [35]

incassum fusos (verse 15) = to have been spent in vain
transcribi (verse 16) — from *transcribere,* to hand over
coniugium (verse 17) = bride
dotes (verse 17) = dowry
heres (verse 18) = heir
Haec (verse 21) — the object of *fari* (verse 22)
in arma (verse 24) = to battle
Caelestum (verse 26) = of the heavenly gods
fatetur (verse 27) — from *fateri,* to consent

2. Answer *all* of the following:

a. Give the syntax of each of *three* of the following: *cunctis* (verse 2), *inrise* (verse 19), *flumine* (verse 24), *sentiat* (verse 28). [3]

b. Scan verses 22 and 27, indicating the quantity of syllables and the division into feet. [4]

c. What special name is given to words formed like *Laomedontiaden* (verse 2)? [1]

d. Give the usual prose form of *patiere* (verse 15), *periclis* (verse 19), *consedere* (verse 25). [3]

e. Quote from memory the *four* lines immediately following *O passi graviora, dabit deus his quoque finem.* [4]

f. Explain each of *three* of the following terms: diminutive, metonymy, tmesis, hiatus. [3]

g. To whom does *each* of the following refer: *Dardanii, Danai*? [2]

Answer EITHER question 3 OR question 4.

3. Answer *each* of the following:

a. What part does Anna play in the story of Dido and Aeneas and why does Vergil include her among the characters? [2]

b. Give a function and an attribute of each of *four* of the following: Aurora, Parcae, Ceres, Mars, Neptune. [*Example:* Jupiter — king of heaven and earth—the thunderbolt] [4]

c. For what reason did Vergil fail to complete the *Aeneid*? [1]

d. What is the subject of the fifth book of the *Aeneid* and what does it contribute to our knowledge of the character of Aeneas? [2]

e. In which book of the *Aeneid* does Vergil portray his conception of the lower world? [1]

4. Answer *each* of the following:

a. State the interest attaching to each of *four* of the following: Acestes, Cassandra, Sinon, Helen, Olympus. [4]

b. To what kind of poetry do the *Georgics* belong? The *Eclogues*? [2]

c. In what ways does Aeneas fulfil the role of the principal character in a heroic epic? [3]

d. *Sum pius Aenaes, fama super aethera notus.* How do you justify this apparently boastful statement from the lips of Vergil's hero? [1]

VERGIL

January 23, 1936

Answer three questions.

1. Translate the following passages into English:

[Filled with grief, Aeneas makes preparations for the funeral of his young friend Pallas.]

1 Haec ubi deflevit, tolli miserabile corpus
2 imperat, et toto lectos ex agmine mittit
3 mille viros, qui supremum comitentur honorem
4 intersintque patris lacrimis, solacia luctus
5 exigua ingentis, misero sed debita patri.
6 Tum geminas vestes auroque ostroque rigentes
7 extulit Aeneas, quas illi laeta *laborum*
8 ipsa suis quondam manibus Sidonia Dido
9 fecerat et tenui telas discreverat auro.
10 Harum unam iuveni supremum maestus honorem
11 induit arsurasque comas obnubit amictu,
12 multaque praeterea Laurentis praemia pugnae
13 aggerat et longo praedam iubet ordine duci;
14 addit equos et tela, *quibus* spoliaverat hostem.

—*Aeneid,* XI, 59-63; 72-80 [35]

comitentur (verse 3) = attend
intersint (verse 4) = share
solacia (verse 4) = comfort
ostro (verse 6) = purple
telas discreverat (verse 9) = had embroidered the fabric
obnubit (verse 11) = (he) veils
Laurentis (verse 12) = Laurentian
aggerat (verse 13) = he heaps up

[Juno reproaches Venus for her constant help to Aeneas and the Trojans and claims for herself the same right to help Turnus and the Rutuli.]

15 Tu potes *Aenean* manibus subducere *Graium*
16 proque viro nebulam et ventos obtendere inanes:
17 nos aliquid Rutulos contra iuvisse nefandum est?
18 Aeneas ignarus abest: ignarus et absit.
19 Est Paphus Idaliumque *tibi,* sunt alta Cythera:
20 quid gravidam bellis urbem et corda aspera temptas?
21 Nosne tibi fluxas Phrygiae res vertere fundo

22 conamur? nos? an miseros qui Troas Achivis
23 obiecit? quae causa fuit, consurgere in arma
24 Europàmque Asiamque, et foedera solvere furto?
25 Me duce *Dardanius* Spartam *expugnavit adulter,*
26 aut ego tela dedi, fovive cupidine bella?
27 Tum decuit metuisse tuis: nunc sera querelis
28 haud iustis adsurgis et inrita iurgia iactas.

—*Aeneid,* X, 81-95 (abridged) [35]

subducere (verse 15) = *eripere*
pro (verse 16) = in front of
nebulam (verse 16) = cloud
obtendere (verse 16) = to spread out
contra (verse 17) = in turn (adverb)
gravidam (verse 20) = teeming
fluxas (verse 21) = tottering
fundo (verse 21) = from the very bottom
adulter (verse 25) = seducer
inrita iurgia (verse 28) = groundless accusations

2. Answer *all* of the following:
   a. Give the syntax of each of *two* of the following: *laborum* (verse 7), *quibus* (verse 14), *tibi* (verse 19). [2]
   b. What is the force of the prefix in *expugnavit* (verse 25)? [1]
   c. Scan verses 24 and 25, indicating the quantity of syllables and the division into feet. [4]
   d. Explain each of *two* of the following terms: ictus, elision, hiatus. [2]
   e. What war is referred to in verses 23 and 24 and who is the *Dardanius adulter* referred to in verse 25? [2]
   f. Mention a stylistic device used in the following:
   Interea magno misceri murmure caelum
   incipit. [1]
   g. What would be the purely Latin (not Greek) form of *Aenean* (verse 15)? The ordinary prose form of *Graium* (verse 15)? [2]
   h. Quote from memory the four lines immediately following *Excudent alii spirantia mollius aera . . .* [4]
   i. Why were Cassandra's prophecies not believed? What fate befell Laocoon and his sons? [2]
   j. The following quotation is taken from the *Eclogues*:
   "Mantua, vae, miserae nimium vicina Cremonae!" (Alas for Mantua, situated too near wretched Cremona!)
   What event in Vergil's life caused him thus to commiserate with the city of Mantua? To what kind of poetry do the *Eclogues* belong? [2]

Answer EITHER question 3 OR question 4.

3. Answer *each* of the following:

   a. Write a brief explanatory note on each of *four* of the following, showing its connection with the *Aeneid*: Cumae, Ithaca, Tenedos, Hesperia, Sidon. [4]

   b. Using one sentence for each, show what *four* of the following have to do with the story of the *Aeneid*: Anchises, Sinon, Lavinia, Creusa, Cerberus. [4]

4. Answer *each* of the following:

   a. Show by mentioning *three* specific episodes the attitude of Juno toward the Trojans as Vergil represents it. [3]

   b. On the basis of the quotation "*Tantaene animis caelestibus irae?*" what do you think was Vergil's *personal* view of the gods? [1]

   c. Give *two* reasons for the immediate success of the *Aeneid.* [2]

   d. Name *two* non-Latin epics strongly influenced by the *Aeneid.* [2]

VERGIL

June 18, 1936

Answer three questions.

1. Translate the following passages into English:

[Before the war that is to win for the Trojans a home in Latium, Aeneas has a dream beside the river Tiber.]

1 Nox erat, et terras animalia fessa per omnes
2 alituum pecudumque genus sopor altus habebat,
3 cum pater in ripa gelidique sub aetheris axe
4 Aeneas, tristi turbatus *pectora* bello,
5 procubuit seramque dedit per membra quietem.
6 Huic deus ipse loci fluvio Tiberinus amoeno
7 populeas inter senior se attollere frondes
8 visus; . . .
9 tum sic adfari et curas his *demere* dictis:
10 "O *sate* gente *deum,* Troianam ex hostibus urbem
11 qui revehis nobis aeternaque Pergama servas,
12 exspectate solo Laurenti *arvis*que Latinis,
13 hic tibi certa domus, certi — *ne absiste* — Penates;
14 neu belli terrere minis; tumor omnis et irae
15 *concessere* deum."

— *Aeneid,* VIII, 26-41 (abridged) [35]

alituum (verse 2) — irregular genitive plural of *ales, alitis*
Tiberinus . . . senior (verses 6-7) = old Father Tiber (the river god)

amoeno (verse 6) = pleasant

populeas (verse 7) = poplar, of the poplar (tree)

demere (verse 9) — from *demo,* take away, remove

exspectate (verse 12) — same construction as *sate* (verse 10)

Laurenti (verse 12) = of Laurentum (the city of King Latinus)

absiste (verse 13) — from *absistere,* to withdraw, to hesitate

terrere (verse 14) — passive imperative

tumor . . . et irae (verse 14) = swollen wrath (hendiadys)

[The friendship of Nisus, son of Hyrtacus, and Euryalus, who were among the followers of Aeneas in the war against the Latins and the Rutulians]

16 Nisus erat portae custos, acerimus armis,
17 Hyrtacides, comitem Aeneae quem miserat Ida
18 venatrix, iaculo celerem levibusque sagittis;
19 et iuxta comes Euryalus, *quo* pulchrior alter
20 non fuit Aeneadum Troiana neque induit arma.
21 His amor unus erat, pariterque in bella ruebant;
22 tum quoque communi portam statione tenebant.
23 Nisus ait: "Dine hunc ardorem mentibus addunt?
24 Aut pugnam aut aliquid iam dudum invadere magnum
25 mens agitat mihi, nec placida contenta quiete est.
26 Cernis quae Rutulos *habeat* fiducia rerum.
27 Lumina rara micant, somno vinoque soluti
28 procubuere, silent late loca. Percipe porro,
29 quid dubitem et quae nunc animo sententia surgat."

— *Aeneid,* IX, 176-191 (abridged) [35]

Ida venatrix (verses 17-18) = Ida, the huntress

pariter (verse 21) = side by side

statione (verse 22) = on sentry duty

ardorem (verse 23) = eager desire

addunt (verse 23) — from *addere,* to put into

aliquid . . . magnum (verse 24) — Translate as "some great deed"

rara (verse 27) — Translate as "only a few"

porro (verse 28) = then

dubitem (verse 29) = I ponder

2. Answer *all* of the following:

a. Explain the syntax of each of *four* of the following: *pectora* (verse 4), *demere* (verse 9), *sate* (verse 10), *quo* (verse 19), *habeat* (verse 26). [4]

b. Point out *two* patronymics that appear in the second passage. [2]

c. Give the usual prose form of *deum* (verse 10) and *concessere* (verse 15). [2]

d. In prose syntax how would *each* of the following usually be expressed in Latin: *arvis* (verse 12), *ne absiste* (verse 13)? [2]

e. Scan verses 24 and 25, indicating the quantity of syllables and the division into feet. [4]

f. In what respect are a simile and a metaphor alike? In what respect are they unlike? Define a spondee. [3]

g. Quote from memory the three and a half lines beginning *Tros Anchisiade, facilis descensus Averno . . .* [3]

Answer either question 3 or question 4.

3. Answer *each* of the following:

a. At what point in Aeneas's wanderings does the story of the *Aeneid* begin? What deity came to the rescue of the Trojans at that time? [2]

b. Write a *brief* account of *one* of the following: Anchises, Dido, the Cumaean Sibyl. [2]

c. Why was Aeneas called *pius?* [1]

d. Who was "the Ithacan" and why was he so called? [2]

e. What circumstances of Vergil's boyhood explain his frequent use of ants, bees and snakes as the subjects of his similes? [1]

f. Write a brief explanatory note on each of *two* of the following: Creusa, Calchas, Atridae. [2]

4. Answer *each* of the following:

a. What was the main purpose of the *Aeneid?* [1]

b. Mention a Latin or a Greek epic poem earlier than the *Aeneid.* [1]

c. What were the circumstances of Vergil's death? Where is he supposed to have been buried? [2]

d. What is the meaning of the name *Hesperia?* [1]

e. Name the Roman deity who presided over *each* of the following: wine, the sea, grain, Hades, fire, hunting. [3]

f. Write a brief explanatory note on each of *two* of the following: Elysium, Icarus, Cytherea, Janus. [2]

VERGIL

January 21, 1937

Answer three questions.

1. Translate the following passages into English:

[Latinus, the aged king of Latium, reluctantly yields to his people's demand for war against the Trojans and reproaches Turnus.]

1 Cuncti contra omina bellum,
2 contra fata deum, perverso numine poscunt.
3 Certatim regis circumstant tecta Latini;
4 ille velut pelagi rupes immota resistit.
5 Verum ubi nulla datur caecum exsuperare potestas
6 consilium, et saevae nutu Iunonis eunt res,
7 multa deos aurasque pater testatus inanes,
8 "Frangimur heu fatis" inquit "ferimurque procella!
9 Ipsi has sacrilego pendetis sanguine poenas,
10 O miseri. Te, Turne, nefas, te triste manebit
11 supplicium, votisque deos venerabere seris.
12 Nam mihi parta quies, omnisque in limine portus;
13 funere felici spolior." Nec plura locutus
14 saepsit se tectis, rerumque reliquit habenas.

—*Aeneid,* VII, 583-586, 591-600 [35]

perverso numine (verse 2) = inspired by an evil influence
Certatim (verse 3) = emulously, eagerly
multa (verse 7) = many times
procella (verse 8) = storm (of civil commotion)
sacrilego (verse 9) = sacrilegious, impious
omnisque in limine portus (verse 12) = I am quite at the entrance of the harbor
saepsit (verse 14) = from *saepire,* to enclose, shut up

[Daedalus, the artist, confined by King Minos in Crete, plans to escape by making wings for himself and his son.]

15 Daedalus interea Creten longumque perosus
16 exsilium tactusque loci natalis amore,
17 clausus erat pelago. "Terras licet" inquit "et undas
18 obstruat: at caelum certe patet. Ibimus illac.
19 Omnia possideat, non possidet aëra Minos."

20 Dixit, et ignotas animum dimittit in artes,
21 naturamque novat. Nam ponit in ordine pinnas,
22 atque ita compositas parvo curvamine flectit,
23 ut veras imitetur aves. Puer Icarus una
24 stabat et, ignarus sua se tractare pericla,
25 ore renidenti modo quas vaga moverat aura,
26 captabat plumas, flavam modo pollice ceram
27 mollibat, lusoque suo mirabile patris
28 impediebat opus.

— Ovid, *Metam.*, VIII, 183-189, 194-200 [35]

perosus (verse 15) = hating, detesting
licet . . . obstruat (verses 17-18) = he (Minos) may make impassable
illac (verse 18) = there, by that way
novat (verse 21) — from *novare,* to make new, change
tractare (verse 24) — The verb *tractare* means to handle, touch
renidenti (verse 25) = beaming, cheerful
vaga (verse 25) = wandering, uncertain
plumas (verse 26) = feathers
pollice (verse 26) = with his thumb
ceram (verse 26) = wax
mollibat (verse 27) — from *mollire,* to soften, mould
luso (verse 27) = by his play, playing

2. Answer *all* of the following:
   a. Scan verses 9 and 12, indicating the quantity of syllables and the division into feet. [4]
   b. Explain the syntax of *each* of the following:
      funere (verse 13), *loci* (verse 16), *imitetur* (verse 23), *tractare* (verse 24). [4]
   c. What is the special force of such a verb as *captabat* (verse 26)? [1]
   d. Give the more usual prose form for *deum* (verse 2), *pericla* (verse 24), *mollibat* (verse 27). [3]
   e. Discuss the meaning of the English words *perverse* and *tact,* in view of their Latin derivation. [2]
   f. Name the figure of speech in verse 14. Explain alliteration and onomatopoeia. [3]
   g. Quote from memory a verse and a half of Laocoon's remarks about the wooden horse. Complete the verse beginning:
      Una salus victis, . . . [3]

Answer either question 3 or question 4.

3. Answer *each* of the following:
   a. Mention *two* names by which Vergil refers to the Greeks. [1]
   b. Give Vergil's explanation of the origin of *two* of the following names: Julius, Avernus, Byrsa. [2]
   c. Define and locate *each* of the following: Tenedos, Elysium. [2]
   d. Identify briefly each of *four* of the following: Achates, Andromache, Cassandra, Lavinia, Menelaus, Sinon. [4]
   e. What was the reason or occasion for holding the athletic games described in the fifth book of the *Aeneid?* [1]

4. Answer *each* of the following:
   a. What qualifies the *Aeneid* to be considered a national epic? In what special way did the *Aeneid* contribute to the glory of the family of the Caesars? [2]
   b. Name *two* of Vergil's best friends. [1]
   c. What was the subject matter of the *Eclogues* and of the *Georgics?* [2]
   d. Name the Roman deity who presided over *each* of the following: trade, the winds, the dawn, the hearth. [2]
   e. For what was Hercules chiefly noted? What is the significance of the name Alcides? [1]
   f. What is Olympus? Why should it have been considered the home of the gods? [1]
   g. State briefly how Vergil was regarded in the Middle Ages. [1]

VERGIL

June 17, 1937

Answer three questions.

1. Translate the following passages into English:

[Queen Amata protests to King Latinus against giving their daughter Lavinia in marriage to Aeneas instead of to Turnus and claims that Turnus, too, may be considered a foreigner.]

1 "Exsulibusne datur ducenda Lavinia Teucris,
2 O genitor? nec te miseret nataeque tuique?
3 Nec matris miseret, quam primo aquilone relinquet
4 perfidus, alta petens abducta virgine, praedo?
5 An non sic Phrygius penetrat Lacedaemona pastor
6 Ledaeamque Helenam Troianas vexit ad urbes?
7 Quid tua sancta fides? Quid cura antiqua tuorum
8 et consanguineo totiens data dextera Turno?
9 Si gener externa petitur de gente Latinis,
10 idque sedet, Faunique premunt te iussa parentis,
11 omnem equidem sceptris terram quae libera nostris
12 dissidet, externam reor, et sic dicere divos.
13 Et Turno, si prima domus repetatur origo,
14 Inachus Acrisiusque patres."

—*Aeneid,* VII, 359-372 [35]

Exsulibus (verse 1) — from *exsul, exsulis,* an exile
Ledaeam (verse 6) = daughter of Leda (literally, of Leda)
Quid (verse 7) = Of what avail?
consanguineo (verse 8) = kinsman
sedet (verse 10) = is fixed, is your firm resolve
Fauni (verse 10) = from *Faunus -i,* m., Faunus (The oracle of Faunus, deified father of King Latinus, had said that Lavinia should be married to a foreigner.)
libera . . . dissidet (verses 11-12) = is free and separate
Inachus and *Acrisius* (verse 14) — These were two early kings of Argos

[Laodamia, wife of Protesilaus, a Greek who was fated to die at Troy, urges him to be cautious in battle, so that he may come home to her alive.]

> Note that the shorter, alternate verses are not hexameters. Note also the frequent use of the imperative.

15 "Hectora, quisquis is est, si sum tibi cara, caveto:
16 signatum memori pectore nomen habe.
17 Hunc ubi vitaris, alios vitare memento,
18 et multos illic Hectoras esse puta;
19 et facito ut dicas, quotiens pugnare parabis,
20 'parcere me iussit Laodamia sibi.'
21 Si cadere Argolico fas est sub milite Troiam,
22 te quoque non ullum vulnus habente cadat.
23 Pugnet et adversos tendat Menelaus in hostis:
24 hostibus e mediis nupta petenda viro est.
25 Causa tua est dispar. Tu tantum vivere pugna,
26 inque pios dominae posse redire sinus.
27 Parcite, Dardanidae, de tot, precor, hostibus uni.
28 Non est, quem deceat nudo concurrere ferro,
29 saevaque in oppositos pectora ferre viros.
30 Fortius ille potest multo, quam pugnat, amare.
31 Bella gerant alii; Protesilaus amet."

— Ovid, *Heroides*, XIII, 64-84 (abridged) [35]

Hectora (verse 15) — accusative
caveto (verse 15) = you must beware of (future imperative). Note also *memento* and *facito* (verses 17 and 19)
memori (verse 16) — an adjective with *pectore*
vitaris (verse 17) — shortened form of *vitaveris*
facito (verse 19) — Translate as "you must see to it"
nupta (verse 24) = a bride
dispar (verse 25) = different
dominae (verse 26) — genitive; translate here as "wife"
quam (verse 30) = than

2. Answer *all* of the following:
   a. Explain the syntax of *each* of the following: *tui* (verse 2), *Turno* (verse 13), *Pugnet* (verse 23), *vivere* (verse 25). [4]
   b. Why do the forms *Lacedaemona* (verse 5) and *Hectora* (verse 15) end in *-a*? [1]
   c. Who were: *perfidus praedo* (verse 4), *Phrygius pastor* (verse 5), *Menelaus* (verse 23)? [3]
   d. To whom does the word *nupta* (verse 24) refer? [1]
   e. Scan verses 4 and 11, indicating the quantity of syllables and the division into feet. [4]
   f. Define hiatus, as used in verse; what does the word literally mean? [2]
      What is meant by the terms: syllaba anceps, patronymic, zeugma, metaphor? [2]
   g. Quote at least *three* lines of the passage beginning: *Excudent alii . . .* [3]

Answer either question 3 or question 4.

3. Answer *each* of the following:
   a. How did Aeneas receive his first information that the Greeks had captured Troy? [1]
   b. For what sacrilegious act was Laocoon killed by the serpents? [1]
   c. To whom and about whom did Venus say, *"dux femina facti"*? [2]
   d. Mention briefly the principal topic in *each* of the following books of the *Aeneid:* II, IV. [2]
   e. Locate the following: Carthage, Lavinium, Cumae, Styx. [2]
   f. Write a brief acount of *each* of the following: Cassandra, Creusa, Daedalus, Minos. [2]

4. Answer *each* of the following:
   a. About how long was Vergil occupied in writing the *Aeneid*? [1]
   b. Mention *two* places, other than Rome, where Vergil lived. [2]
   c. In what important respect is the *Aeneid* like the *Odyssey*? [1]
   d. Mention *two* ways in which the *Aeneid* was designed to add to the dignity of Rome. [2]
   e. What is the meaning of the term "Elysian Fields"? [1]
   f. What did *each* of the following deities stand for in the Roman religion: Diana, Mercury, Pluto, Vulcan? [2]
   g. What is meant by *Sortes Vergilianae*? [1]

VERGIL

January 27, 1938

Answer three questions.

1. Translate the following passages into English:

[Aeneas and his men, newly arrived in Latium, explore the country in different directions (*diversi*), begin a settlement and send an embassy to the king.]

1 Postera cum prima lustrabat lampade terras
2 orta dies, urbem et fines et litora gentis
3 diversi explorant: haec fontis stagna Numici,
4 hunc Tiberim fluvium, hic fortes habitare Latinos.
5 Tum satus Anchisa delectos ordine ab omni
6 centum oratores augusta ad moenia regis
7 ire iubet, ramis velatos Palladis omnes,
8 donaque ferre viro, pacemque exposcere Teucris.
9 Haud mora, festinant iussi rapidisque feruntur
10 passibus. Ipse humili designat moenia fossa,
11 moliturque locum, primasque in litore sedes
12 castrorum in morem pinnis atque aggere cingit.
13 Iamque iter emensi turres ac tecta Latinorum
14 ardua cernebant iuvenes, muroque subibant.

—*Aeneid,* VII, 148-161 (adapted) [35]

lampade (verse 1) — from *lampas, lampadis,* a beam of light
haec (verse 3) and *hunc* (verse 4) — After each of these supply *esse* (depending on "they find that" understood)
stagna (verse 3) = still waters, pool (accusative)
Numici (verse 3) = of the Numicius (a small river)
satus Anchisa (verse 5) = the son of Anchises
oratores (verse 6) = envoys
augusta (verse 6) = stately
festinant (verse 9) — from *festinare,* to hasten
humili (verse 10) = shallow
designat (verse 10) — from *designare,* to mark out
molitur (verse 11) — from *moliri,* to arrange
in morem (verse 12) = after the fashion of
pinnis (verse 12) = battlements (ablative)
emensi (verse 13) — from *emetiri,* to traverse
subibant (verse 14) — from *subire,* to approach

[Vergil here describes a series of prophetic scenes pictured on the shield made by Vulcan, the fire god (*Ignipotens*), for Aeneas at the request of Venus.]

15 Illic res Italas Romanorumque triumphos,
16 haud vatum ignarus venturique inscius aevi,
17 fecerat Ignipotens, illic genus omne futurae
18 stirpis ab Ascanio, pugnataque in ordine bella.

---

19 Nec procul hinc Romam et raptas sine more Sabinas
20 addiderat, subitoque novum consurgere bellum.

---

21 In summo custos Tarpeiae Manlius arcis
22 stabat pro templo et Capitolia celsa tenebat.

---

23 Haec inter tumidi late maris ibat imago;
24 in medio classes aeratas, Actia bella,
25 cernere erat; totumque instructo Marte videres
26 fervere Leucaten, auroque effulgere fluctus.
27 Hinc Augustus agens Italos in proelia Caesar
28 cum patribus populoque, Penatibus et magnis dis,
29 stans celsa in puppi.

—*Aeneid,* VIII, 626-680 (abridged) [35]

Illic (verses 15 and 17) = there (on the shield)
hinc (verse 19) = from here (on the shield)
sine more (verse 19) = lawlessly
Sabinas (verse 19) = the Sabine women
In summo (verse 21) = at the top of the shield (with *clipeo* understood)
Tarpeiae (verse 21) = Tarpeian (from *Tarpeius, -a, -um*)
Haec inter (verse 23) — Note the postpositive preposition
aeratas (verse 24) = trimmed with bronze
Actia (verse 24) = of Actium
erat (verse 25) = it was possible
Leucaten (verse 26) = Leucate (accusative) (A promontory near Actium)
effulgere (verse 26) = glitter
Hinc (verse 27) — Translate as "here"
stans (verse 29) — Translate as if it were "*stat*"

2. Answer *all* of the following:
   a. Scan verses 1 and 6, indicating the quantity of syllables and the division into feet. [4]
   b. Explain the syntax of each of *four* of the following: *habitare* (verse 4), *Anchisa* (verse 5), *Teucris* (verse 8), *muro* (verse 14), *aevi* (verse 16). [4]

c. Why does *ramis Palladis* (verse 7) mean "olive branches" and why were they worn on this occasion? [1]

d. What do you understand to be the difference between "great gods" (verse 28) and minor ones? [1]

e. To what incident in Roman legend does *raptas sine more Sabinas* (verse 19) refer? [1]

f. Name the figure of speech in *instructo Marte* (verse 25). [1]

g. Who was *Ascanius* (verse 18). [1]

h. Give a Latin synonym for *Teucris* (verse 8). [1]

i. Define hendiadys; explain the difference between simile and metaphor. [2]

j. Under what circumstances were the following words spoken: *"O socii (neque enim ignari sumus ante malorum)"?* [1] Quote at least *three* more lines of this speech. [3]

Answer either question 3 or question 4.

3. *a.* What incident in the *Aeneid* brought Aeolus and Neptune into conflict? [1]

b. According to legend, what caused the Greeks to attack Troy? [1]

c. In Book VI of the *Aeneid,* what great wars does Vergil foreshadow? [1]

d. Locate Ithaca and Carthage. [2]

e. Why did Sinon speak of his escape as "sinful"? [1]

f. Who was each of *four* of the following: Hecuba, Atrides, Lavinia, Achates, Laocoon? [4]

4. *a.* What is an epic poem? Mention *two* respects in which the *Aeneid* meets the requirements. [3]

b. What *two* poetical works had Vergil written before the *Aeneid?* [2]

c. Was Vergil a Roman citizen by birth? Explain your answer. [1]

d. State briefly the circumstances of his death. [1]

e. Why was his original farm taken from him? [1]

f. What later Italian poet was especially influenced by Vergil's account of the descent into the Lower World? [1]

g. Explain briefly the relationship of Maecenas and Vergil. [1]

VERGIL

June 23, 1938

Answer three questions.

1. Translate the following passages into English:

[Camilla, warrior queen of the Volscians (*Volsci*), proposes to Turnus, the Rutulian king, that she should lead her cavalry against the Trojans, leaving Turnus to defend, on foot, the city of Laurentum.]

1 Cingitur ipse furens certatim in proelia Turnus.
2 Obvia cui, Volscorum acie comitante, Camilla
3 occurrit, portisque ab equo regina sub ipsis
4 desiluit, quam tota cohors imitata relictis
5 ad terram defluxit equis; tum talia fatur:
6 "Turne, sui merito si qua est fiducia *forti,*
7 audeo et *Aeneadum* promitto occurrere turmae
8 solaque Tyrrhenos equites ire obvia contra.
9 Me sine prima manu temptare pericula belli:
10 tu pedes ad muros subsiste, et moenia *serva.*"
11 Turnus ad haec, oculos horrenda in virgine fixus:
12 "O decus Italiae virgo, . . .
13 tu Tyrrhenum equitem conlatis excipe signis;
14 *tecum* acer Messapus erit, turmaeque Latinae."
15 Sic ait, et paribus Messapum in proelia dictis
16 hortatur sociosque duces, et pergit in hostem.

—*Aeneid,* XI, 486-521 (abridged) [40]

certatim (verse 1) = eagerly
Obvia (verse 2) = to meet
desiluit (verse 4) — from *desilire,* to leap down
imitata (verse 4) — from *imitari,* to imitate
ad terram defluxit (verse 5) = dismounted
sui (verse 6) — objective genitive with *fiducia,* confidence
merito (verse 6) = justly
turmae (verses 7 and 14) — from *turma,* a troop of cavalry
Tyrrhenos (verse 8) = Etruscan (The Etruscans were allies of Aeneas.)
sine (verse 9) — imperative mood [Note frequent other imperatives following.]
pedes . . . subsiste (verse 10) = stay as a footsoldier
horrenda (verse 11) = awesome
excipe (verse 13) = withstand (imperative)
Messapus (verse 14) — an ally of Turnus and the Latins

[Evander mourns over the body of his son, Pallas, who had fallen in his first battle while aiding the Trojans.]

17 At non Evandrum potis est vis ulla tenere;
18 sed venit in medios. Feretro Pallanta reposto
19 procubuit super, atque haeret lacrimansque gemensque,
20 et via vix tandem voci laxata dolore est;
21 "Non haec, O *Palla,* dederas promissa parenti,
22 cautius us saevo velles te credere Marti.
23 *Haud ignarus* eram, quantum nova gloria in armis
24 et praedulce decus primo certamine *posset.*
25 Primitiae iuvenis miserae, bellique propinqui
26 dura rudimenta! et *nulli* exaudita deorum
27 vota precesque meae! Tuque, O sanctissima coniunx,
28 felix *morte* tua, neque in hunc servata *dolorem!*"

—*Aeneid,* XI, 148-159 **[30]**

potis est (verse 17) = *potest*
Feretro . . . reposto (verse 18) = when the bier had been set down
laxata . . . est (verse 20) = was opened up
cautius (verse 22) = more cautiously
quantum . . . posset (verses 23-24) = how compelling . . . was
praedulce (verse 24) — *prae* is intensive; translate as "very . . ."
Primitiae (verse 25) = first efforts
rudimenta (verse 26) = beginnings

2. Answer *all* of the following:
   a. Scan verses 7 and 13, indicating the quantity of syllables and division into feet. [4]
   b. Explain the syntax of each of *five* of the following: *forti* (verse 6), *serva* (verse 10), *Palla* (verse 21), *posset* (verse 24), *nulli* (verse 26), *morte* (verse 28). [5]
   c. To what or to whom does *each* of the following refer: *te* in tecum (verse 14), *dolorem* (verse 28)? [2]
   d. What figure of speech does *Haud ignarus* (verse 23) illustrate? What familiar figure of speech appears in verse 20? [2]
   e. How does the meaning of *Aeneadum* (verse 7) differ from the usual patronymic meaning? [1]
   f. Quote from memory the first *four* lines of the Aeneid. [4]
   g. Define metaphor and metonymy. [2]

Answer either question 3 *or question* 4.

3. *a.* What other deity did Venus resemble when she met Aeneas near Carthage? [1]
   b. According to Aeneas' own statement, what was the main reason which made him abandon Dido? [1]
   c. Write brief explanatory notes on each of *four* of the following: Acestes, Creusa, Daedalus, Menelaus, Tartarus, Vulcanus. [4]

d. Write a brief general heading for the subject matter of *each* of Books I, II, IV and VI of the *Aeneid.* [4]

4. *a.* Write briefly about Minos and his kingdom. [1]
   b. Why did Vergil wish to have the *Aeneid* destroyed? By whose order was it preserved and published? [2]
   c. State briefly the relation of the Trojan War to the history of Rome. [2]
   d. Locate Vergil's boyhood home and name *two* places besides Rome where as a youth he went to school. [3]
   e. To what deity would a Roman pray for *each* of the following: prosperity in business, success in war, good crops of grain, a plentiful crop of grapes? [2]

VERGIL

January 24, 1939

Answer all three questions.

1. Translate the following passages into English:

[The people of King Evander, at a ceremonial feast, are startled by the appearance of the Trojan ships. Aeneas, accosted by Evander's son, Pallas, replies with disarming friendliness and is welcomed as a guest (*hospes*).]

1 Terrentur visu subito, cunctique relictis
2 consurgunt mensis. Audax quos rumpere Pallas
3 sacra vetat, raptoque volat telo obvius ipse,
4 et procul e tumulo: "Iuvenes, quae causa subegit
5 ignotas temptare vias? quo tenditis?" inquit.
6 "Qui genus? unde domo? pacemne huc fertis, an arma?"
7 Tum pater Aeneas puppi sic fatur ab alta,
8 *paciferae*que manu ramum praetendit olivae:
9 "Troiugenas ac tela vides inimica Latinis;
10 Evandrum petimus. Ferte haec, et dicite lectos
11 *Dardaniae* venisse duces, socia arma rogantes."
12 Obstipuit tanto perculsus nomine Pallas:
13 "Egredere o quicumque es," ait, "coramque parentem
14 adloquere, ac nostris succede *penatibus hospes.*"

—*Aeneid,* VIII, 109-123 (abridged) [35]

vetat (verse 3) = forbids *obvius* (verse 3) — Translate as "to meet them" *subegit* (verse 4) — from *subigere,* to drive, to induce *genus* (verse 6) — an accusative of specification *paciferae* (verse 8) = symbolic of peace *Troiugenas* (verse 9) = Trojans *Ferte* (verse 10) — equivalent to *nuntiate* *socia arma* (verse 11) = armed alliance *perculsus* (verse 12) = very much impressed *Egredere* (verse 13) = disembark (imperative) *coram* (verse 13) = face to face *succede* (verse 14) — from *sub+cedo,* come to, approach

[Atlas, in fear of all strangers (*externi*) because of a prophecy, refuses hospitality to Perseus despite his claim to be a son of Jupiter. Atlas is about to eject him forcibly when Perseus shows him Medusa's magic head, the sight of which transforms Atlas into a mountain.]

15 Id metuens solidis pomaria clauserat Atlas
16 moenibus et vasto dederat *servanda* draconi
17 arcebatque suis externos finibus omnes.
18 Huic quoque "Vade procul, ne longe *gloria* rerum,
19 quam mentiris" ait, "longe tibi Iuppiter *absit*";
20 vimque minis addit manibusque expellere temptat
21 cunctantem et placidis miscentem fortia dictis.
22 *Viribus* inferior (quis enim par *esset* Atlanti
23 viribus?) "At quoniam parvi tibi gratia nostra est,
24 accipe munus" ait, laevaque a parte Medusae
25 ipse retroversus squalentia protulit ora.
26 Quantus erat, mons factus Atlas: nam barba comaeque
27 in silvas abeunt, iuga sunt umerique manusque,
28 quod caput ante fuit, summo est in monte cacumen,
29 ossa lapis fiunt.

— Ovid, *Metamorphoses,* IV, 646-660 [35]

pomaria (verse 15) = orchards *draconi* (verse 16) — from *draco, draconis,* a dragon *arcebat* (verse 17) = was excluding *Huic* (verse 18) — refers to Perseus *Vade* (verse 18) = go *mentiris* (verse 19) — from *mentiri,* to claim falsely *longe . . . absit* (verse 19) = be of no avail *minis* (verse 20) — from *minae, minarum,* threats *cunctantem* (verse 21) — from *cunctari,* to delay, to linger *parvi* (verse 23) = of little account *retroversus* (verse 25) = turning his back *squalentia* (verse 25) = squalid, disgusting *protulit* (verse 25) = he displayed *Quantus erat* (verse 26) = Great as he was *barba* (verse 26) = beard *abeunt* (verse 27) — Translate as "change" *cacumen* (verse 28) = peak

2. Answer *all* of the following:

a. Scan verses 10 and 11, indicating the quantity of syllables and division into feet. [4]

b. Explain the syntax of each of *six* of the following: *penatibus* (verse 14), *hospes* (verse 14), *servanda* (verse 16), *gloria* (verse 18), *absit* (verse 19), *Viribus* (verse 22), *esset* (verse 22). [6]

c. Why did Perseus turn his back (verse 25)? [1]

d. Give the formation of the word *paciferae* (verse 8). [1]

e. Explain the origin and meaning of the name *Dardaniae* (verse 11). [1]

f. What figure of speech appears in the use of *penatibus* (verse 14)? [1]

3. Answer *four* only of the following groups:

   a. Where was Vergil's boyhood home and where, besides Rome, was his home during his later life? Describe briefly *one* of his works other than the *Aeneid.* Quote the line in which Aeneas reminds his men that their painful experiences may sometime afford a pleasant memory. [4]

   b. State briefly how the *Aeneid* was helpful to Roman patriotism. Mention at least *two* reasons for Juno's hatred of the Trojans. Write a brief explanatory note about Hector. [4]

   c. State the circumstances which made Dido a widow. Why was Juno willing that Dido should fall in love with Aeneas? Define alliteration and onomatopoeia. [4]

   d. How, according to Vergil, did Avernus get its name? Who said *"Equo ne credite"* and on what occasion? Describe the part which Aeolus took in the action of the *Aeneid.* [4]

   e. What is the difference between elision and hiatus? For what reason was Cassandra especially celebrated? Write a brief explanatory note about *each* of the following: Cerberus, Menelaus. [4]

   f. Why is the first half of the *Aeneid* often compared to the *Odyssey* and the second half to the *Iliad?* What was the more usual name of *Pelides?* What is the meaning of the name *Pelides?* [4]

   g. Write a brief explanatory note on *each* of the following: Diana, Janus, Mercury, Vesta. [4]

VERGIL

June 22, 1939

Answer all three questions.

1. Translate the following passages into English:
[When Romulus, after his career on earth, was deified and taken up to heaven as the god Quirinus, Juno sent Iris, goddess of the rainbow, to his bereaved wife, Hersilia, and made her divine, under the new name of Hora.]

1 Flebat ut amissum coniunx, cum *regia* Iuno
2 Irin ad Hersiliam descendere limite curvo
3 imperat, et viduae sua sic mandata referre:
4 "O et de Latio, O et de gente Sabina
5 praecipuum, *matrona,* decus, dignissima tanti
6 ante fuisse viri, coniunx nunc esse Quirini,
7 siste tuos fletus, et si *tibi* cura videndi
8 coniugis est, *duce me,* lucum pete, colle Quirini
9 qui viret, et templum Romani regis obumbrat."
10 Paret, et in terram pictos delapsa per arcus,
11 Hersiliam iussis compellat vocibus Iris.
12 Nec mora;
13 ingreditur colles; Romanae conditor urbis
14 excipit, et priscum pariter cum corpore nomen
15 mutat, Horamque vocat, quae nunc dea iuncta Quirino est.

—Ovid, *Metamorphoses,* XIV, 829-851 (abridged) [35]

ut amissum (verse 1) = him as one lost (refers to Romulus) *limite curvo* (verse 2) = the curving path (of the rainbow) *viduae* (verse 3) = widow, the bereaved one *praecipuum* (verse 5) = special, chief (modifies *decus*) *matrona* (verse 5) = matron, lady *fuisse* (verse 6) — After this word supply *coniunx* *duce* (verse 8) — not the verb *lucum* (verse 8) — not from *lux* *colle Quirini* (verse 8) = on the Quirinal hill (where the temple of Quirinus was) *viret* (verse 9) — from *vireo,-ere,* to be green *obumbrat* (verse 9) = shades *pictos delapsa per arcus* (verse 10) = gliding down along the colored arch *compellat* (verse 11) = addresses *ingreditur* (verse 13) — The subject is Hersilia *conditor* (verse 13) = the founder *priscum* (verse 14) = original, former (modifying *nomen*)

[After a disastrous battle two factions arose among the Latins. One faction, led by Drances, demanded that Turnus meet Aeneas in single combat.]

16 Dirum execrantur bellum Turnique *hymenaeos;*
17 ipsum armis, ipsumque iubent decernere ferro,
18 qui regnum Italiae et primos sibi poscat honores.
19 Ingravat haec saevus Drances, solumque vocari
20 testatur, solum posci in certamina Turnum.
21 Multa simul contra variis sententia dictis
22 pro Turno; et magnum reginae nomen obumbrat;
23 multa virum meritis sustentat fama tropaeis.
24 Hos inter motus, medio in flagrante tumultu,
25 ecce super maesti magna Diomedis ab urbe
26 legati responsa ferunt: *nihil* omnibus actum
27 tantorum impensis operum; *nil* dona neque aurum
28 nec magnas valuisse preces; alia arma *Latinis*
29 *quaerenda,* aut pacem *Troiano* ab *rege* petendam.
30 Deficit ingenti luctu rex ipse Latinus.

Aeneid, XI, 217-231 [35]

execrantur (verse 16) — from *execrari,* to curse (Supply as subject, "The bereaved Latins") *hymenaeos* (verse 16) = wedding *decernere* (verse 17) = to fight it out *Ingravat* (verse 19) — from *ingravare,* to aggravate *solum(que)* (verse 19) — modifies *Turnum,* understood *testatur* (verse 20) — from *testari,* to declare, to assert *contra* (verse 21) = on the other hand *obumbrat* verse 22) = protects (him) *sustentat* (verse 23) — a synonym of *sustineo* *tropaeis* (verse 23) = trophies *flagrante* (verse 24) = blazing, excited *super* (verse 25) — the adverb *maesti* (verse 25) — modifies *legati* (verse 26) *omnibus . . . impensis* (verses 26-27) — Translate "by all the outlay" *operum* (verse 27) = efforts *Deficit* (verse 30) = collapses, grows faint

2. Answer *all* of the following:

a. Scan verses 17 and 18, indicating the quantity of syllables and division into feet. [4]

b. Explain the syntax of each of *four* of the following: *matrona* (verse 5), *tibi* (verse 7), *duce* (verse 8), *Latinis* (verse 28), *quaerenda* (*esse*) (verse 29). [4]

c. Point out and explain an example of hiatus in verse 4. [1]

d. Explain the significance of *regia* (verse 1) as applied to Juno. [1]

e. Who is referred to as the intended bride in *hymenaeos* (verse 16)? [1]

f. To whom does *each* of the following refer: *me* (verse 8), *Troiano rege* (verse 29)? [2]

g. Why does Vergil use *nihil* in verse 26 and *nil* in verse 27? [1]

3. Answer *four* of the following groups:

   a. With what particular character in Roman mythology is each of *four* of the following associated: ruling the winds, forging thunderbolts, ferrying spirits of the dead, presiding over the lower world, founding the city of Rome? [4]

   b. Quote from memory *four* consecutive lines of the *Aeneid.* [4]

   c. What is the general theme of *each* of Books I, II, IV and VI of the *Aeneid?* [4]

   d. In which one of the works of Vergil was Maecenas especially interested? Why did the writing of this work appeal to Vergil? Why has it been called a "Farmer's Manual"? Give the subject of *one* of the four divisions of this work. [4]

   e. What character of the *Aeneid* is meant by each of *four* of the following: *Anchisiades, dei iussu non umquam credita Teucris, deus omnipotens, dux femina facti, Maiā genitum?* [4]

   f. How did the incident of the "golden apple" lead to the Trojan War? What incident led to the death of Laocoon? What priestess helped Aeneas discover the *aureus ramus?* What war was apparently prophesied in Dido's curse upon Aeneas? [4]

   g. Write a brief explanatory note on each of *four* of the following: Ascanius, Cyclops, Creusa, Sinon, Tenedos. [4]